We the People

A Story of Internment in America

ラ
ヲ
子

Arigato!

Mary Tsuruko Tsukamoto
(ラ ヲ 子)

We the People

A Story of Internment in America

by

Mary Tsukamoto
and
Elizabeth Pinkerton

Best wishes to you —
Elizabeth Pinkerton

Laguna Publishers

1988

First printed in September, 1987

Library of Congress: 87-205205
ISBN: P: 0-944665-42-X

Manufactured in the United States of America
Second Printing, April 1988

WE THE PEOPLE

Dedication

Al
Tom
Marielle
Mike
Connie
Pat
Tim
Sarah
John William

Mary's Mentors:
Mable Barron – American Cultural Heritage
Kohana Sasaki – Japanese Cultural Heritage

ACKNOWLEDGEMENTS

We began work on this book in August of 1979. If we had known it would take us eight years, we might not have attempted the task. However, we have been encouraged by many and we have encouraged each other, and so the months passed by. Although we are the writers, books, like many other creative ventures, include the ideas, suggestions, and research of many. It's time to say thanks to all of them.

Gratefully, we acknowledge the assistance provided by members of the Florin Japanese American community who freely shared their experiences and their priceless photographs and documents. The amazing recollections of Mr. Joichi Niita are included in the text, and we thank all the Issei for thier wonderful memories. We thank the Nisei soldiers for sharing their wartime experiences. We thank the Jan Ken Po Gakko children and parents for their contribuitions, and we are indebted to the JACL for their support.

We are thankful that Dorothea Lange (now deceased) had the sensitivity she did in photographing Florin residents as they prepared for evacuation. We are grateful that Frances Compston brought her camera with her to work on May 29, 1942, thus capturing forever the sad scene at the Elk Grove train station with the only photographs in existence to remind us of that day.

To Mary's Japanese mentor, Kahana Sasaki, and her American mentor, Mable Barron, we convey much gratitude from the both of us. Our many thanks to Fumiko L. Sato whose graceful brush drawings highlight the main sections of the book with the plum, bamboo, and pine. Our appreciation to Henry Sugimoto for the use of his marvelous paintings from Fresno and Jerome.

We thank our typists and technicians: Lois Nakashima and Sharon Gravert who typed for Mary before she got her computer; Sandy Chapman who did all the word processing; and Sarah Pinkerton who pitched in when there was no one else. We thank Al Beechick, Tina Stauss, and Jacklyn Boor for their technical assistance and editing.

Elk Grove Unified School District Board of Education, Superintendent Bob Trigg, Bart Lagomarsino, and Anna Kato – your support has sustained us. We greatly appreciate the insights of Don Larson who as an eighth grader in 1942 anguished with his classmates when they were taken away. Dave Morse, we were encouraged by your support and suggestions.

Eldon Penrose and Robbye Lamb - thanks for your careful guidance; Sarah Levine, Alice Kubo, and Kimi Kaneko - we appreciate your confidence and encouragement; Carole Sacre - our thanks for quiet writing time at your Lake Tahoe cabin.

We thank the exhibit preparers from the Smithsonian Institution: Dr. Thomas Crouch, Selma Thomas, Jennifer Locke, Geoffrey Howard, and especially Dr. Harold Langley whose comments are included in our introduction. We are grateful for the introductory remarks provided by Mayor Anne Rudin of Sacramento and Congressman Robert Matsui.

John Marshall, your critiques were excellent, and we so appreciate your encouragement and support as well as your expertise in everthing Japanese. Marielle, your guidance from beginning to end straightened us out when we didn't know where we were going; Al Tsukamoto and Tom Pinkerton, without you two there would be no book at all. Thanks for your encouragement, patience, and understanding.

Mary Tsukamoto
Elizabeth Pinkerton

CONTENTS

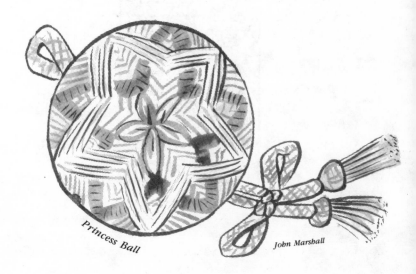

Princess Ball   *John Marshall*

John Marshall

PREFACE

This is the story of a most remarkable woman. Though she is frail and crippled with arthritis, she stands tall in her 72nd year and she speaks out for America. Her voice is strong and crystal clear; fire burns in her eyes as she stands before her audience to tell her story. Soon there are no dry eyes anywhere. We cry, not for Mary Tsukamoto, but for our nation.

Mary Tsukamoto brims over with a patriotic fervor that knows no rest. She is a teacher of children and adults who in her youth attended a segregated school for Japanese children. In her senior years, Mary has dedicated herself to righting a tragic wrong, a violation of our greatest document, the U.S. Constitution. The story of internment in America, the sending of thousands of innocent men, women and children to American concentration camps during World War II, has become Mary's personal grievance. It is her redress, and she seeks to set the story straight. The internment was part of her life as it was for 110,000 persons of Japanese ancestry who lived on the west coast of the United States in 1942. If enough people know the story, it will never happen again to any Americans anywhere!

How could our country, the great nation of Jefferson and Lincoln, have allowed its citizens to be treated so sadly? How could we have let people be rounded up like criminals, sent to armed camps, and kept there for months and even years? How could all this have happened without there having been any crimes committed? Without charges having been filed? Without trials or juries? Doesn't the Constitution guarantee due process?

These questions are finally being asked after more than forty years have passed. Americans are questioning the legal system that allowed such a shocking chapter of history to occur. They are searching through old records and what was once secret information to find the answers. They are finding many of the participants long dead and others with fading memories, but the truth will prevail as it always

1

does in America.

On October 1, 1987, the Smithsonian Institution will open a new exhibit to celebrate the 200th anniversary of the U.S. Constitution. Worldwide attention will be focused upon the little known story of the Japanese internment, a time when the Constitution failed its citizens. Mary Tsukamoto, spokesperson for Florin, California, will be part of that exhibit. You will hear her voice when you view a collection of artifacts from the strawberry and grape growing farms that once covered the countryside in south Sacramento County.

When did our lives come together—this intense little lady whose mission overcomes everything that stands in its path—and I, who just happened to be in Florin and Elk Grove at the right time to help save some pieces of their history from oblivion?

I came to Samuel Kennedy School one evening in 1963 to attend a university extension class, and that's when I first met her. She was still there, correcting her papers after a long day, and fixing up her classroom so that the children would find it exciting and motivational. Some time later, I heard that she had tuberculosis and had to go to a sanatorium. We didn't meet again until 1970 when I sent a student to interview her for an oral history project. I listened to Bonnie's tape over and over again and then went to see her. This was really the beginning of our friendship and association. I found the story of internment simply incredible. No history class of mine had even hinted at this chapter of our country's past.

As I listened to Mary, I remembered Tom Nakashima who had been in my seventh grade class when I first came to Elk Grove. We had been studying about immigration, and someone mentioned how there had been many Japanese families in Florin and Elk Grove before the war. Most students didn't know anything about the internment, nor did I, but a few including Tom seemed to know quite a bit. I was surprised that I knew so little about this part of American history but I was even more surprised the next morning when one of my students approached me with a message from her parents. "They don't think you should be talking about the Japanese in class," she reported. "It will only cause problems."

I was so stunned at her comments that I didn't even ask her what they meant. Instinctively, I knew that this was a topic that needed to

2

be handled carefully. There was an intensity in her eyes that warned me, and I realized that she too was caught up in the middle of something she did not understand. I backed off, but working with Mary for these many months, was like starting again where I had left off in 1962. There was an obligation to set the story straight, to present the facts as they appeared to be, and let each one judge for himself.

The question lingers though—where does the community stand? Is there anyone left who cares? The answer is yes, both in Elk Grove and Florin and in the many, many communities across California, the story is the same. There are many who care, but there has been very little discussion on the topic since 1945.

As Japanese American families drifted back to their old homes the few who did only wanted to put the past behind them, forget what had happened, and start to live all over again. That's what was needed for the healing to begin, but a collective guilt settled down upon those who were taken away and those who quietly stood aside and let it happen.

There was little anyone *could* have done. The President had signed the order, and the U.S. Army took them away, but in hundreds of homes there was confusion about what was taking place and conflicting loyalties about how to act and what to say. A high school student at the time explained, "I cried for nights when my best friend left. My mother wouldn't even let me write to her because we were afraid of the FBI. Everyone was scared to death."

Those who were supportive of the plight of the internees rarely made their views known openly for to do so was to invite nighttime visitors up to no good. "Everyone knew where we stood," a rancher told me. "One night a car came up our lane and left a crudely lettered sign saying 'Jap Lover.' We were scared, but my dad knew he was right."

I listened to another viewpoint: "Everyone suffered during the war. They weren't the only ones. Every serviceman went through the same thing." True. But how many soldiers went to camp with their wives, babies, teenagers and old parents? How might it have been to endure the indignities of camp life not only for one's self but for one's loved ones as well?

Another opinion: "They had to be taken away for their own protection. And some of them really were spies." In the face of mountains of facts, these words run counter to constitutional rights. In 1987 we recognize lack of due process and what was a gross violation of civil rights. Treatment of alien parents is one story (and it is true that some Italians and Germans had their movements restricted and some even were interned for a time), but the other story is the treatment of citizens. The native born children of immigrants, the Nisei, were citizens—nearly two thirds of the internees! It is this issue that disturbs scholars of the Constitution. What indeed is to prevent a similar situation with some other group if this wrong is not corrected?

The truth, they say, will always prevail, and that is the foundation of this book. Mary and I opened trunks that had not seen the light of day since the Tsukamotos came home from camp in 1945. Inside were journals, letters, diaries, and an incredible variety of materials to refresh fading memories. Some of these will be in the Smithsonian exhibit in Washington, D.C. It is amazing how the "junk" of yesterday becomes today's historical treasure, and how fortunate that Al and Mary never succumbed to the temptation to throw it all out, as so many of us are inclined to do with stuff that piles up.

As we approach the ending of this writing venture, it is Mary's wish and mine that children in our schools will always be taught the truth about what happened in America, not just about the internment, but all parts of our history. Children need to know how their lives and their future will be affected by our past. When hundreds of children walk through the Week of Remembrance exhibit sponsored by Elk Grove Unified School District and listen to Mary tell about internment, I can't help but think about my seventh graders of so long ago. Your son, Tom Nakashima, is finding a different world in his classroom than you did 25 years ago, and that is why America is so great.

Elizabeth Pinkerton
July 27, 1987

INTRODUCTION—
Congressman Robert Matsui

1942 was a dark year for Japanese Americans. The bombing of Pearl Harbor had catapulted the United States into war with Japan and created an atmosphere of wartime hysteria that was sweeping the nation. Suspicion and paranoia greeted Japanese Americans at every turn, and before the year was over, the U.S. Government had ordered the evacuation of thousands of Japanese Americans to armed detention camps.

It was an incident that fractured the lives of thousands of American citizens. But surprisingly, during the war years and decades later, the internment of Japanese Americans remained a largely untold chapter in American history. Like the atomic bombing of Japan it was an incident that Americans had accepted but were anxious to forget.

Then, in 1980, President Jimmy Carter, House Speaker Thomas P. "Tip" O'Neill, and Senate Majority Leader Howard Baker appointed the Congressional Commission on Wartime Relocation and Internment of Civilians to reopen the history books. It was this Congressional Commission that reported for the first time the fateful chain of events that led to the detention of over 120,000 Japanese Americans.

During World War II, the Government had claimed that the internment was a necessity of war, and that claim was even upheld by the U.S. Supreme Court. But documents unearthed by the Commission clearly acknowledged that there was no military necessity for the mass detention of Japanese Americans. No such detentions were conducted against German or Italian Americans—or even against Japanese Americans living in Hawaii, some 3,000 miles closer to the actual fighting.

Japanese Americans were not spies nor agents of Imperial Japan, and they posed no threat to the national security of the United States. They were loyal American citizens who solely because of their

5

ancestry were uprooted from their communities and their homes and imprisoned without trial or jury.

When the Commission on War Relocation issued its report, it brought to light documents and details about the internment that had been hidden for years. But the real story of the internment—the story of how thousands of lives and families were shattered under the pretext of protecting the national security of the United States—has never been fully told.

It is in this book, *We the People, A Story of Internment in America,* that the window into the past is finally opened wide. In telling about her personal experiences, Mary Tsukamoto goes beyond the clinical details of the Commission's report to reveal the enormity of a tragedy that can only be measured in the dimensions of individual suffering.

In 1942, I lived with my family in Sacramento, California, only minutes from Mary's home in Florin. I was only 10 months old when my family was evacuated to a detention camp at Tule Lake, California, but the experience changed my life and the lives of my family and friends forever. For those of us who lived through the internment, *We the People* brings back painful memories. Mary Tsukamoto and Elizabeth Pinkerton recount the images and emotions from those years more powerfully and more eloquently than any congressional commission ever could.

We the People paints a vivid picture of the internment as a story of betrayal. It is a story of how the U.S. Government betrayed its own citizens—and the very foundations of our constitutional government in the process. It is a story of how the U.S. Government, in depriving Japanese Americans of their liberty and freedom, violated the most fundamental rights under our Constitution.

But in the end, it is also a story of the courage and religious conviction of Japanese Americans. Although families were separated and dreams were shattered, it was their courage and strength that enabled Japanese Americans to withstand the shame of being labeled traitors to and by their own country. For thousands of Japanese Americans, it was their religious convictions that steered them through the nightmare of the internment.

Some of the American soldiers cried as they evacuated Japanese Americans from their homes, and I think that they were expressing a sentiment at the time that was indicative of the moral strength of the American people. Many Americans knew from the beginning that the internment was wrong, and as individuals they tried to keep the nation's moral compass rooted firmly in a sense of what was right.

To this day, the U.S. Government has yet to atone for the internment and has opposed efforts to provide redress to Japanese Americans both in Congress and in the courts. But as more and more Americans begin to understand the tragic dimensions of the internment, perhaps the American people themselves can balm the wounds that still have not healed from so long ago.

ROBERT T. MATSUI
Member of Congress

MAYOR ANNE RUDIN—
City of Sacramento

We The People is a moving portrayal of a piece of American history that we ignored for too long. Written without rancor or vengefulness by one who had reason to be much less forgiving, it is a story of the hopefulness and faith of which the noblest human spirit is capable.

It is a story of personal sacrifice, beginning with Pearl Harbor and Executive Order 9066, and concluding with current efforts to obtain redress of grievances for Japanese Americans. Throughout, it is a sad reminder that constitutional government may be set aside and constitutional protections abridged, when we transfer our feelings of hatred of the enemy to symbols of the enemy. Under the pressures of war, reasonable people do unreasonable things, undermining traditional values of freedom and democracy.

We know the costs of war in lives lost; we know the costs of war in dollars and property wasted. This story brings to our attention the costs of war in our loss of humanity. But, if it shows the depths to which humanity can plunge, it also shows the heights to which it can ascend, as old friends stood loyally and unselfishly by their Issei and

Nisei neighbors, caring for their property and belongings during their long internment, without fear of consequences to themselves.

We learn of the remarkable courage of those in the camps who had given up everything for which they had spent their lives; who filled the dreary days with meaningful pursuits for survival of body and spirit. In addition to dealing with their own physical maintenance, the internees developed and maintained a social structure that kept alive the traditions that characterized their lives and culture.

Those Californians of Japanese ancestry never gave up hope. Mary Tsukamoto's own innately positive outlook shines through, reminding us of something Camus once said: "In the midst of winter, I finally learned that there was in me an invincible summer."

It is a strong statement that we must all work to preserve the peace in order to preserve democracy.

ANNE RUDIN
Mayor of Sacramento

DR. HAROLD LANGLEY—
Curator, Smithsonian Institution

This is the story of a great national tragedy as seen through the eyes of a woman of Japanese ancestry. For most of her early life, Mary Tsukamoto's world was centered around the family's strawberry farm in Florin, near Sacramento, California. It was hard, physically demanding work, but Mary's family was confident that their situation would improve.

The tranquility and order of the Florin community were shattered in the weeks that followed the Japanese attack on Pearl Harbor and America's entry into World War II. Suddenly the Japanese Americans were identified as the "enemy" in the eyes of the Caucasian majority. In California there had long been an anti-Asian attitude that had led to the passage of the alien land laws and segregated schooling arrangements earlier in the 20th century. Now old prejudices were reenforced by new suspicions of treachery, based on

8

misinformation.

The hatred and fear of the majority made no allowances for age, education, sex, health, political motivations, financial conditions, or the absence of evidence of disloyalty and sabotage on the part of the Japanese minority. All were under suspicion, and all were to be removed from their homes and businesses on the West Coast and placed in special camps in remote inland areas. Furthermore, they would be allowed to take only what they could carry with them.

News of the relocation order came as a tremendous shock to Mary and Al Tsukamoto. How could this happen in America, a nation governed by the Constitution, a nation that has respect for the rights of the individual? Where were the voices of dissent? Why was there no outcry from churches, civic organizations, college and university spokesmen, or from leaders of the land?

Surely this outrageous order could not stand the test of judicial review!

But the order remained, and it was implemented. The Tsukamoto family, along with all their relatives, neighbors and friends joined hundreds of other Japanese Americans in hastily built internment camps in isolated inland regions in America. Many adjustments had to be made - adjustments to basic needs for survival such as shelter, food, and clothing, as well as adjustments to climate, social organization, and the total lack of privacy. As irritating as all these were, the most debilitating thought of all was that there was no rational reason for such suffering. People of all ages were being punished without any proof of guilt and without any trials. Even after the possibility of a Japanese invasion of the mainland of the United States faded, the internment continued.

Although deeply humiliated, the Tsukamotos modified their living conditions and began working to improve the schools and day-to-day activities. For Mary the months in camp were a time of testing her belief in the Constitution and the American way of life as well as her faith in God. Day by day she drew strength from the words and example of others. For the sake of her daughter, husband, and family, she projected a happy and optimistic exterior; duty and habit gave her the added stamina to overcome the hardships and disappointments they faced. Mary emerged from the ordeal a deeper and more sensitive person.

As the war against Japan progressed, and eventually victory became more apparent, restrictions against the Japanese Americans were gradually lifted. The Tsukamoto family moved to Kalamazoo, Michigan and worked in a bakery. In this pleasant environment they made new friends and strengthened their feelings of self worth.

When the Pacific War was ended, Japanese Americans were allowed to return to their homes in California. The Tsukamotos returned to Florin. Blessed with good friends and neighbors who had looked after their property, their return was welcomed. Adversity had made them strong, and when they found that the days of raising strawberries and grapes were gone, both Mary and Al turned to other ways of making a living. Mary became a public school teacher, working in her own classroom with children of many nationalities and cultural backgrounds. She watched her daughter grow into a fine young woman and go off to college, and when Marielle went to Japan to teach, Mary and Al had the opportunity to visit the land of their grandparents.

As Mary grew older, she reflected more and more upon the wrongs that her family and other Japanese Americans had suffered. She began to participate in the effort to make the U.S. government acknowledge that it had done a great wrong when it forced Japanese Americans into the relocation camps. Many years have gone into the redress effort, but the goal has not yet been achieved. Mary Tsukamoto will continue the struggle as long as she has the strength.

Readers of this volume will come to know a remarkable woman. She is cast in the heroic mold that we normally associate with our pioneering ancestors. Here is a citizen whose faith in and love of her country have been tested in the fires of adversity and are unbreakable. Her story has a special meaning today as Americans of all ages and classes struggle to define their values, their priorities, and their futures.

Harold D. Langley, Ph.D.
Curator
National Museum of American History
Smithsonian Institution

10

FOR GREATER UNDERSTANDING . . .

Commission on Wartime Relocation and Internment of Civilians
Congressional commission that investigated the World War II actions of the United States government following Executive Order 9066. President Jimmy Carter signed the bill that established the commission in 1980. The commission concluded its investigation in 1983.

Executive Order 9066
This order was signed by President Franklin Delano Roosevelt on February 19, 1942. It gave the U.S. Army unprecedented powers over civilians and allowed the removal of all persons of Japanese ancestry who lived on the west coast of the United States and their placement in internment camps during World War II. President Gerald Ford rescinded the order on February 19, 1976.

Internment Camps
There were ten camps established for the purpose of containing the Japanese Americans who were evacuated from their West Coast homes in 1942. The camps were in Tule Lake and Manzanar, California; Gila and Poston, Arizona; Topaz, Utah; Heart Mountain, Wyoming; Granada, Colorado; Jerome and Rohwer, Arkansas; and Minidoka, Idaho. The camps were open from 1942 until 1946.

Issei, Nisei, Sansei, and Yonsei
These are the terms used to refer to each generation of Japanese Americans. The Issei were the first, the immigrants. Their children are known as Nisei or second generaton. The third generation are the Sansei and the fourth are Yonsei.

JACL
The Japanese American Citizens League, organized in 1930, is a nationally known cultural heritage organization that works to foster "Better Americans in a Greater America."

Ojiisan, Obaasan

These are respectful terms used within a family for the grandfather and grandmother. They are translated literally as "old man" and "old woman." With the substitution of "chan" for "san," a special feeling of endearment is added to the name similar to dear grandpa or dear grandma (Ojiichan, Obaachan).

Redress

The U.S. Constitution, Amendment I, allows citizens the right of redress if they have a grievance or complaint. Japanese Americans are seeking redress for the wrongs committed against them by the U.S. government during World War II.

Wartime Civil Control Administration (WCCA)

This group supervised the evacuation of the Japanese Americans in 1942 from their homes to temporary assembly centers. Its director was Major Karl Bendetson of the U.S. Army.

War Relocation Authority (WRA)

This agency was created by President Roosevelt to assist persons who were being interned at relocation centers. Its first head was Milton S. Eisenhower.

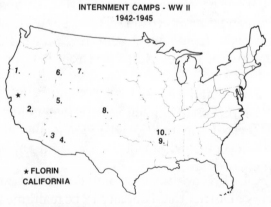

INTERNMENT CAMPS - WW II
1942-1945

★ FLORIN
CALIFORNIA

1. Tule Lake, California
2. Manzanar, California
3. Poston, Arizona
4. Gila, Arizona
5. Topaz, Utah
6. Minidoka, Idaho

7. Heart Mountain, Wyoming
8. Granada, Colorado
9. Jerome, Arkansas
10. Rohwer, Arkansas

12

Elk Grove Unified School District
BOARD COMMUNICATION

From the Office of the Superintendent   Date <u>February 17, 1987</u>

To The Board of Education   BC No. _____

Regarding: <u>Day of Remembrance</u>

Prepared By: <u>Anna T. Kato</u>

WHEREAS, on February 19, 1942, President Franklin D. Roosevelt signed Executive Order 9066, allowing the incarceration of 120,000 people of Japanese ancestry during World War II; and

WHEREAS, this incarceration was carried out without charge or trial was not an isolated incident but the culmination of decades of discrimination on the West Coast; and

WHEREAS, this tragic event in our History must be remembered as a lesson on how racism, economic and political exploitation and expediency can undermine the constitutional and human rights of both citizens and aliens alike; and

WHEREAS, there is a need to ensure that young people are provided factual information about events such as the incarceration of people of Japanese ancestry in order that they can be prepared to make judgments and decisions in the future that are free of bias; show an understanding of the needs for due process; and exhibit an awareness of the constitutional and human rights of all people;

BE IT RESOLVED by the Governing Board of the Elk Grove Unified School District that February 19 be reaffirmed a "Day of Remembrance" with March 14 designated a day for teacher inservice education and March 23 through 27 designated days for a commemorative exhibition open to the public.

Long Ago

in the ancient country of Japan,
there was a wise man who found the essence of life
heralded in the natural world around him.

His philosophy has been translated in the term
Sho-Chiku-Bai:
the plum blossom, the bamboo and the pine.

These are the elements of nature that
represent the most valued
qualities of life.

They
are the
ultimate expression
of harmony
and
maturation
from
youth to adulthood,
and
from
adulthood
to
old age.

The Years of the Plum

Childhood

The Pre-War Years

The delicate flower of early spring
dares to bloom in harsh weather.
Its exquisite beauty breaks forth
in the springtime
as it struggles
bravely and innocently
to understand
the mysteries of life .

Chapter 1

Pearl Harbor

"Christmas brings us hope, but where is that hope tonight?"

It was Sunday morning as the last ringing chords of "Joy to the World" echoed through our little Florin church. The Christmas lights twinkled merrily in anticipation of the joyful season about to come. I looked around at the faces of my family and friends, and a sense of inner peace came over me.

"Surely this must have been the heavenly music that was heard in Bethlehem when Christ was born," I thought.

The church door was suddenly flung open and Al rushed in. I had never seen my husband so frightened and shocked. What was he doing here? Why was he interrupting our church services? "Pearl Harbor has been bombed," I heard him shout. "I just heard it on the radio. We are at war with Japan." We sat in stunned silence not knowing how to comprehend this strange message. Joy to the world was forgotten as we sat and looked at one another fearing the worst, but not knowing what to fear. The news of the bombing extinguished the light from our lives. Never was the world so dark as on that Sunday morning of December 7, 1941.

No one spoke as we sat there afraid to move, too frightened to leave our little sanctuary, fearful of what might greet us outside the doors of our little church. All the faces inside were Japanese; fear had already leaped into our hearts. The four walls of our tiny church sheltered us from the rest of the world and from the rest of Florin, California, but the refuge would not be for long.

America, our country, was at war with Japan, the country of our

16

ancestors and parents. Al and I were American citizens (as were all who had been born in the U. S.), but still we feared—for ourselves as well as for our parents who had not been able to become citizens because of discriminating laws. What would happen to them? What would happen to us?

One by one, each family ventured out and went home. We huddled in our houses all day listening to every word of the radio broadcasts. "Japs bomb Pearl Harbor." "American ships have been sunk." Each word rang in my ears and etched itself onto my soul.

In our little farming community of Florin, California, as in other towns and villages all over California, FBI agents, armed with the lists of their suspects, acted swiftly on that December Sunday. Thinking our elderly parents to be enemy agents, they pounded on doors, arrested fathers and grandfathers and took them away. By late afternoon, fearful rumors ran through Florin like water from a broken dam.

When evening came, we returned to church just as we did each Sunday, but this was no ordinary Sunday evening in this church filled with Japanese faces. Our new youth minister, Reverend James Sasaki, comforted us with soothing words and tried to calm our fears. In the crowded church we wept and prayed together. As I worshipped, I tried to understand the impact of this day. I sensed the despair and fear shared by all of us who were Japanese, but I wondered what effect this tragic bombing had upon our Caucasian neighbors here in Florin and in all of California.

Suddenly, Reverend Sasaki surprised us by turning out all the lights in the church. He spoke softly of the time when angels first sang of the Holy Child's birth and told us how people of that time had been in great despair. He explained how mankind had been ravaged all through the ages by sorrow, slavery, poverty, war, and desolation, and how always there had been great suffering. "But always," he said, "there were some whose vision and faith kept the light of Christ burning—no matter how great the obstacles placed before them; no matter how dark the world had become."

Dramatically, our pastor brought before us the darkness of the world on that tragic day. Through the shadows of the church, we saw our brave minister light one little candle, and we saw indeed how the

17

light seemed to push the night away. We were struck with awe and wonderment. We realized that all the darkness of the world indeed could not blot out the light of one candle.

Reverend Sasaki's quiet, courageous words, filled with faith, brought us calm. "Christmas brings us that hope. We who have met here and touched the light of Christ must keep the radiant light of hope shining through our attitudes, our actions, and our lives. We must be the source of strength to others who may be shattered by what may come to us. We must be strong because we live in America at this time and because we have Japanese faces."

Over and over again in the days that followed, when I felt there was nowhere to turn, I heard Reverend Sasaki's words. I heard them when I was frightened to death of tomorrow, when I felt as if I were dangling in mid-air not able to touch the ground and when I did not know what would happen to me or why. When I was afraid or humiliated because of my Japanese face, I said the wondrous words to myself. They reminded me to have faith, to believe and to endure, and eventually, I began to believe that I could be the candle that pushed back the darkness. I convinced myself that my fears were groundless. Life would go on, and we would do what we could for the war effort because our country needed us. I was ready for whatever sacrifice my country demanded.

As I think back upon this still vivid scene drawn from my memories of 45 years ago, I realize how naive I was, and how naive I continued to be throughout the years that followed. I experienced leaving my home, the relocation, internment, and living as a refugee in a strange city. I returned finally, frightened and bewildered, to my home. Perhaps I am still naive to think that my story would be of interest to anyone else, but I am compelled as a citizen of this great and wonderful country to place into the record of the history of America the experiences of one individual through most of the 20th century. My life it seems has been shaped by world and national events, many of which I knew little until years later when I delved into the history of America and the political forces before, during, and after World War II. On that Sunday evening, however, in December of 1941, I knew nothing—only that my country was at war with Japan, and I was more frightened than I had ever been in my life.

Mary's Journal

Chapter 2

Executive Order 9066

"Each day brings new rumors of what will happen to us. I fear for all of us—elderly Issei parents and all the rest of us who are American citizens by virtue of our births."

The morning after Pearl Harbor, Al and I found out that many prominent men, leaders of our Florin community, had been arrested during the night. FBI agents had suddenly appeared at their doors and taken them away, leaving their families behind closed doors with their sorrow. The men they took were respected business and community leaders, grandfatherly figures, active in Florin's strawberry and grape industry and involved with social and service activities. Surely they had done no wrong, but we were amazed how they had been taken so quickly and without anyone knowing why. Their families did not know where they had been taken or if they would ever be back. They feared the worst—that their loved ones had been imprisoned and would be executed.

Al told me about one of our neighbors, a long-time farmer, just beginning to recover from his Depression losses.

"Mary, he was terribly scared by the arrests and rumors, and he was recovering from a stroke. When the FBI came and quizzed him to make him tell about other people, he was not able to speak English well, and he was so afraid that he had implicated others that he hung himself to spare his family grief and shame."

Shock waves reverberated throughout our Florin community. We sensed that this would not be the only death resulting from this tragic time.

Fear permeated our humble homes as each day's rumors added fuel to the fires of anxiety and terror. We heard that agents were searching through personal belongings looking for contraband. Frantically, we tore through the possessions of Al's parents, looking desperately for anything that might arouse suspicion of being pro-Japan. In a backyard bonfire, we burned all of Grandpa's books, photographs, newspapers, certificates and anything that had connections to Japan. Precious family records of historical value went up in the smoke of family fires in Florin's back yards. A frenzy of fear had enveloped us all.

We became more and more frightened as we read in our daily newspaper what people thought of us. Columnists like Henry McLemore demanded our removal from our homes:

"I am for the immediate removal of every Japanese on the West Coast to a point deep in the interior...Let 'em be pinched, hurt, hungry and dead up against it... Let us have no patience with anyone whose veins carry his blood. Personally, I hate the Japanese and that goes for all of them..

(*Sacramento Union, January 30, 1942*)

The attitude that "a Jap is always a Jap" set the stage. President Franklin Delano Roosevelt acted on February 19 by signing Executive Order 9066. This greatly added to the time of terror and trauma for American citizens of Japanese ancestry. It was the spark that ignited a serious constitutional error for the United States of America by allowing us to be taken from our homes and locked up in prison camps.

The President through Executive Order 9066 gave unprecedented powers to the Secretary of War. The hate mongers in the nation and state were supported by the President's action, and what we had feared most became a reality. Newspapers kept up the barrage of anti-Japanese rhetoric, deeply rooted in the alien land laws and the exclusion legislation. "JAPS MUST GO" signs began to appear all over California and Sacramento County. We knew it was just a matter of time before the racists would have their way.* We wanted so badly to believe in America—to believe that our country would not bow to the pressures for our removal or internment. Al and I wanted to be needed, not cast off like excess baggage. We wanted to help win the war, but we had no idea of the sacrifice our country would extract from us before it was over.

By the end of March, the Florin JACL (Japanese American Citizens League) of which I had been hastily appointed as emergency executive secretary, took charge of urgent tasks related to the impending evacuation. We worked frantically with the U.S. Army, the WCCA (Wartime Civil Control Administration), the Federal Reserve Bank, Farm Security Agency and social welfare workers to coordinate the needs of Florin evacuees.

Everything happened so fast it was hard to keep track of each new development and the many problems involved with suddenly relocating so many people. There were 2500 men, women and children in the Florin-Elk Grove area designated for evacuation. In the town of Florin, more than two-thirds of its people, all those of Japanese ancestry, prepared to leave in the spring of 1942.

Public Law 77-503, passed by Congress in March, made it a criminal offense to violate military restrictions, so we didn't dare not do what we were told. We were placed under the direct orders of the U. S. Army for evacuation, and we did everything they told us to do. We heard about the residents of Terminal Island and how they were evicted with only 24 hours notice to pack up and leave. Fear was our daily companion as we walked around our Florin farms and wondered what would be our fate.

A nighttime curfew was established by General DeWitt, commander of the 3rd Army Division. We had to be in our homes by 8:00 p.m. Travel was restricted to a five mile radius. In a rural area like Florin this meant that we couldn't even go to Sacramento to a doctor unless we had a special permit. Even more confusing was the fact that we had to go to Sacramento to get the permit. Our precious freedoms were being taken away, and we hardly noticed it at all. There was no

---

* Even though there were Caucasians who disagreed with what took place, it was dangerous for them to speak out. Many years later, I found out about the risks taken by a handful of our white neighbors in Florin and Elk Grove.

time to worry about freedom. Our immediate concerns focused upon what was going to happen to us on a day to day basis rather than the daily loss of our personal liberties and their long range status.

In our little farming communities of south Sacramento County, all Japanese American families went about the task of preparing for evacuation. Many of these communities would never exist again— Mayhew, Taishoku, Walsh Station, and California Vineyard. Others such as Pleasant Grove, Sierra Enterprise, Sloughhouse, Elk Grove, Florin and Perkins would never be the same. Amazingly, we lifted no voices in protest. As good citizens, we felt it was our duty to cooperate in this hour of need. Our President himself had signed the order; we had no choice other than to obey. None of us considered doing anything less.

Many of us worked devotedly with our local Red Cross chapter rolling bandages and doing our utmost for the war effort. Some of our soldier sons, caught in the midst of governmental confusion over their status, were sent home to join their families and work in the fields with them as they prepared to leave. They were discharged and re-classified 4C, "enemy aliens ineligible for service," a strange interpretation by military bureaucracy. The visibility of these boys and others who came on furlough to help their families pack, added to the perplexity of our confusing situation. The sight of a young man in the uniform of our country helping his aged mother pick the last berries before being sent away to camp was hard to explain to anyone.

In a way, we found it hard to believe that we would actually be forced to leave. Nor could we anticipate what lay ahead of us. Our destination was referred to as "camp," so many of us interpreted that to mean that we would be going off to the mountains somewhere. We bought boots to protect us from snakes, a real fear!

I gathered clothing, toilet articles, utensils and packets of food that would help us survive the coming ordeal. I packed heavy coats and blankets, not knowing that we would end up in hot Fresno and then in humid Arkansas where we would have other needs. I searched in vain for some type of overalls for the women of my family, Grandma, Nami and Marielle. I was determined that my family would survive this evacuation no matter what it turned out to be.

One day we found out from Harry French, the acting sheriff of

Florin, that any cameras in our possession had to be registered. Al took his old camera and turned it in. They made him think he would get it back, but somehow, we doubted it would be so. Fortunately, the camera we had then was not of much value, but photographs of our unique journey and the events that followed would have become historical treasures.

My anxiety was compounded by grave concerns for each member of my family. Grandpa (*Ojiisan*), Al's father, was 75 years old; Grandma (*Obaasan*) was 63, a little younger than her pioneering husband. They had struggled for nearly fifty years, toiling in the fields of Florin as they raised strawberries and grapes. Their life goal was to give their children a beginning in their chosen country. How could anyone think these two elderly Issei (immigrants, first generation) could be dangerous enemy aliens? Everywhere, however, their names were marked as "aliens ineligible for citizenship." They would have given anything for the privilege of being American citizens. Ironically, the same laws that denied them citizenship because of their foreign birth also denied them ownership of land because they were not citizens. Their new country, of which they were so proud, must have indeed been perplexing to them at times.

Then there was Nami, Al's quiet, courageous younger sister, so pale and thin. She had been under doctor's care for tuberculosis for three years. I was concerned about her recovery because I knew that several of her friends were buried in our little cemetery. Death was often the sad aftermath of this dread disease. How could I be sure that Nami had the medical care she needed as we began our journey to wherever we were to go?

My greatest concern was for our dependable leader, my handsome husband Al, smiling and warm. He was the one we all looked to for support, guidance, and detailed decisions. Al was our tower of noble strength, our pillar of family stability. Without him, we knew we could not survive the ordeal ahead. We looked to Al with gratitude as each new order came our way and decisions had to be made.

Not long after Pearl Harbor turned our little world into darkness, I panicked one night as Al whispered to me, "Mary, I'm bleeding. I've been coughing up blood."

We hurried the next day to see Dr. Ito, quietly guarding this secret

24

from our family. How fortunate that Dr. Ito was only three miles from us or we would not have been able to see him due to travel restrictions. Al was ordered to bed for rest. Worry, anxiety and physical strain had broken old scars of pleurisy which had nearly cost him his life when he was twelve. I wondered if the rigors of the coming months would be more than he could endure.

In addition to my cares for each of my loved ones, I harbored the longings of a young mother. God had given us a precious gift, a beautiful daughter. Marielle was not yet five years old and the joy of our lives. How difficult it was to face such a blinding move into an insecure future just as my child was ready to go off to school and begin her important education. I found myself controlled by fear, my anxious prayers were unceasing, and my inner source of strength sorely tested with each new wave of fear and uncertainty.

In the midst of tending to property arrangements, storing, selling and packing of belongings, I discovered that we were going to be separated from our friends and neighbors. Our little farming community of Florin was designated for division into four groups for our mass removal. It was a shocking development that none of us had anticipated, and the news reached us just a few days before our departure. Military orders showed four separate and distinct groups divided by the railroad tracks and Florin Road. Each group had a different destination. New fears were suddenly thrust into our hearts. Was it by design that families and friends faced never seeing one another again—an elaborate scheme to keep us separate? Or was it the first of what were to be many decisions from high authorities that were irrational, illogical, or lacking of common sense?

Soldiers came one day and tacked our orders onto telephone poles. They quickly went about their task not knowing the great turmoil they left in their wake.

As JACL Executive Secretary, I unexpectedly found myself the victim of vicious accusations by people in the community who were being evacuated. I was accused of plotting to take all my relatives with me to Fresno. Of course it was not true for I had no such influence, but distraught people could not understand what was happening to them, so they reached for answers even when there were none to find.

There was no way to avoid splitting up families for when the 500 places allocated for each group were gone, the next places were assigned to the next group. These were the mechanics of evacuation that did not take into account our suffering as individual human beings.

There were many who were in need of special considerations, and I wondered what would become of them. Mr. Fujii had to be hospitalized the day before his departure because of an attack of bleeding ulcers. His family was assured that he would join them when he recovered, but we worried if he ever would.

I will always remember Mrs. Kurima. She had to leave behind her eldest child, Toyoki, whom she had lovingly cared for since his birth 32 years ago. Toyoki was never able to attend school, for he needed the special care of an infant. Mrs. Kurima bravely cared for him on their strawberry farm, fed him and loved him as only a mother could. When the WCCA ruled that Toyoki could not be taken, it became my sad duty to tell the tired Issei that her son would be sent to an institution. I wept as I spoke but she continued to hoe her strawberries, not able to acknowledge the pain my words conveyed to her. I felt a part of me shrink away as I absorbed the sorrow of this fine mother of five sons who now had to part abruptly with the child who needed her the most. What, I wondered, would become of this manchild who had never been away from his family, who could eat only Japanese food, and who understood only the Japanese words of his loved ones? I embraced Mrs. Kurima, and together we wept bitter tears in the strawberry fields of Florin.*

The WCCA officials of the evacuation knew nothing of the extended Japanese family unit. Nor did they know of the bonds of friendship established by people from the same village or prefecture of Japan, as close as blood with immigrant people who had left their families far, far across the ocean. Separation from some friends could be endured, but not so the sundering of village friends and close neighbors—nor parents from their married children and brothers

---

*Several weeks later, after we were settled into our new life in barracks and stables at the Fresno fairgrounds, we received the message of Toyoki's death. Forty-five years later, tears still come to my eyes and my heart still grieves when I think of the anguish of Mrs. Kurima.

from their sisters.

In our hectic, last days, Al's sister Edith and her family, trying to keep their family together, had far more to do than there were hours left to do it in. Edith was bookkeeper for her husband's company, Northern California Farms. Harold Ouchida and his partner had agreed to pay farmers for every crate of strawberries brought to them even though they had outstanding loans. On the last day before we were to leave, Edith worked until midnight doing her books and writing checks to keep the accounts accurate. Exhausted and numb from the day's frantic pace, she finally went home to get her family of five and Grandpa Ouchida ready for the next day's departure. The Fujii family of eight from across the tracks had moved in with them. Sleeping children filled the living room. How she managed to pack clothes and bedding and report to the train station the next morning, I will never know. Mary McComber, a friend of Edith's, cleaned up her house and mailed packages to her until the family had what they needed to survive. Edith, my sister-in-law, was the sainted heroine of our departure.

Our 35 acre farm was placed in the dependable hands of Bob Fletcher. Al's hard working, caring friend agreed to run our farm along with that of two adjoining ones, those of Al's cousin and a neighbor. Bob had the proper papers drawn up to make the arrangement legal. He insisted that the profit would be shared equally with the absent owners for as long as they would be gone. No other farms in Florin had such a good business agreement. I have always cherished finding Bob Fletcher in our time of need.

Some families had only brief hours before they had to leave. The Otake family planned to spend their last day picking berries. As they sat around the table trying to enjoy the last hasty meal they would have together as a free family, a military patrol car drove into the yard.

"The orders have changed," reported the M. P. who came to the door. "You are to report to Elk Grove today. You are going to Manzanar. Please hurry."

The Otakes had planned to stay up all night to pack and clean so their house would be left in good order. Now they had only two hours to get ready to leave. Food was left partly eaten and the dishes unwashed as they hurried to get things together. In anger and bitterness they left with no time to say good-bye to anyone.

Our orders told us to be at the Elk Grove train station by 9:00 a.m. on Friday, May 29, 1942. Our family number was #22076. Each one of us had a letter along with the number. We wore these on our clothes and also marked them on our baggage. Our destination, at least temporarily, was Fresno, about 150 miles south of Florin in the San Joaquin Valley. We were relieved to know where we were going, but still we went through the last days on edge never knowing when new orders would place new obstacles in our lives.

The first groups left Florin hurriedly early in the week. I went to see them off. Those who lived west of the tracks and south of Florin Road waited anxiously in the parking lot of the train station. Busses were there to take them to Arboga near Marysville. Later they were to go to Tule Lake in northern California. I ran frantically through the large, sad crowd, speaking to as many as I could.

"Goodbye, goodbye."

"Peace be with you until we meet again."

"God bless you all."

My words seemed so inadequate. What was there to say to these friends, grown so dear in our little farming community?

Together we had survived the poverty of the worst Depression years. We had shared our anguish over continuing racial tensions. And now, we faced this great separation, so devastating to us because we were bound by unique cultural bonds that made us one.

I watched the severing of the ties established over time in our church family, and I realized that the carefree days of joyous weddings and births were gone. As each dear person stepped sadly onto the bus, I cried until my eyes were swollen. It was so hard to let them go.

Who was to blame for this seemingly unnecessary division of loved ones? Trusting in my government, the United States of America, I sincerely believed there was no intent to hurt any of us. As unpleasant as the evacuation task was, Al and I were convinced that it had to be done. As JACL secretary, my job had been to relay messages from WCCA to families telling them they would not be separated. Now here were orders that were leading to inhumane treatment of sensitive people. I felt personally responsible for the pain and heart-ache I saw around me. How was I to know that the government would not do what they said?

How could we say goodbye to the Kushis? Tommy's father was Grandpa's nephew and Al's cousin. Grandpa was the one who had encouraged the Kushis to come to Florin from Hiroshima; now they were on their way up north somewhere, and we might never see them again. How could we tell Al's parents of this heart-breaking situation? Everything I wanted to say choked up inside of me.

We pained even more for the 50 Nisei (second generation) soldiers from our Florin area who served in the U.S. Army at our time of crisis. A few who had been discharged to go home were even more confused than the rest of us because they had been humiliated and treated as aliens even though they were proud American citizens in the U.S. Army.

Quick sales had taken care of much of the evacuees' property. We had to be satisfied with whatever we could get. A few of us had trusted Caucasian friends to care for our land and belongings. Most, however, had no one, so in desperation and with time running out, they just boarded things up and walked away.

The majority of Florin's farmers had pulled through the lean years of the 1930s and bound by mortgages, they hoped to be soon free of debt. Some believed the government would confiscate their property and they would lose everything they had worked so hard to get. The Federal Reserve Board, the government's custodian for property, assured them that everything would be kept safe. In all the confusion and mixed-up communication, however, it was hard not to doubt that word.

Wonderful Caucasian friends quietly offered their help in this time of despair. Mary McComber brought over casseroles and cakes to our homes. Roy Learned, our former high school principal, a sensitive and caring person, offered to store our precious wedding gifts, our dining room table and chairs and our piano. Little by little these friends helped us dispose of kitchen items, clothes and furniture. How grateful we were for these gestures of friendship that helped ease our pain and make our tasks lighter.

How grievous to be at war with Japan, the land of our ancestors.

Though we all had family members who had not come to America, and our thoughts were with them from time to time, our only real concerns were for our American families and friends. Together we had survived the bad times. Now it seemed as if the times ahead would be even worse.

NOTICE

Headquarters
Western Defense Command
and Fourth Army

Presidio of San Francisco, California
May 23, 1942

Civilian Exclusion Order No. 92

1. Pursuant to the provisions of Public Proclamations Nos. 1 and 2, this Headquarters, dated March 2, 1942, and March 16, 1942, respectively, it is hereby ordered that from and after 12 o'clock noon, P. W. T., of Saturday, May 30, 1942, all persons of Japanese ancestry, both alien and non-alien, be excluded from that portion of Military Area No. 1 described as follows:

All that portion of the Counties of Sacramento and Amador, State of California, within the boundary beginning at a point at which California State Highway No. 16 intersects California State Highway No. 49, approximately two miles south of Plymouth; thence southerly along said Highway No. 49 to the Amador-Calaveras County Line; thence westerly along the Amador-Calaveras County Line to the Amador-San Joaquin County Line; thence northerly along the Amador-San Joaquin County Line to the Sacramento-San Joaquin County Line; thence westerly along the Sacramento-San Joaquin County Line to the easterly line of the right of way of the main line of the Southern Pacific Railroad from Lodi to Sacramento; thence northerly along said easterly line to its crossing with California State Highway No. 16; thence easterly along said Highway No. 16 to point of beginning.

2. A responsible member of each family, and each individual living alone, in the above described area will report between the hours of 8:00 A. M. and 5:00 P. M., Sunday, May 24, 1942, or during the same hours on Monday, May 25, 1942, to the Civil Control Station located at:

Masonic Hall,
Elk Grove, California.

3. Any person subject to this order who fails to comply with any of its provisions or with the provisions of published instructions pertaining hereto or who is found in the above area after 12 o'clock noon, P. W. T., of Saturday, May 30, 1942, will be liable to the criminal penalties provided by Public Law No. 503, 77th Congress, approved March 21, 1942, entitled "An Act to Provide a Penalty for Violation of Restrictions or Orders with Respect to Persons Entering, Remaining in, Leaving or Committing Any Act in Military Areas or Zones," and alien Japanese will be subject to immediate apprehension and internment.

4. All persons within the bounds of an established Assembly Center pursuant to instructions from this Headquarters are excepted from the provisions of this order while those persons are in such Assembly Center.

J. L. DeWITT
Lieutenant General, U. S. Army
Commanding

31

WESTERN DEFENSE COMMAND AND FOURTH ARMY
WARTIME CIVIL CONTROL ADMINISTRATION

Presidio of San Francisco, California
May 23, 1942

INSTRUCTIONS
TO ALL PERSONS OF
JAPANESE
ANCESTRY

Living in the Following Area:

All that portion of the Counties of Sacramento and Amador, State of California, within the boundary beginning at a point at which California State Highway No. 16 intersects California State Highway No. 49, approximately two miles south of Plymouth; thence southerly along said Highway No. 49 to the Amador-Calaveras County Line; thence westerly along the Amador-Calaveras County Line to the Amador-San Joaquin County Line; thence northerly along the Amador-San Joaquin County Line to the Sacramento-San Joaquin County Line; thence westerly along the Sacramento-San Joaquin County Line to the easterly line of the right of way of the main line of the Southern Pacific Railroad from Lodi to Sacramento; thence northerly along said easterly line to its crossing with California State Highway No. 16; thence easterly along said Highway No. 16 to point of beginning.

Pursuant to the provisions of Civilian Exclusion Order No. 92, this Headquarters, dated May 23, 1942, all persons of Japanese ancestry, both alien and non-alien, will be evacuated from the above area by 12 o'clock noon, P. W. T., Saturday, May 30, 1942.

No Japanese person will be permitted to move into, or out of, the above area after 12 o'clock noon, P. W. T., Saturday, May 23, 1942, without obtaining special permission from the representative of the Commanding General, Northern California Sector, at the Civil Control Station located at:

Masonic Hall,
Elk Grove, California.

Such permits will only be granted for the purpose of uniting members of a family, or in cases of grave emergency.

The Civil Control Station is equipped to assist the Japanese population affected by this evacuation in the following ways:

1. Give advice and instructions on the evacuation.

2. Provide services with respect to the management, leasing, sale, storage or other disposition of most kinds of property, such as real estate, business and professional equipment, household goods, boats, automobiles and livestock.

3. Provide temporary residence elsewhere for all Japanese in family groups.

4. Transport persons and a limited amount of clothing and equipment to their new residence.

The Following Instructions Must Be Observed:

1. A responsible member of each family, preferably the head of the family, or the person in whose name most of the property is held, and each individual living alone, will report to the Civil Control Station to receive further instructions. This must be done between 8:00 A. M. and 5:00 P. M. on Sunday, May 24, 1942, or between 8:00 A. M. and 5:00 P. M. on Monday, May 25, 1942.

2. Evacuees must carry with them on departure for the Assembly Center, the following property:

(a) Bedding and linens (no mattress) for each member of the family;

(b) Toilet articles for each member of the family;

(c) Extra clothing for each member of the family;

(d) Essential personal effects for each member of the family.

All items carried will be securely packaged, tied and plainly marked with the name of the owner and numbered in accordance with instructions obtained at the Civil Control Station. The size and number of packages is limited to that which can be carried by the individual or family group.

3. No pets of any kind will be permitted.

4. No personal items and no household goods will be shipped to the Assembly Center.

5. The United States Government through its agencies will provide for the storage, at the sole risk of the owner, of the more substantial household items, such as iceboxes, washing machines, pianos and other heavy furniture. Cooking utensils and other small items will be accepted for storage if crated, packed and plainly marked with the name and address of the owner. Only one name and address will be used by a given family.

6. Each family, and individual living alone, will be furnished transportation to the Assembly Center. Private means of transportation will not be utilized. All instructions pertaining to the movement will be obtained at the Civil Control Station.

Go to the Civil Control Station between the hours of 8:00 A. M. and 5:00 P. M., Sunday, May 24, 1942, or between the hours of 8:00 A. M. and 5:00 P. M., Monday, May 25, 1942, to receive further instructions.

J. L. DeWITT
Lieutenant General, U. S. Army
Commanding

SEE CIVILIAN EXCLUSION ORDER NO. 92

Chapter 3

May 29, 1942

*"I knew this day would come, but deep inside I wished somehow that
our last night in our little house would never end."*

May was always such a beautiful month in the Sacramento Valley.
The summer heat was yet to come; days were usually bright and clear.
Fields were green from the winter's rain, and flowers bloomed
everywhere. May was also harvest month for Florin's strawberries.
The delicious, but fragile, red berries were ready to be placed in
boxcars and shipped to Seattle, Portland and other major cities. In
May of 1942, however, there were only a few Florin strawberries
shipped to the breakfast tables of America. Florin's berries rotted in
the fields that spring because there was no one to pick them, pack
them, or ship them away. The work force that would have harvested
them was boarding busses and trains for a journey that would take
them far away. For many it was a final farewell to Florin's strawberry
fields.

The day we left is like a crystal memory in time. In the darkness
I heard my husband call to us. It was time to get up even though the
day was yet too early for the sun.

For a sweet fleeting moment, my body tingled with excitement. I
remembered other mornings when I had been awakened in just this
way, when Al had surprised us by transforming ordinary events into
memorable adventures for the Tsukamoto family. That day, though
it would be memorable, was not an ordinary day at all. It was the day
of our departure.

The cold wetness of my pillow shocked me into reality, and my sleepy state was gone in an instant. Suddenly, I realized what was to come as the horror of the day dawned and my heart began to pound like thunder. My body was weak from fright, my throat, dry and sore from yet another night of weeping. Though I had cried deep inside for months, as a mother and responsible member of my family, I dared not let my loved ones know how sick at heart I was. My angry tears came forth only at night when there was no one there to see.

That last night, I heard my husband, usually so brave and strong, sobbing under the blanket in the privacy of the quiet night. How hopeless it was, and how helpless we were! Our only course was to follow the orders of the military.

With only a few hours left, we had much to do before it was time to surrender the last bit of our freedom. Blessed sleep had for a brief moment erased the nightmare in which we were gripped, the nightmare that controlled our destiny and clutched at our very souls. Every person of Japanese ancestry on the west coast of the United States of America, in California, Washington, Oregon, and Arizona in the winter and spring of 1942 was caught up in that torment.

My muffled heart begged to cry out again and again—why? why? why? What have I done? Why is this happening to me? What did I do? What did we do?

I was an American citizen. So were my husband and my tiny daughter. We had broken no law, committed no criminal act. We were law-abiding citizens, farmers, growers of strawberries and grapes. We loved our country and only asked to prove our loyalty if we could but be given the chance.

On this day we were to leave our homes—leave our farm and our lives. No one knew where we were to go nor for how long we would be gone. We were to take only what we could carry and be at the train station at nine or go to prison for crimes we knew nothing of. Our orders were clear and supported by our president; it was our sad duty as residents of California in May of 1942. We were labeled as criminals because our faces were Japanese.

Shocked into reality, I rolled off the mattress and touched the bare floor. I quickly remembered why I had spent this night sleeping on a mattress on the floor. Our furniture was already stored on the second floor of our barn. This morning we had only enough time to put the mattresses away, pack our bedding and eat the last breakfast in our house.

I packed a lunch for us to eat on the train, and we cleaned the house thoroughly from end to end. This ritual of cleaning was important for we could not bear to leave our dear home dirty. This humble place had given us warmth and security, and as we brought back memories of past griefs and joys, our little house was made more dear to us. Here we felt safe; we belonged. We would no more know this feeling.

It was almost time to leave. I swept the kitchen floor for the last time daring not to think about a return. Al mopped up each tiny bit of dust, and each family member did something to tidy up. We all wept silently, reluctant to leave. With this final act, we prayed to God that in His infinite mercy He would bless us to return to Florin and our farm home once again.

In Japanese, Ojiisan spoke the last words. "It is the darkest day of our lives. We are about to lose our treasured liberty. Will we ever see this dear place again?"

Margaret and George Feil, our good friends, came to take us to the train station in Elk Grove, eight miles away. Marielle hugged Uppie, her little dog, and fed him for the last time. Uppie was a perky, white dog with black spots, his tail especially curly as he pranced about the yard. I turned away with a lump in my throat knowing the grief that would tear our little daughter's heart. The orders were firm in regard to pets; Uppie was to be left behind.

"He'll miss us, Mommy," cried Marielle. "And I'll miss him too. He'll feel forsaken here all alone."

"Not as forsaken as we feel," I replied, cheered somewhat by my daughter's compassion and her brave attempt to use adult words. I could not think of any adult words that would explain to her the enormity of this day and what was taking place among us.

The last things were put away. Al loaded the numbered duffel bags into the truck Bob Fletcher brought. There was one bag for each of us, each clearly marked with bright green stripes so we would be able to recognize them easily. On each bag was the military number given to the Tsukamoto family—#22076.

Grandpa stood quietly in the corner of the yard facing his acres of beautiful green grape vines. They were the vines he had planted more than twenty years ago. Beyond him were row upon row of ripe strawberries, ready to be picked.

Grandma was in her garden crying. Lovely flowers bloomed in all their glory in May. Nami and Marielle cried together, and Marielle could not let go of her Uppie. "It's time to go," called Al. "We must not be late. The papers said nine o'clock."

He was right. The stark words from the military posters tacked all over Florin days earlier were vividly imprinted in my mind.

> *No Japanese person will be permitted to move into, or out of, the above area after 12 o'clock noon. . . both alien and non-alien will be evacuated. . . all persons of Japanese ancestry. . . no pets of any kind will be permitted. . . packages limited to that which can be carried by the individual or family group. . .*

Our orders were from the WCCA and the Western Defense Command of the 4th Army. Did we ever consider not obeying? Never. We never questioned it at all. It was our duty, and we had better be there on time.

From the scant information on the posters, we had planned our tentative future and decided what to take with us. Now we were on our way.

We were all gravely silent as we drove away from the Tsukamoto place. We knew it was not polite to weep in the presence of friends. How interesting that age-old Japanese customs controlled our leaving just as they had shaped our lives in bringing us to this tragic situation. Inwardly, we wept as we searched to make sense out of this abrupt departure from everything we loved.

I looked out across the Sacramento Valley, and as I did I caught a view of the magnificent, snow-capped Sierra Nevada Mountains. How often I had looked to the east with joy and faith. Though there was no joy in my heart that day, I looked with faith.

May 29, 1942

Never had the words of the psalmist meant so much to me:
"I will lift up mine eyes unto the hills from whence cometh my help; My help cometh from the Lord who made Heaven and Earth."

With this prayer in my heart, I left Florin enroute to Elk Grove to board a train that would take us on the first part of our long journey into the unknown.

Elk Grove-Florin Road, the seven mile stretch of road between the sister towns of Elk Grove and Florin, was the scene of a strange procession that day. I felt as if I were in a movie theater watching an exodus of a people. But these people were us—families of Japanese ancestry—and we were crowded into the oddest collection of old vehicles I had ever seen. There were huge pick-ups, ancient passenger cars, and trucks loaded to capacity with personal belongings. We joined the strange parade and turned down Main Street. I wanted to laugh, but the sick queasiness in my stomach stopped me. The incredible assortment of vehicles, piled high with colorful suitcases and hand luggage, was like nothing I had ever seen before. Peeking out from among the piles of baggage were the familiar faces of friends and neighbors. They were coming to the station in whatever means of transportation they could manage to find at this late date. Often the new owner of what had been the family car accompanied them, helped them unload and then drove off with his new purchase.

Entire families were on the road—stunned grandparents, some barely able to walk; playful teenagers, more interested in seeing each other than the solemn event taking place; tiny babies and frightened children; and among them all, Nisei parents trying to find order in the confusion of the day.

Everyone was dressed in their Sunday best, men in suits and women in dresses and hats. How strange to see so many wearing coats on such a warm May morning, but with so much to keep track of, it was wiser to wear a coat than to lose it in the crowd.

Children talked excitedly. Most had never been on a train before. Growing up as they had in the age of the automobile, they were thrilled at the prospect of a train ride. Their excitement, however, turned to bewilderment as they saw the old people crying unashamedly as they sat on their suitcases and blankets in the middle of the hubbub. They had been brave before, but now their tears flowed

38

freely, the only semblance of freedom at the station that day.

As each truck and car arrived, many hands helped with unloading. An enormous pile of belongings was being packed into the baggage car. We had been instructed specifically to take only what each of us could carry. I was amazed at the mountain of luggage for the 500 people assigned to our train.

What if the soldiers would not let us take so much? What if they refused to take it all? What would I do? I needed everything I had packed for my family's needs. I had followed the army's instructions to the letter.

It was not my problem, I suddenly realized. My eyes blurred as I gazed at the bizarre drama of people being loaded on the train. It seemed like a dream, but they were all Japanese faces. At that very moment, my consciousness jarred into the harsh realization that we had become evacuees. My tongue turned dry, and I could not speak without choking. We were evacuees, leaving our homes — forever perhaps — and we were prisoners as well. This knowledge rushed through my soul with a jolt. A silent scream echoed through my heart.

Suddenly I noticed the guns! The soldiers were carrying rifles with bayonets as if we were to be shot down if we tried to escape. They were young boys in brisk uniforms, perplexed by what was happening before them. I looked closely at the one nearest to me. He looked just as frightened as I, and there were tears in his eyes too.

Beyond him were the children, with large conspicuous numbers pinned to the front of their clothes. We had all become numbered items for the government file.

In the midst of the crowd, Mrs. Okimoto began to have labor pains and was ordered to the hospital. No one was allowed to go with her, a dismaying realization to her family, wrought with concerns for her well-being and for the child about to be born. There was nothing that could be done, however, for the train was about to leave.

I moved about greeting friends I had known for a long time. I knew not what to say, nor did they, but our collective grief was eased with the knowledge that we were going to the same camp. What a disappointment to hear, "They left for Manzanar two days ago. . ." "She has gone to Walerga . .." "Tule Lake I think." My heart sank a dozen times as I wondered if I would ever see those dear ones again.

There were all sorts of last minute problems in addition to the impending birth. Some were minor, but others could not be ignored as families struggled to find solutions. Expectant mothers, some great with child and exhausted already from the ordeal, were worried and anxious. Elderly parents needed to be made comfortable. Some were ill and had to lie down; special places had to be arranged. Finally, we were ready to go; it was exactly nine o'clock.

Much to our surprise there was a small group of people who had braved criticism to see us off—teachers, neighbors and friends. Some wept openly; others looked confused by what they saw. There was much hugging, but there were few words amidst the mass bewilderment. No one knew what to say in a situation like this.

Just as we were ready to board, Edith's children ran up to us shouting, "Sonny's got the chicken pox."

"Mom says to tell you we can't ride with you."

Sure enough, Sonny had the chicken pox. Patricia Thayer, the social welfare worker, scurried around trying to arrange a special quarantine section for the Ouchida family. It was a hectic last minute emergency, but a solution was found. The entire family would be quartered in the ladies' restroom, the only isolated place that could be found. Women in that car had to use the next car for their toilet needs.

Al had made earlier arrangements for Grandma to have a Pullman car and bed because she always got carsick when she traveled. This meant that she would ride apart from us, but we were pleased she could have the facilities she needed. Our sense of anxiety for each other increased when we were separated in these chaotic hours of our lives, but knowing Grandma was comfortable, we all relaxed a little.

I was grateful for the few, brave Caucasian friends who had come to see us off. They brought us sandwiches and cookies for our trip. It was a marvelous testimony to the bond of friendship that had developed between the Japanese people and their Caucasian neighbors in our rural communities. They brought gifts and mementoes, packages of sandwiches, cakes and cookies, prepared for us with love. I forgot the hateful headlines as I looked out across the faces so different from ours, yet the same in that we were all children of God, and we were all Americans.

Soldiers reminded us that it was time to board the train. I held hands tightly with dear friends who tearfully promised to wait for my safe return. I cried unashamedly as I said good-bye to classmates, teachers, neighbors and friends and stepped on board. I cried until I could hardly breathe. The train moved slowly southward; I strained to catch the last glimpse of the railroad station and the friends who stood transfixed at the spot where we had just parted.

I said goodbye to a part of my life the day we left Elk Grove. I could not comprehend the forces that caused this strange departure from the community we loved. With breaking hearts, we were wrenched away from the only home we knew.

Our painful parting from friends and neighbors was more than we could bear. Deep within all of us, however, invisible threads of friendship were slowly knitting into form. I hoped there would be letters and messages to strengthen our affection. I hoped that our song of faith, hope, and joy would eventually become a great affirmation.

Once again, I remembered Reverend Sasaki's words on that fateful December day:

"All the darkness of the world cannot blot out the light from one candle."

Thus we left Elk Grove and our Florin home. For all we knew it would be forever. I sat in a stupor, exhausted and trembling all over from the emotional ordeal of parting. It was over now; we were on our way, the last people of Japanese ancestry to leave Florin, California on May 29, 1942.

The first-time travelers among us looked eagerly out the windows of the train to watch the changing scenery of this great adventure as the train moved slowly down the San Joaquin Valley. Suddenly, though, there were military police in the cars. Quickly, they pulled down the blinds so we could not see. The lights were turned on so it would not be dark in the cars. Some among us protested and the truth was finally known—"We don't want anyone to see that this is a trainload of Japanese being moved."

Our departure was to be a secret! It was the first of many shocking humiliations. I was sick with despair.

41

Suspected of crimes we never dreamed of committing, there was clearly nothing we could do. We, the people of Florin, of Japanese ancestry, were on our way to become a chapter of American history. We had been singled out along with our brothers and sisters from the western coast of California, Washington and Oregon. There were 110,000 of us, a mass removal unprecedented in the annals of our country's story. How we ached to prove our loyalty to the only country we had ever known! Instead, even though we were American citizens, we were heading for prison because our country was at war with the land of our ancestors. We had been told that it was a military necessity and that we were a threat to national security, but it made no sense at all. Each and every one of us felt the loss of freedom and personal liberties.

I sat with Marielle and Al in the shrouded car and wondered with traces of bitterness, "Where is the justice of it all?"

Bancroft Library, University of California

Painting by Henry Sugimoto

Chapter 4

Strawberry Fields of Florin

*The strawberry fields of Florin seem far, far away as we head south into
the Sacramento—San Joaquin Valley. How can our great California
allow this tragic journey to take place."*

The train lulled my nerves and provided an opportunity for my
emotions to rest while I pondered the reasons for this sorry state of
affairs.

I prayed to God that I would be given the insight to cope with the
days ahead. From childhood stories, the cultural teachings of my
heritage came rushing back to me. "Sho Chiku Bai," I kept repeating
over and over to myself. It explained everything in life—this age old
legend of the pine, bamboo and plum blossom. Had I blossomed forth
with courage and beauty as the legend said? My plum years were now
over, my innocence gone with them; so it was when late spring storms
destroyed the delicate blooms of the plum. Strong, destructive winds
were now upon me. To survive, I must be like the sturdy bamboo that
never breaks no matter how much it is battered and bent. I must dare
to grow tall, gracefully, as I am destined. My dream was to serve
mankind. I must now be useful in a thousand ways, though I knew not
how I could be of use to anyone as a prisoner on a train that was taking
us far, far away from everything in our lives.

I wondered though—was I destined someday to serve others? Was
that perhaps why I had survived the streetcar accident in long ago

San Francisco when I was a toddling child? I often wondered why I had lived for everyone was sure I was dead. Mother and Dad were operating a laundry on Geary Street, and I had wandered out into the street. Suddenly, I was under the streetcar and being dragged along. Traffic stopped. Mother was screaming and everyone came rushing to my aid. They thought I was dead, but when they pulled me out, they found I had only a few bruises I was rushed to the emergency hospital. The doctor gave me a lollypop. "It was a miracle," he said. "The baby is alive; she is a very lucky child."

Not long after that, my family left San Francisco and moved to Turlock where my parents raised melons. There were five of us—I had four sisters; our brother was born after we moved to Parlier in Fresno county. "Finally I have a son," said my mother. "At last I feel like a woman." We enjoyed the country life and picking huge, delicious peaches even though it meant long hours of hard work for all of us.

It was in Turlock that real fear had first come to dwell with me... the fear that comes from bigotry and racial prejudice. Father was greasing the wheels of a wagon one day; I was helping him even though I was not old enough for school yet. I remember Mama telling me that I would sleep thirty times before it was time to go to school.

Suddenly a noisy convertible raced by. I heard loud, violent voices shout out, "God damn you Japs."

Angry boys yelling ugly insults at us—my tiny world shattered with terror. Father sat quietly for a moment, but his eyes betrayed him, and I was even more frightened. Suddenly he dashed forward, threw his hammer into the air and lifted his clenched fist at the car, no longer visible in the dust.

Stark, cold fright enveloped me and froze my heart. There was something taking place that I did not understand, but instinctively, I knew that such fear would live with me forever.

We left the San Joaquin Valley in 1925 and moved to Florin near Sacramento. Ruth was twelve, tall and mature for her age, a quiet, wise big sister to us all. I was ten and thin, long legs and all neck. They teased me because my Japanese name was Tsuruko which meant "stork," so they said I looked like one too. Isabel was eight, a live-wire with a temper that often got us into sisterly fights. Jean at five was gentle, frail and quiet; Julia, three, was a chubby dear little girl, and George, our brother was the dearly awaited first son. Father enrolled us in the Florin Grammar School, a public school in the small country town of Florin. Father took us girls there on the first day. He was shocked to find that every child from the first grade to the eighth was Japanese. Our school was a segregated school, but the teachers were Caucasian.

Father said very little. I could tell that the demeaning message was clear. I wondered what was in his mind. This was the America he was so proud of, the America he had read about in school books in faraway Okinawa, the America he talked incessantly about as we worked together in the fields. What did he think that day in Florin about his hero, Abraham Lincoln? What did he think about the Great Emancipator, as his children enrolled in a segregated school while white children went to the new brick school down the road?

I settled into my new life in Florin, made new friends, and took my studies seriously. Family life left little time for anything other than farm work, school, and church.

One unforgettable day, Father bought us an old piano. We moved the heavy upright into the center of our little farm home. Ruth had been taking piano lessons from Mrs. Anita Wiedeman. Without a piano, however, her practicing had been done at the home of generous, kind-hearted Annie Jenkins, a school teacher and our neighbor. Now we could all listen to Ruth right in our own home as she practiced her lessons! It was a musical education for all of us for 25 cents a week. How my father had conceived the notion that his children should have this luxury I do not know, but somehow he found the money to carry out his plan.

Then one day, Father said to me, "Mary, you go to Mrs. Wiedeman's for the piano lesson." My heart leaped with joy! What could my father possibly mean? Why was I suddenly the chosen one? In my excitement, I forgot about Ruth's love of music as I prepared to become the pianist of my father's dreams. I loved every hour spent practicing, and I played for church services, choir, weddings, and funerals. Whenever I sat down to play, I said a prayer of thanks that this great gift had been given to me and that I had been able to make my father's dream come true.

WE THE PEOPLE

Later I realized why Ruth had been denied the opportunity of becoming a musician. She was my father's expert crate maker. Ruth had learned the craft from watching Takashi Higa's rhythmical pounding and hammering of nails as he made the large slat crates in which cantaloupes were packed in Turlock. Ruth was only eight years old when she learned how to hold the nails just so and with a single effort pound them down. In Florin Ruth was given the important task of making thousands of crates for shipping our strawberries to market. Ruth's hands were calloused and blistered from her chores. Those hammer-wielding hands were too tough and stiff for the intricate exercises of an advanced pianist. This is how I became the one to have the piano lessons in our family.

I know Ruth must have been terribly disappointed, but my great joy concealed my guilty thoughts. My gratitude to Ruth and my father have stayed with me to this day. My sister Ruth was a remarkable person, so unassuming, yet quietly determined. As the oldest child she had been given heavy responsibilities long before she was old enough to shoulder such burdens. Father relied upon her. She was the first Dakuzaku to go to school, the first to come home with marvelous knowledge of the outside world, this great America. And, she was the first in our family to have the ability to read and write in English. This was worth more than gold to my immigrant parents.

The goals my father had for himself when he sailed for America, though modest, were beyond his limitations. He was chained to his farm and growing family, and no matter what he did, he could not free himself from the label placed upon him: "Alien, ineligible for citizenship." Like all Issei immigrants, he was denied the opportunity to own land, and thus his hopes and dreams were thwarted by California's anti-alien land law which was passed in 1913. The law was a severe blow to Japanese farmers in California because they were designated as aliens ineligible for citizenship.

My father could not own land and was therefore destined to work for someone else, forever limited by the whims of landlords.

His children, however, were American citizens by virtue of their birth and we *could* own land. With that legal basis, Father's dreams were realized. Early in Ruth's life, she became the legal owner of the land on which our Dakuzaku family depended upon for our living.

47

Ruth, the maker of boxes and owner of the family's land, though denied music to enrich her life, was the recipient of the most precious gift our family could afford. As the eldest child, it was planned that Ruth would go to the University of California in Berkeley because she wanted to become a bacteriologist. We scraped and saved every penny we could, for as the legal heir, Ruth was to be properly educated. We accepted this as a necessary part of our lives even though no such plans were made for the rest of us girls.

Our Florin childhood was dominated by the daily work that goes into making a living. Only with the combined efforts of each member of the family could my parents hope to provide for basic needs. This is the way it was with all Japanese farm families in Florin; everyone worked in the fields from dawn to dusk. School and church time were the only other priorities of our lives.

Chosei Taro Dakuzaku, my father, had come to America as a teenager from Okinawa. He worked in the sugar cane fields of Hawaii for a time and then set sail for San Francisco. There he opened a laundry on Geary Street with his older brother and three friends. He saved his money and was able to send for his wife, Kame, in 1912. Although they knew little about farming, my parents decided to try their luck in the great farmlands of California. They spent several years trying to raise melons in Turlock and peaches in Parlier. Finally, they moved to Florin in one last attempt to achieve their dreams and aspirations.

The harsh life of a strawberry grower in Florin required a strictly disciplined family. Everyone had to work together just to make ends meet. Father was a model of determination and endurance as he worked in the fields. He cultivated, irrigated, and fertilized his plants, continually looking for signs of insects or disease. One misjudgment meant there was no food for the coming year.

My father's year-round labor crew consisted of the entire family—Ruth, Isabel, Jean, Julia, and me, our little brother George, and our uncomplaining, hard-working mother. We did everything that had to be done.

With careful management and everyone's hard work, Father and Mother hoped to pass their dreams on to us. We were to work hard, study our lessons, go to church, and ignore as much as possible of the outside world. My parents knew the heartbreaks of prejudice and hoped to spare us from them. Attending a segregated school, we had little contact with that ugly, outside world.

The life of a berry worker was a back breaking one. There was only one way to work with strawberries, and that was close to the ground. The hard work went on all day long—stooping, crawling, bending, and picking berries.

The busiest time began about the middle of April. By May, long unrelenting hours were needed to cover every inch of the fields so that not a single berry was missed. Extra field hands were recruited for the harvest. We provided bed and board for them.

My mother had been a servant raised in the palace of Okinawa. She was tiny, not even five feet tall, and had not been prepared for the strenuous life of a farm wife. The hard work that fell upon her slight shoulders is difficult to describe much less comprehend. Mother was responsible for feeding the crew which made her day begin at dawn when she prepared breakfast for the hungry workers. With limited resources, she somehow provided an ample table. After cleaning up and starting the next meal, Mother took her place in the field with the children and workers.

After dinner in the evening, when the family and crew finished their hot Japanese baths, Mother and Father worked in their vegetable garden until dark. This task too was vital to the family's survival. I don't know how my mother found the time for it, but she also had a flower garden filled with a profusion of fragrant blooms—larkspurs, marigolds, daisies, roses and poppies. This was her special place. Here she could breathe in the soul-healing perfumes as she pulled stray weeds and snipped spent blooms. It was as if the flower garden was her luxury, a moment of peace in each difficult day.

We youthful workers of the family had no interest in flowers. Our special time was when we heard Father's welcome words, "*Sukoshi yasumo.*" (Let us rest a bit on this hot afternoon.)

Summer temperatures in Florin reached 110 and more. On these days a little rest was not only desirable, but necessary to our survival. For a short moment, we were free from hard work, free to rest our tired bodies, free to pause and forget the hundreds of berries still out there waiting to be picked.

Most memorable were the few occasions when the temperature was extremely high and Mother would let us eat bowls of the delicious berries with cream, ice cold and refreshing. It was as if nothing on earth could be so sweet, so restoring of hope to childish thoughts. These precious moments were quickly over, however, and then with bonnets back on our heads, we trudged on to the berry fields.

The endless work went on from one season to another. We worked before school and after school, on weekends and on vacations. The routine of weeding, hoeing, and planting of strawberry runners stopped only during the frantic tension-filled harvest days when not even a minute could be wasted in getting the perishable fruit to market. The stakes were high, the toll in family stress and fatigue even higher.

The two highly important crops of strawberries and grapes were the livelihood of hundreds of Japanese families around Florin. Strawberries ripened in May; the grapes were harvested in September. Florin emerged from the Great Depression of the 1930's as a great fruit and berry growing, packing, and shipping center of the state. There were berry fields all over Florin and Elk Grove, a significant agricultural region of Sacramento County. Two thirds of the farms were run by Japanese American farmers and their families.

In the springtime the berry blossoms turned the green fields white. When the berries ripened, the fields were dotted with glimmers of rich red tucked in and around lush leaves. If it weren't for the endless back breaking work, we would have thought the fields were beautiful, balm for our weary souls. Such was the common experience of those who labored in the strawberry fields to bring luscious berries to the tables of America.

Berry growing in Florin had begun before the turn of the century. Each year more and more carloads of fresh strawberries were shipped in ice-packed railroad cars from Florin to distant cities as greater demands for the good tasting berries were made. Enterprising white farmers recruited Japanese laborers to share their crops. By 1941, Florin, California was the largest shipper of fresh strawberries in the United States. If it weren't for Executive Order 9066, it might have gone on forever.

Long before the strawberries, there had been delicate, tiny wildflowers that graced the meadowlands south of Sacramento, California. Each year their beauty burst forth under the hot spring sun. Enriched by winter rains, the flowers covered the fields with color—pink, yellow, pale blue, and violet. The town of Florin, seven miles south of the state's capital, received its name from the pretty little flowers.

The famous California Gold Rush fanned the flames of gold fever throughout the Sacramento area after 1849 and brought the first of many immigrants to the area. The Central Pacific Railroad laid its tracks from Sacramento to Stockton, the two centers of gold activity, and a name was needed for a railroad stop in the middle of the flower-filled fields. Judge E. V. Crocker thought of the Spanish "flor" and thus was christened Florin. By 1878, there was the beginning of a small community there.

Florin's fame, however, came with the demise of the wildflowers. Their places were soon taken by lush fruits and berries including the renowned Tokay grape, first planted in Florin by the English carpenter, James Rutter. Florin's climate and soil were perfect for the new grape, and before long the viticulture of these fine table grapes spread throughout the Florin area. The flame red Tokays ripened early, and the new rail lines were there to take them to eastern markets. Florin Tokays consistently won ribbons at fairs; and the ensuing publicity increased their value in a significant way.

Along with grapes, Florin became noted for its strawberries. Chinese workers, brought to America to build the railroad, were tossed into the labor force when the transcontinental line was completed. Some drifted to Florin and became the first to plant strawberries there. By 1890 they were joined by Japanese immigrants who began an extraordinary venture as they planted strawberries between the grape vines for quick cash crops. The companion crops were an excellent combination for Florin's hot sun and clay soil. Little did these immigrants from the crowded Japanese islands know they were founding a great berry enterprise that would last through nearly half of the 20th century.

Nor did the Japanese immigrants realize that within the shadow of California's capitol, they would be subjected to a hateful campaign of racial prejudice. It did not matter that their victimization had been

51

inherited from the Chinese who had preceded them; the Japanese immigrants became the easy targets of bigots and racists, many of whom were associated with the state's leading industry, agriculture.

By the late 1800s the Chinese had been singled out in the passage of the Chinese Exclusion Act. Hatred and discrimination were easily transferred from one Asian group to another. These were the atti- tudes found by the first Japanese to leave Japan after the island nation opened its doors to the West in 1885.

My husband's father, Kuzo Tsukamoto, was one of the first young men to leave Japan. He left his native Hiroshima to search for a better life during the first year of emigration. Kuzo was on the second boat to leave Japan enroute to Hawaii and a new life. Eventually, Kuzo came to Florin where he labored in the vineyards. Work was plentiful, the rural setting agreeable, and the young men from Japan began to think about setting down their roots. Some went back to Japan to find wives. Others sent for so called "picture brides." This is how the immigrant families began to build the community of Florin.

The Issei, or first generation, worked hard, and in spite of great obstacles, they transformed Florin into a great place for growing and shipping grapes and strawberries.

They accomplished this in spite of the fact that they could not own property. Because they were foreign born Asians, they could not become citizens; and because they were not citizens, they could not own property. Life in the new country appeared to be one hindrance after another in the path of success.

The Issei learned to overcome such obstructions. They waited until their children were old enough to read and write and became of age; then with money they had saved, they bought land in the names of their children who, being native born, were citizens.

The Issei were committed to two goals. The first was their dedication to the land that had sustained them, and the second was to their goal of education for their children. With hard work and education, they knew they could achieve their dream of greater opportunities for their children in America.

In addition to their transition from sharecroppers to landowners, the Issei also founded businesses and churches and set up private language schools to keep their culture alive. In Florin, Japanese language schools were an important part of life every Saturday morning, no matter how much we tried to convince our parents that we'd rather not go. None of us knew that this cultural commitment would be cause for suspicion in the dark days of 1942.

The Issei parents expected their children to attend the best colleges and universities, and the entire family was dedicated to carry out these ambitious goals. In many schools, however, the Nisei students were ostracized, limited to participation in student activities and prevented from taking part in student affairs. Worse yet, upon graduation, professions for which they were trained were not open to accepting those of another race. Attitudes implanted in these formative years helped the pre-Pearl Harbor kettle boil over and result in the actions that took place through Executive Order 9066.

The Japanese American families, however, revered the ideals of democracy and America and discussed them with pride. Issei could not believe their good fortune in their adopted country. They accepted their status as non-citizens and the inconveniences of difficult laws. They persevered because they knew it would be different for their children who were American citizens. They believed it was a small price to pay for the privilege of living in America.

In the same manner, they ignored the racial taunts, ostracism, and newspaper attacks. Culturally conditioned to turn the other cheek, Japanese Americans stayed close to each other in their little communities. What they did not know was that these very actions seemed to emphasize inability to assimilate, and that this would be interpreted as signs of treason and disloyalty; they would be labeled as traitors, disloyal to America in her time of crisis.

As Florin grew in the 1920s and 1930s, the Japanese minority grew until it became the majority population of the community. Many, it seems, must have watched with alarm at the growing number of Japanese names on local property lists. Most of the racial agitation, however, came from outside of Florin. A few farmers raising fruit in an area had not been noticed, but when the few became hundreds, outsiders began to take note.

When stores and businesses began to be taken over by Japanese proprietors, and five of the seven shipping companies were being operated by Japanese, even those who were unprejudiced found it difficult to meet the arguments of the hate preachers who wanted to limit the newcomers.

"They are getting too powerful."

"We're going to have to put a stop to this."

"They're taking over Florin."

Growing up in Florin during this time was difficult for us Nisei children. Some of us developed lifetime scars from ostracism and racial tension. Others, like me, learned a kind of timidity that clung to us and made us fearful and careful not to step on anyone's toes. Though we were the majority culture of Florin, we found ourselves isolated, wrapped up in a protective, sheltering existence. Children have a way of knowing the meaning of stares, whispers, pointing, and hurtful comments. We learned to avoid those who cursed, threatened us, and approached us in aggressive ways. We traveled in groups and stayed close to home within the safety of family and friends. Our associations with others were limited to those who made attempts to reach out to us.

The segregation of the Florin Grammar School had a lot to do with our attitudes and perhaps those of others toward us too. It had come about quietly in the fall of 1923, a mute expression of the ill-will festering within the community. The vicious anti-Oriental propaganda in the state and nation was perpetuated by a profit seeking press. It was easy for ambitious politicians to use it to their advantage and carry the banner for pressure groups. These groups were well organized in their efforts to rid the West Coast of unwanted foreigners who they felt were crowding the land.

The passage of the California anti alien land law (the Webb Act, 1913) was encouraged by these bigots, and soon other states passed similar laws. The act prohibited "aliens ineligible for citizenship" from purchasing or leasing land for longer than three years.

The problems in Florin were blown into senseless proportions. In 1923 Governor Hiram Johnson and U. S. Secretary of State William Jennings Bryan came to Florin. Imagine having important political figures such as these visit a tiny agricultural town! They were concerned about what they called the "troublesome Japanese problem" in California. Such public attention fanned the fires of racism

54

and bigotry in Florin.

COMES TO TOWN

April 28, 1913
THE PRESIDENTS ENVOY IS GOVERNOR'S GUEST

BRYAN'S MESSAGE

Will Be Governor's Guest at Executive Mansion During His Stay in Sacramento	Secretary of State Tells Legislators How President Wilson Views Proposed Anti-Alien Land Law	MET AT DEPOT BY GOVERNOR Democratic Legislators Also Guest Secretary of

Sacramento Bee

Joichi Nitta, our neighbor and kin from Hiroshima, was a young man when he heard Bryan speak at the Florin railroad station. Many years later, he still spoke vividly about the fiery words and the crowd reaction to them. "It was frightening to behold," he recalled. "There was such anger in the eyes of so many. I thought it best to slip quietly away. I stayed in my house all day."

After the passage of the Japanese Exclusion Act of 1924, the banner of discrimination was waved openly in Florin. It seemed as if American sentiments toward the Oriental people of the world were suddenly revealed. Children of immigrant Oriental parents experienced what it meant to be second class citizens.

The segregation of the Florin School followed these events. A new brick building was built at the west end of town. Some people knew what it was for. One day, all the white children were paraded out of the Florin School. They carried American flags and marched down the muddy road. School was held for them at the church hall until their classrooms were ready in the new West School. The Japanese children stayed at the East School.

The teachers justified the segregation of the children.

"The Japanese children are so far behind."
"Children from homes where Japanese is spoken need a different teaching program."
"The school cannot handle such insurmountable linguistic and cultural problems."

55

The previous year, every Japanese child to the fifth grade had been held back. Issei parents were shocked to find this out. However, they held educators in such high esteem that they believed what they were told.

Those whites who had anti-Japanese feelings used the school issue as justification for further agitation. Their leaders were those who found the problem one of economic competition. Support for their propaganda was found in the McClatchy and Hearst newspapers and active organizations such as the American Legion and the California Grange.

The children, however, had no idea of what was taking place until they heard their parents talk about it.

Al remembered the day very well. "I was in the primary grades when we split up. One day the white children were there; the next day they were not. I missed some of my playmates. The thing I remember most after that is that the teacher gave us a lot of recess."

As long as we stayed on the edge of poverty, we were disregarded for we posed no threat to the majority population. As we improved our land, however, and as we used our carefully saved nickels and dimes to raise the standard of our living, the voices of opposition came from all corners. We broke all the rules of successful race relations in a community. We moved from the minority population to the majority, and we moved away from total poverty. There would be a price to pay for this.

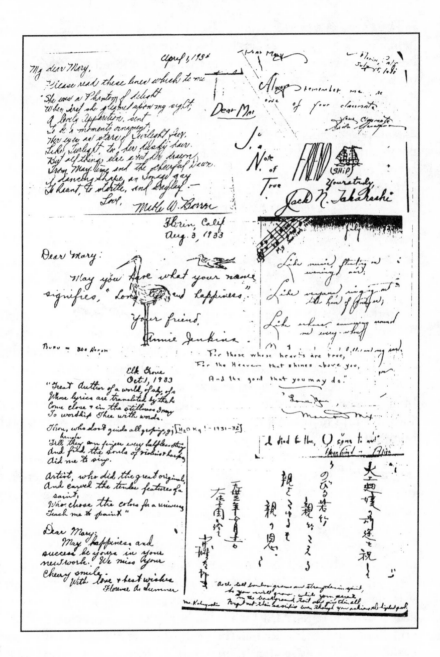

Pages from Mary's autograph book.

Chapter 5

The Bitter Fruit of Segregation

*"I am thinking about Mable Barron as our train creeps along toward
Fresno. I wonder what she would say if
she could see me now."*

In the fall of 1929 I enrolled in classes at Elk Grove Union High
School. There were about 250 students in the school; about 20% of
us were Japanese Americans.* Most of us lived in Florin and the
surrounding area and were bussed to high school.

The effects of segregation stay with a child for a long time.
Memories of my early years still bring a choking tightness to my
throat. I find myself having to fight past those feelings of fear and
humiliation.

A few Caucasian friends transformed school into a wonderful,
bright world. It seemed that Florin was changing too as my generation, the Nisei, was able to communicate in English. We began to
find that there were many fine Caucasian people in Florin and the
surrounding area.

One person stood out in my high school years as being able to
understand the need for children to grow and develop, even if they
were Japanese and poor and their parents didn't speak English. She
was Mable Barron, a rare and magnanimous teacher who bounced up
and down the halls of Elk Grove High. Her presence meant laughter
and happy voices for she had the greatest sense of humor any person
could have. We were all attracted to this caring woman who looked

---

*By 1942 our numbers had increased to nearly 50%.

at us with generous, blue eyes and made us feel her boundless capacity to love and understand.

Mrs. Barron was short, rather plump, and had hair somewhere between blonde and brunette, cut short with bangs that were pushed aside. Her dresses were ill-fitted as if they were hastily sewn by a lady who had more important things to worry about than her clothes. It didn't matter what she looked like. When you were around Mrs. Barron, you knew you belonged, and you knew you could do anything you set your mind to do. That's the effect she had upon you.

I signed up for public speaking. It was as if the gentle hand of Providence was at work to bring me to Mable Barron. How could I, a shy, withdrawn child of Japanese farmers, know what would result from that unusual and inspirational class? How could I know how it would change the course of my life?

One spring day we were given an exciting assignment. It was an oration about our great state of California. I worked hard to research the lives of prominent Californians who had made contributions to our state. Finally, I selected John Muir, the first conservationist of our natural beauty.

Mrs. Barron worked to help us develop a variety of speaking skills. She made it clear that she expected us to be excellent orators. Finally came the try-outs. From the tension, I came to realize that this was more than a classroom activity. Children of long-time residents bubbled over with anticipation, hoping to be one of the nine finalists on the stage.

Such thoughts were far from my mind. I only wanted to live through the ordeal that had dominated my life for the past weeks. When it was my turn, I finished with great relief, deciding that public speaking was not for me. Even up there on the big stage, I was the farmer's daughter from Florin—little, terribly shy, and barely able to speak.

Several days later, I was called from my class to report immediately to the Principal's office. Accusing eyes of my classmates turned toward me; I was so embarrassed I could hardly walk. My face turned strawberry red as I bolted out the door. What could this mean?

Our principal, Mr. Wells, and Mrs. Barron were waiting for me. On their faces were troubled expressions. Mrs. Barron had been crying, but she was as angry as she was distressed. "Can't we do something to change this?" she demanded. I was perplexed as they painstakingly told me what had happened. Though I had been one of the nine finalists in the oratorical contest, the organizers, the Native Sons of the Golden West, would not allow children of immigrants to participate. Even though I was a native Californian, I was disqualified because of my parents.

Mrs. Barron was outraged; she felt it was unfair and personally humiliating to me that I could not take part in what was one of the highlights of the year at Elk Grove High.

I, however, was greatly relieved. I had already decided that I was not going to become a public speaker. I was happy to dismiss the matter.

"Let it be," I heard myself saying. "I don't want to create an incident."

My protests were ignored as their discussion grew more and more heated. They talked about equality, fair play, and how education had a responsibility to give a child opportunities to develop to the fullest potential.

I began to realize why this gifted teacher was so angry. This really did affect me whether I realized it or not. As I walked away, I smiled, but I was stunned inside. I quivered with hurt. Somehow I should have known that things like this could happen. The racial turmoil in the state and nation could hardly go untouched in Elk Grove and Florin. How could I have been so naive to think that all injustices could be overcome? I was sixteen years old that spring day in 1931. I wanted to crawl into my childhood shell and die. At this vulnerable time in my life, this revelation was devastating.

My soul was penetrated by this painful experience. Deep wounds from my childhood were touched, and I could not hide from the hurt. Emotion-packed incidents from my growing up years, experiences I had almost forgotten as I hid them deep inside of me, surfaced and threatened to overwhelm me with their intensity. I felt like a delicate flower, trampled and crushed beyond hope, deeply scarred and surely never to be the same. My ever sensitive teachers noticed the change in me, the disappearance of my usual bubbling enthusiasm.

"What is wrong with Mary?" I heard them ask.

"Her voice is barely audible."

"What has happened to her?"

My world of innocence was destroyed—that's what happened to me. I was doomed to a humiliating life because my name and ancestry were with me forever. I began to resent my parents. I hated being Japanese. I felt crowded and pushed into a tiny dark shell, and I never wanted to come out. I wished my life could be snuffed out. There was nothing ahead for me. Why should I live?

Divine Providence, however, once again intervened into an insignificant, sixteen year old life. Florin's Methodist Youth Fellowship, the Epworth League, was invited to participate in a speaking contest sponsored by the Sacramento Junior College Students' club.

"Mary, you must enter this oratorical contest. Represent the Epworth League of Florin. I will help you."

Mrs. Barron knew this was what I needed. Japanese American clubs were springing forth on college campuses in response to discrimination of Nisei students. Denied opportunities to participate fully in campus social life, the students were seeing a need for acceptance of the awareness of being uniquely Japanese. They dared to proclaim their self-identity.

I needed to put my energies into a productive venture like this. Mrs. Barron was there to help me. No orator ever received more support and encouragement than I did. My tutor spent long hours helping me re-write and correct my oration. I marveled at her understanding of my problems and her ability to develop the content of my speech. Her masterful strokes transformed my simple words into an eloquent oration. With her skilled, patient coaching, I was turned into a confident, poised, young orator.

"Stand erect, Mary. Smile as though you are on top of the world...Pause briefly when you smile...Emphasize that last phrase... Make it sound convincing...."

I must have done everything she told me to do because I came home with first prize. It was an electric clock, and I had tasted the joy of being a winner. I knew it would not be my last. The clock was placed proudly on the piano where it could be admired by all who entered our home.

A rash of contests, oratorical and essay, suddenly came to my attention. It seemed as if every Japanese American club was becoming involved with such worthy endeavors. I worked hard. I wrote a religious essay called "Teach Us To Pray" for the annual Young People's Christian Conference, and it won me a picture of Christ praying at Gethsemane. I took every class I could from Mrs. Barron including English literature which I came to love.

Then a great challenge was tossed to me. The Japanese Students' Club of the University of California sponsored an oratorical contest to be held at the Reformed Church in San Francisco. It was the church where I had begun nursery school at the age of three and where I had taken my first toddling steps into Christianity. I could hardly wait to begin work on the topic: "What can we leave for the next generation?"

Again, Mrs. Barron committed herself to me although no teacher was busier than she. In addition to her teaching duties, she coached drama productions with endless rehearsals. Her trusty old flivver tore down country roads picking students up for practice and taking them home again late at night. With practically no budget at all in those depression years, she improvised, borrowed, and somehow found ways to get the jobs done. Once she even used a loaned truck to haul her own living room furniture to school to use in a play.

With boundless energy, Mrs. Barron helped me with this oration. I memorized every word, practiced my delivery in front of a mirror and then in her presence, polished my words with gestures and pauses. As my speaking voice improved, I paid attention to my diction and phrasing. Never was an orator given such careful preparation.

A master craftsman of word power and prudent in her conception of what my future could be, Mrs. Barron taught me more than how to have a winning speech. Her strong faith in democracy and her vision of what the ideal life could be in American culture created for me a lasting confidence in the country of my birth. Mable Barron made me see the valuable heritage of my ancestors. She knew I needed to accept my roots so I could serve as a bridge between the culture of my parents and that of my country, America. I began to see in my destiny the proud possession of the best of both cultures, and I would have to blend them successfully in this vast new land of the United States of America.

I still thrill to remember these stirring words from my oration:

> *Our heritage must be built day by day, hour by hour, by shaping our own lives, homes, work and recreation, toward the end of ensuring a suitable environment for our children. We are the parents of tomorrow: the homes we establish will be our children's environment. When beauty, truth and self-sacrifice dominate our lives; when spiritual values are ever present in our homes; when the high ideals of reverence, patriotism and devotion to duty given us by our parents predominate, then we know that the heritage of the third generation is secure.*

Exhausted from the triumphant weekend, I returned home late on Sunday evening. Wearily, I got off the train that brought me back to Florin from Oakland. Every minute of my San Francisco experience was etched into my heart and soul. I clutched my dearly-won trophy—the Consul-General Wakasugi Silver Cup. I had carried it all the way home, reluctant to put it into my suitcase. I was so overwhelmed with what I had done; I had won the perpetual trophy for the Florin's Epworth League. I was beside myself with joy in this most thrilling moment of my life.

My only regret was that my family had not been able to be with me as I gave my talk. It was April, and the strawberry fields needed every hand that could be found. I was lucky to have been spared the weekend. I stayed with my aunt and uncle in Oakland, and their whole family went with me on the ferry boat and streetcar to the Reformed Church where they cheered for me.

That victorious experience had a remarkable effect upon the young Nisei girl I was, but there was a rainbow of bright years yet to come.

Unknown to me, Mrs. Barron had been making inquiries at the College of the Pacific, her alma mater in Stockton, fifty miles south of Florin. Bob Burns, the student recruiter, came to Elk Grove High School one warm day in May to interview me. I was excited and impressed with him, but I realized that such a prestigious college was much too costly for me to even think about. One semester's tuition was $600. This was more than my family's profit from a full year on our little farm.

In 1933, the effects of the Great Depression were felt by all Americans. My folks were barely able to make a living for our family of eight. We had Ruth at the University, so I decided not to trouble them with my impossible aspirations. Bravely, I tried to dismiss the notion of going to college.

Mrs. Barron, however, was not so easily deterred. I have no idea how many trips she made to Stockton to see Dr. Tully Knoles, the college president. She was determined to find a way for me to attend the College of the Pacific.

During spring vacation she invited me to spend a week with her family in Lodi. I was a companion to her two daughters, Betty and Mary, and helped her sew many colorful pieces of fabric together to make two quilt comforters. This amazing woman was also an accomplished seamstress. A pile of old clothes was stacked in a corner of the room, and from it she selected pieces that she cut and sewed. Occasionally, she called me over for a fitting; and I began to realize that this assortment of clothes was going to be a wardrobe for me.

Tirelessly, and one step at a time, Mrs. Barron worked out the strategy she had in mind for me. She seemed oblivious to the formidable task ahead.

I graduated from high school with the Class of 1933 and settled down into the routine of farm work. One hot day in July, Mrs. Barron drove into our farm yard. She was greatly excited as she announced, "Mary, Dr. Knoles, the president of College of the Pacific, has faith in you. He is offering you a scholarship for $125."

Mrs. Barron spoke to my father. She asked him if he would release me from working on the farm so I might have the privilege of a college education. Her plans were carefully thought out; she was prepared to assume full responsibility for me. She was confident that other scholarships would follow. Helen Householder, also a teacher at Elk Grove High School, would contribute $10 each month for me. The college planned to find me a home where I could work for my room and board. A complete wardrobe had been sewed for me.

My father was so moved he could not speak. This great teacher cared so much for his daughter that she had taken infinite pains to manage this awesome responsibility in the middle of the terrible depression. Even with two children of her own to care for, Mrs. Barron planned to do this for me. I was overjoyed. Her expression of confidence astounded me. But, it was such a huge amount of money. How could it ever come to be?

"Father," I said reluctantly, "you cannot spare me from the fields. Ruth is at Berkeley. It would not be fair to the rest of the family for me to be gone."

I could hardly believe what I was saying, but I knew my responsibility to my sisters and mother. I knew that my father wanted me to go to college, but there was just no way that it could be done.

My heart stopped as I waited for my father's answer. On his face I saw the look I remembered when he told me I would go to Mrs. Wiedeman's for piano lessons. My sisters held their breaths as they wondered what Father would say.

No one spoke. Mrs. Barron waited expectantly. She had already presented all the details of her plan. The searing heat of summer pressed against us all. Finally, my father bowed with deep humility and said, "Yes. Mary may go."

My spirit immediately found wings with no bounds to my flight. I was ready to fly! I had been lifted up and allowed to see my destiny. Mable Barron had opened doors that would lead to thrilling opportunities for me. Everything I would ever become I would owe to this beautiful teacher and friend who sparked a light in me that I would never allow to be extinguished.

As for my father, this immigrant strawberry farmer found a heart of American gold in Mrs. Barron. It was a thrilling privilege he never dreamed would be possible. His joy and faith in the country of his choice had been restored. The ideals of Abraham Lincoln that he cherished as a young boy were present in his great country, the United States of America, the country for all its people.

I enrolled at the College of the Pacific in Stockton, California in the fall of 1933. It was a well-known liberal arts school, an ideal climate for a young mind and a sheltered environment for a timid, young woman from Florin. Its church centered curriculum offered possibilities in missionary work, a field I was allowed to consider rather than teaching which I preferred. Realistically, pursuits of life work in education for Oriental women were limited, as my counselors explained to me.

The beautiful campus was a shady haven far from the rigors of the strawberry fields. The picturesque Gothic characteristics of the music conservatory symbolized the religious base of my new school. I was proud to know that the College of the Pacific was one of the first schools of higher education in California.

In my eighteen years of growing up, I had never known anything like COP. I walked down the path leading to the red brick buildings on September 6, 1933, and I could not believe I was there.

It was incomprehensible. Though penniless and in the midst of the worst depression the country had every known, a shy, frightened, American girl with a Japanese face was going to attend a prestigious college. How could I dare dream such dreams? How could the daughter of an illiterate Japanese immigrant farmer dream of doing something other than toil endlessly in the family grapes and berries? My life, it seemed, had blossomed forth into a thing of great beauty, far beyond my greatest expectations.

Everyone at COP looked at me with great personal interest, and as thrilled as I was, I was terrified and frightened to death at the same time. Each experience turned me into a bundle of nerves. I wondered if I really did belong in this friendly, free atmosphere. Perhaps it was always like this when dreams came true.

There were many new friends to meet so I had to keep myself from being afraid. My energies needed to be focused on study and school activities just as they had been at Elk Grove High School.

The trauma of registration presented many situations, seemingly ordinary for most students, but for me they were filled with unbelievable tension. Emily Knoles, the president's wife, gave a tea for incoming freshmen. I had never been to a tea, never been to a president's house; I had no idea what to expect. I looked at the invitation a hundred times to make sure the date and time were right. As I walked toward the door, I thought I would faint before I reached it. My blue rayon two-piece dress, cleverly altered by Mrs. Barron, seemed right for the occasion. Out of appreciation for the woman who made all this possible, I mustered up every bit of courage in me

66

to walk up those stairs and ring the bell.

Mrs. Knoles, a lady with a radiant, kind face, was a most gracious hostess. I felt warmly welcomed as I stood among new friends. As I looked around, I was happily reassured when I saw how the other girls were dressed.

With a smile I received the tea, served in a delicate cup and saucer. Miraculously, the hot liquid did not spill as my clumsy hands held the dainty cup. I smiled and responded to introductions and friendly voices. At the same time, I prayed I could hold onto the shaking cup and balance the little cake.

The room dazzled my eyes. Thoughtful attention had been given to every detail. Tall, golden yellow candles in silver holders graced the centerpiece arranged as an exquisite autumn bouquet. The lace table cloth was complete with shining crystal and silver. Delicious little cakes, ever so tiny, were artistically placed on magnificent silver trays. I could not have imagined a tea like this. Nothing in my life had prepared me for such an occasion. I felt uncomfortable and strangely out of place.

Then I heard soft, heavenly music played by a fine pianist. I recognized Chopin's "Nocturne", one of my favorite pieces. At once I was relaxed and happy, and as I listened to the familiar sounds, I knew I really did belong. I was a student at the College of the Pacific. This was my new home.

Through those first days, I was given the kindest of receptions from everyone I met. I completed the registration process with apprehension knowing that only the $125 scholarship had been paid. I still owed the college a lot of money, and I had none in my purse to pay. A huge, cold lump placed itself inside of me. I tried to be as optimistic as Mrs. Barron would have wanted me to be. Were there secret plans that would allow me to stay and find a rightful place on this wonderful campus? I desperately wanted to stay. Higher education was my hope for the future; already I knew the strawberry fields were not for me.

Somehow I found the faith and believed that it could be done. The weeks and months of that first year were dominated by frightening summonses to see the comptroller. Kindly, Mr. Ritter explained to me how much more I owed on my account as I sat there red-faced and frantic with fear. Each time I prayed desperately that somehow dollars would be placed by my name to free me from this humiliating ordeal.

And miraculously they were! Some days notes were delivered to me telling of anonymous gifts designated for a "worthy student." Angels from somewhere came to my rescue time and again. I owed so much to these loving, caring friends. Somehow I struggled through the first semester. Then a student work program allowed me to work for my tuition. I donned a work apron and rose while it was still dark to sweep, dust and mop the classrooms. I worked frantically, determined to finish before the other students arrived. No matter how hard I worked though, there was never enough money to equal the insurmountable sum needed each semester.

On weekends, vacations and summer days, I washed windows, scraped grimy stoves, and cleaned filthy apartments my fellow students had left behind. I was determined to get an education and vowed not to let anything get in my way.

I continued through my sophomore and junior years at College of the Pacific and found time to meet the rigorous academic requirements in spite of the many hours I worked each week at several outside jobs. Eventually, the Scholarship Committee voted me the entire tuition as a show of confidence in my potential to succeed. I continued my speaking engagements and took up dance as another way to express myself.

The protected Christian environment appeared to be safe from prejudice. I felt secure with good friends in a place where everyone knew everyone else. I knew where I could go and from where it was best to stay away. Staring eyes and little frowns reminded me when I stepped too far from where I was welcome. Sororities and certain clubs were not for me, but I was content to enjoy that part of college life in which I was allowed to participate.

My background provided others with an opportunity to learn about diversity, and slowly I came to appreciate my cultural heritage. As chairman of the international dinner in my junior year, we planned a gala sukiyaki dinner complete with Japanese dances and music.

As soloist for the annual Dance Drama, I used my Florin friends

68

and relatives as resources in arranging a production of "One Fine Day" from Madame Butterfly. I borrowed kimonos and introduced my Caucasian friends to the intricacies of Japanese culture and dance. The racial unrest that was burning its way across California was practically unknown on the sheltered campus in Stockton in the mid 1930s.

I struggled on somehow, determined to finish my education, but it was so difficult. One day Mrs. Barron came to visit me.

"Mary," she asked in her quiet way, "Why do you have rubber bands on your shoes?"

I looked down in embarrassment at my worn out brown shoes realizing that those bright blue eyes I knew so well had discovered my secret.

"They have holes," I finally managed to say. "I cut pieces of cardboard to cover the holes so my socks won't get dirty. The rubber bands hold my shoes together. They're all right; really, they are."

I didn't want her to see how bad my shoes were. She'd buy new ones for me, and she shouldn't because her own daughters needed the little money she had. But, she went out and bought me a new pair of shoes, and I had a hard time feeling good about it.

My arthritis, which had become a part of my life while I was at COP, got worse and worse in my junior year. The physical demands of my cleaning jobs inflamed my joints until the pain was excruciating. I could hardly bear it.

Dr. Minerva Goodman, the physician at the infirmary for women students, and my personal friend with whom I lived and worked for my room and board, sent me to UC Medical Hospital for all the tests and X-rays, but there was nothing known to them then that could be prescribed. Dr. Goodman read about a new serum that was being tried by a physician in London. She sent for it and I tried it for a while. My infected tonsils were removed and decayed teeth pulled, but there was no cure for arthritis in the 1930s.

With no money and in constant pain, I reluctantly realized that I could not continue with my schooling. My future was unsure even with a college education. What was I to do as a missionary or social worker? I said goodbye to college and went back to my father's strawberry farm.

There was one ray of hope for my future, however. Throughout my Stockton years, while I had kept my ties to Florin and my family, I had also kept in touch with my high school boyfriend, Alfred Tsukamoto. Al had been raised in Florin like me; he graduated from Elk Grove High in 1931, and he was one of the most popular boys in the school. He played on the football team and seemed to know everyone. Like most Japanese boys, he worked on his father's berry and grape farm.

Al was handsome and always seemed to be in charge. His gentleness and kindness were genuine, and I was always so happy when I was with him. He understood what I was going through, but he wanted me to go to college if that's what I wanted to do. When I decided to come home, Al was waiting for me, and before long, we were married and began our wonderful life together.

Al and I entered the mainstream of life in Florin. On the Tsukamoto farm there were grapes, boysenberries and, of course, strawberries. Al worked for Florin Fruit Growers Association, and we became active in the JACL (Japanese American Citizens League). Little did we know that our days in Florin were numbered as the prewar days drew to a close.

The lulling motion of the rolling train made me realize how dark the days ahead would be. They would be dark days for the people of America and even darker days for Americans of Japanese ancestry. There were dark days coming for the nation itself.

Pages from the Tsukamoto Family Album

I was only a few months old in this picture. We lived in the laundry on Geary Street in San Francisco. After the street car accident, they said I was a very lucky baby!

Here we are—my father's work crew! Even baby brother George picked berries. The work went on day after day and never stopped. The sun was so hot!

I don't know how my mother worked so hard in the strawberry fields in Florin. She was the hardest worker I ever knew.

Grapes were the other important crop in Florin. This picture was given to us by Bill Okamoto. Most of the grapes raised were Flame Tokays which put Florin on the agricultural map in the 1920s and 1930s.

I won the Silver Cup for my oration! If it hadn't been for Mable Barron, I would not have been able to open my mouth. This was the highlight of my high school life! The beautiful silver cup was donated by Consul-General Wakasuki, and I still have it.

I wouldn't have made it to the College of the Pacific if it hadn't been for Mable Barron either.

They used this photo in the school yearbook. The Tsukamotos brought me the kimono from their visit to Japan.

Al often came to see me while I was at school. He was a handsome fellow, and I thought I was pretty lucky to have such a fine boyfriend.

National Archives

Pearl Harbor changed all of our lives forever. We had only a few days to get ready to leave our homes. Strawberries were ripe in the fields, but there was no one to pick them. Ted Miyata, a U.S. Army soldier, was sent home to help his mother prepare for evacuation.

This photograph was taken by the famous photographer, Dorothea Lange, who worked for the U.S. Government. It has been published many times, but Mrs. Miyata and Ted are never identified. Neither is the fact that the photo was taken in Florin, California.

May 29, 1942

These pictures were taken by Frances Cumpston of Elk Grove on the day of our departure. We boarded the train at the Elk Grove Station. There were 500 of us; 2000 others left from Florin and Elk Grove days earlier.

A small crowd of friends and neighbors saw us off. There were tears everywhere

It was the first day of losing our freedom.

Our destination was Fresno, in the San Joaquin Valley—a hurriedly constructed camp at the Fresno fair

photos by Frances Campiston

The Years of the Bamboo

World War II
and
Post-War Years

Strong storm winds bend the sturdy bamboo
and it is threatened,
but it does not break
as it bends
to meet the demands of life.
Versatile and admirable,
it dares to grow tall
gracefully
as it is destined
to assist mankind
in a thousand useful ways

80

Flame Tokays of Florin

Chapter 6

Relocation at the Fresno Fairgrounds

*"It is not like anything I could have imagined- this strange home
so far away from home, a barrack city of 5000 souls, all of us
tired and weary, fearful, humiliated, and in tears."*

I felt old at twenty-seven as I looked out like a caged animal, captured and placed behind a barbed wire fence that seemed to stretch forever. The sound of the camp gates closing behind us sent a searing pain into my heart. I knew it would leave a scar that would stay with me forever. At that very moment my precious freedom was taken from me.

Earlier that day, on our way to Fresno, our train had approached a town when suddenly, an excited young voice near me cried out, "Look, aren't those Japanese standing there?"

Dusty, sun-tanned figures were crowded up to the fence to peer at our train as it went by. Some waved with excitement as they recognized the tragic cargo and understood our destination. I saw row after row of ugly, black, tar-paper covered buildings in the barren desert; there was not a single green tree to be seen.

This sorrowful picture was stamped in my heart, and as I looked around, I realized that this camp looked exactly the same. The nightmare of internment suddenly became a stark reality, not only for me, but for all the people of Japanese ancestry who were imprisoned here.

The Fresno County fairgrounds was a somewhat logical place to set up a temporary relocation center for thousands of people. The fairgrounds' fences and gates had been easily converted to a guarded center. The site was far enough out of town that it did not create problems for the city; yet it was close enough that resources were available.

From the ominous watch tower, an unmistakable uniformed figure looked down upon us frightened, confused evacuees as we entered the compound and looked for our new quarters. The glint of the rifle in the guard's hands sent terror through our hearts. We huddled in little groups, forlornly waiting to find out what this new life would be.

Tired and numb from such an emotional day, our family stood in a long line waiting to be processed into the strange new place. Our identification was checked, and we were given room assignments. All the while, Al, Marielle and I were greeted and embraced by sisters and cousins who happily welcomed us. Our relatives had left Florin earlier and arrived at camp two days before us.

We were loaded onto trucks that rushed down the dusty roads between the tar-paper covered barrack buildings. A surprise row of fig trees with lush green leaves broke the monotony of the barracks. Inmates were seated under the welcome shade looking like a group of happy picnickers instead of the prisoners they actually were.

The truck stopped, and we were told to get off. Our familiar suitcases and bundles were thrown onto a huge pile of luggage. Part of the camp was fitted into the oval space where cars and horses had raced during the annual fair. Such festive occasions were in poignant contrast to what was taking place before us in the spring of 1942. Twenty neatly regimented and precisely measured long barracks stood, ten in a row, in each of the eleven sections. At one end were barrack buildings to be used as a mess hall, laundry, shower room, and two little huts for latrines.

I had never seen so many Japanese faces in such a small area. Some were already sun-burned; their skin and clothes were covered with dust. I could not believe how we were crowded together and how many of us there were!

As we were picking up our things from the pile of luggage, Marielle suddenly cried out, "Where's Obaachan? Where's Ojiichan? Where's Namichan? They're not here!"

We searched frantically around Sections H, I, J, and K! Friends and relatives helped out, but Grandma and Grandpa, our two old ones, and Nami were nowhere to be found.

How could we have become separated? Each of us had our tags, #22076, attached to us since we had gone to the Elk Grove station early this morning. Moments ago, I had stood by Grandma and Grandpa as we waited in line to be processed into this chaotic place. How could they be lost?

I clung frantically to Marielle's hand, determined not to lose her too. Al and I had vowed to look after our three helpless ones to spare them undue stress. How could this have happened so soon after our arrival?

Al ran to the front office to find out which quarters they had been assigned. Marielle cried and I worried for what seemed hours. Finally, Al returned with our loved ones. Our family's anguish in the first hour of internment was over. Somehow, Grandma, Grandpa and Nami had been assigned to Section A with 24 single men who arrived with our group. Al found them on the opposite end of the fairgrounds. We quickly learned the consequences of not being absolutely careful. It would never happen again.

We dragged our luggage to the barrack as best we could— anxious to have some private space where the six of us could be by ourselves for the first time all day. We found, however, that the room assigned to us was already occupied. What a surprise! The Hideo Kadokawa family was in our tiny room. It was already dusk, so we decided to stay together for the night. The Kadokawas were cousins, so it seemed a shame to send them out. With nine cots, a baby crib, and a huge pile of luggage, there was not much room, but we managed to fit every-one in.

Each family was assigned a portion of the black tar-paper covered barracks. The floor was asphalt and still smelled strong, as it had been finished only recently. The penetrating heat of the Fresno sun turned the asphalt into a soft substance by midday. The floor sank when we stepped on it, and when we sat on our cots the legs penetrated the soft asphalt.

No one slept very much that first night. Searchlights blinked continuously in the darkness. The sounds of voices never stopped and kept everyone awake. One of the Kadokawa children became sick and cried with pain. She could not be quieted, and the commotion got everyone out of bed. Screams of other children reverberated to the roof and across the barrack to torment all five families assigned to our building.

In the morning the Kadokawas moved into a room of their own. We surveyed our quarters in Section H. For the six of us we were assigned a large room that measured 20 by 25 feet. The room was as large as our kitchen back home. Our six cots took up most of the space. The walls were of a cheap grade of knotty pine wood. I could see the roughly finished roof with its wooden beams and the tar-paper covering on the outside. The tar was already beginning to drip onto the cots as the morning sun melted it.

The walls that separated us from the rooms of our neighbors were open at the top and unfinished. There were no ceilings. The partitions were so thin that even a whisper could be heard through the walls. Gaps between the boards and knotholes destroyed whatever privacy there was supposed to be.

Families eventually tried to create some measure of private dignity in whatever ways they could. Orange and apple crates from the garbage pile behind the mess hall were fashioned into tables and cupboards. Scraps of poles were turned into corner closets and covered with bedspreads. Wires were strung across the rooms and hung with sheets to create individual spaces.

Our basic needs at camp were provided by the military who had jurisdiction over us. Although they were accustomed to caring for adult males, camp authorities had no experience in dealing with women, the elderly, or children including teenagers and infants. This created innumerable problems, each of which we had to patiently resolve and maintain our emotional and mental stability.

The food was a problem for all of us. The mess hall was hotter than anywhere else in camp because they cooked for so many people. Eating in such a crowded, hot place with so many strangers, all in a hurry, was enough to ruin most appetites.

Our first meal was hot stew. My plate took my appetite away: smelly mutton stew with jello melting into it, a distasteful mess. I tried to eat the buttered bread, but streams of perspiration ran down my face and would not stop. I gulped a salt tablet, which we were told to take regularly, but with my empty stomach, I was immediately nauseated. I hurried out of that noisy, crowded place that smelled so bad and rushed to our barrack. I was glad I had packed some soda crackers and jam to quench my hunger.

The bathrooms created another problem that we had to get used to. My first encounter left me smarting from the shameful insult to my modesty. I waited as long as I could before I finally went. The latrine was in an open public area with no privacy at all, and there was a long, long line queuing to the small shack. I heard water running, and at intervals, there was a great splashing sound like something heavy being knocked over. I tried to figure out what it was, but no bathroom I had ever seen made noises like that. When I got closer, I was shocked to find that the latrine's walls were only screens. I could see people sitting in a row. There was nothing private about it at all!

The door opened, and it was my turn to go in. I entered reluctantly with a very red face. Nothing in my life had prepared me to share my humanness with all these strangers. Five ladies sat back to back with no partitions, their tan bodies exposed, and almost touching each other. The banging came again just as I sat down. There was another great splash; then a large, wooden box spilled water that rushed through the trough beneath me. Raw sewage, putrid and unbearable, splashed out of the seat on the end, next to where I sat. The odor was overpowering. I thought surely I would faint. I ran out clutching my stomach and throwing up along the way, unable to cope with the stench. I never complained about the smell of the stew again.

Even the beds were hard to get used to. We were told to put straw in canvas bags for our mattresses, and a huge amount of straw was piled in the middle of an open area for this purpose. Most of us thought that the more we stuffed into the bags, the more padding would be provided. We were wrong, but we didn't find out until we kept rolling off our cots that first night. We couldn't sleep on top of the lumpy mounds. Every move we made was accompanied by the harsh rubbing sound of coarse straw as we tossed through the night. Away from the privacy and comfort of our homes, we new residents of this strange community tried to sleep, but most of us could not. Like the food and the latrines, it took us a while to adjust.

Chapter 7

Children's Needs Come First

*"Our children are our hope for the future. we must have a
school to provide them with their all important education."*

Early on our first morning in camp, Marielle came running to me
with a bright red popsicle in her hand.

"Where did you get that?" I asked. "Where could you posssibly
have found a popsicle here?" My little girl was smiling happily for the
first time in two days.

"Obaasan found it in the little shack over there," she motioned
with her hand. "She waited a long time and bought one for each of
us."

For this brief moment, my child's tears were gone. It seemed as if
Marielle had cried steadily since the day before when Uppie had been
left behind. She witnessed our shocking departure when even adults
could not hold back their tears, and she wept with us as we entered
this place of confinement.

How grateful I was for Grandma's consuming passion to express
her joy and love for her grandchildren. She told us how she had found
the tiny store in our makeshift city, the PX, and waited in line for an
hour. She inched her way closer and prayed they would not run out
of popsicles before she reached the window. How thrilled Grandma
was to make her purchase with Marielle and two cousins hovering
around while she anticipated their rare treat. Obaasan must have
breathed a sigh of relief as she passed out the icy cold popsicles. How

lucky she had been to get there when she did for others right behind her were turned away when the popsicles were gone.

Our concern for our children was a common one. As evacuees and residents of this temporary assembly center, we wondered what would become of our children. Mature adults might be able to adjust to this strange life, but what of the children? The very young ones reacted in predictable ways. They cried a lot and demanded attention. Older ones were noisy and quarrelsome; teenagers acted wild and tried to be independent. A few angry, rebellious youths caused problems for all of us. They stayed out past curfew, ran around shouting loudly, refused to obey regulations, and generally embarrassed us.

With so much free time on their hands and the loss of their structured community with societal rules and limits, young people were at a loss on how to conduct themselves. Their families were in stress, and for a while at least, there was no one to guide them, provide counsel and help them adjust to this confusing situation.

Nisei parents had a heavy burden upon their young shoulders. Most were even younger than Al and I who were 27 and 30; yet we had the responsibility of not only ourselves and our children, but our parents and their children. We had to be strong. Our future depended upon our strength. This responsibility could not be ignored.

There were so many things that were impossible to explain to children. Marielle, still in pain over the loss of Uppie, discovered that Mrs. Hiyama, right next door to us, had with her a cuddly white dog with a bright ribbon on its fluffy head. What could I tell her? The WCCA had emphatically refused to give permission for any of us from Florin to take even a child's pet. In other areas, there was inconsistency in the enforcement of the rules which resulted in such unfair treatment. Marielle was puzzled by this world around her, and so was I.

"I want my Uppie, Mommy. Let's go back home to Uppie. Let's go back home to America."

For a long time, I kept her strange, helpless pain in my throat and chest. I did not know how to tell my five year child that this strange, mixed-up situation *was* happening in America.

The first days and weeks of camp life continued to bring tensions to our lives. Many of these increased as we adjusted to lives of boredom. We were people who were accustomed to working long hours every day, and suddenly we found ourselves with nothing to do in a place where time stood still. Individual endeavor came to a halt. We felt numb and lost as evacuees. Some of us just stood around dazed; others sat lost in thought. The initial shock left us all helplessly spent.

Then anger and bitterness began to surface over the proceedings of the evacuation. As Florin's JACL Executive Secretary, I was singled out as a target of people's frustrations. There were those who accused me of wrong-doing.

"Mary took care of her family."

"The Tsukamotos and Dakuzakus were not separated."

These confrontations interrupted the necessary tasks needed for us to settle into a routine of life within the confines of this camp. It was unfortunate, but predictable, in the kind of existence we had been thrown into.

There were bitter arguments that could be heard blocks away. Constant nagging and foul language engaged in by some families were endured by their suffering neighbors. The worst in us was exposed as we were forced to give up our dignity. We thought angry, ugly thoughts, particularly in our first days at camp. The quiet, gentle family life we knew in Florin faded as we became accustomed to the perpetual clamor that invaded our lives. There was no solace even when we sought refuge in the only place in the entire place we could call our private home, our little crowded room.

There were people everywhere, and we could hear their voices through the walls. It was a time when Al and I yearned for each other having been married only seven years. We desperately wanted the privacy of a happily married couple but this was denied us. All six of us—three generations—shared one room. During the day there were always voices and people near by. If I wanted to say endearing words to Al, I had to whisper. We smiled and our eyes met; we held hands in our evening walks among the crowd or at a movie.

Every morning, the sound of bugles at dawn woke up the camp. By seven o'clock, dish pans banged at eleven mess halls. Quickly, long queues formed in front of the doors. When we first arrived we had stood there self-consciously, especially the graying grandparents, but eventually, we became used to it as we did with everything else.

We lined up for each meal with colored cards in our hands. Only 250 could be accommodated with each meal shift, so blue, yellow or red cards indicated our time to eat.

Eventually the mess halls improved and we were fed amply. We missed the satisfaction that a free person has in being able to provide favorite dishes to suit the tastes of each member of the family. And, most importantly, we missed the personal effort that accompanied the preparation of food for our loved ones.

Some found it hard to adjust to the military food because they were used to eating Japanese cooking and seasoning. The Issei especially were accustomed to eating rice with lots of vegetables. Rumors circulated throughout the camp of older people who had trouble with the food and could not eat.

We heard about an elderly grandmother who was aghast at the breakfast served one day. Her quarters were in a former horse stall, and she saw before her that day a bowl of shredded wheat cereal.

She cried, "First they place us in horse stalls and give us mattresses of straw to sleep on. Now they feed us like horses too with little bundles of hay." Although the incident was somewhat amusing, it was another indication of cultural shock and the loss of self-esteem and dignity in this prison camp. The strange cereal went uneaten by many of our elderly.

Al came home to our little room all excited one day. The words rushed out as he told me what had happened to him.

"Mary, I got a job today. I was hanging around the recreation hall in Block H, playing bridge, when Dick Masada, the director, asked me if I would like to be in charge of Block H Recreation Room.

"I told him I was not supposed to lift anything, but he said there wasn't that much to do. All I had to do was open the place up every day at eight o'clock, schedule the club and game groups, keep everything posted on the bulletin board, and lock the place up after the evening event was over. I think I'll take it. I get paid $12 a month, and he already gave me the key. What do you think, Mary? I'm a working man!

I was so proud of my smiling husband. He always came through and had a knack for being in the right place at the right time.

Marielle came running in to tell me, "Daddy was helping the people give us milk at the hall today. He told us to line up and all the little boys and girls will get milk every day at 10 o'clock." She was so proud of her Daddy!

By the end of July, our lives as Fresno Assembly Center inmates were settled into a routine. We had organized a summer school program for 1200 children. Teachers and pupils came together to use their hours for study. The government paid a standard camp wage of $16 per month to the teachers. These dedicated people worked under impossible conditions, but they provided some semblance of schooling for the children.

Our successful summer school was the work of a slender, rather tall, young woman, Inez Nagai. A remarkable teacher, Inez became the superintendent of education at the center. A competent leader, she had been a physical education teacher at Edison Junior High School in Fresno. It was this woman's superb organization that resulted in the fine summer school program that involved so many of us.

Evacuee children had been checked out of their schools before the school year ended. They had not been allowed to finish the term because of the evacuation. We had no idea how long our incarceration would last, so continuation of schooling was imperative.

A few inspired leaders motivated others until we had a cadre of volunteers to serve as teachers. Anyone with at least one year of college was recruited. Though we had no furniture, books, materials, and even no classrooms, the challenge was there for those who rose to meet it. Classrooms were created in sheds, unfinished shower rooms, laundry rooms, along the shady sides of buildings, and even under the row of fig trees. Fine art work and creative crafts resulted from scrap materials, plenty of time, and the ingenious minds and hands of creative people. Despite the relentless summer sun and constantly changing living conditions, the school was begun and continued through the summer weeks.

A tiny corner of a room became the school office. It was over-crowded with busy typists and mimeographers and served as the center of this awesome endeavor. Inez moved calmly about the cluttered place directing the details of the operation. She projected a warm, friendly attitude and encouraged those who did not know where to begin. Though she was dressed casually in a crisp, short-sleeved, white shirt and shorts, her actions were professional and her dedication contagious. Hidden talents were uncovered to open up exciting courses for students—youth and adults as well. Before long, many of us were caught up in the pioneering spirit of the summer school plan.

I was called to the tiny office one day and asked if I would help to teach the children. "You've been to college," I heard Inez saying to me. "We really need teachers if the children are going to get anything out of this summer session."

I was amazed. All I had ever taught was a Sunday School class. "I don't know how to teach," I found myself protesting. "I can remember how hard it was to keep my Sunday School boys in their seats long enough to tell them about the important values of their Bible lessons."

Inez was very persuasive. Before long she made me forget that I didn't know anything about teaching methods and children's educational needs. I wanted to believe that we could meet the urgent need for education, and I knew it would take all of us to do it.

I heard my voice weakly volunteering, "I'll teach public speaking for high school students."

Immediately after these brave words, I realized what I had done as I shook in my boots and wondered if I had gone mad under the Fresno sun. How did I dare to think I could teach! My public speaking classes of high school and college had been years ago. How was I to begin? What was there to teach each day? How could I have been so foolish to volunteer for something I could not do?

I walked back to Section H with my head spinning. I could not even tell Al what I had done. I sat on a corner of my cot and watched the tar drip down from the roof onto the floor. I could not do it. The assignment was overwhelming. I would tell Inez in the morning, but even as I sat, I knew I would be too embarrassed to do that. I searched for words and tried to summon the courage to admit my weakness, but I could not find a gracious way out of my promise. I had no choice but to teach the class.

I knew I could not do so without help, so I wrote letters to Mrs.

Barron and other former teachers and principals in hopes of receiving help with lessons and plans. In a very short time, encouraging words and packages arrived. My prayers, once again, had been heard and the help I needed was on the way.

I struggled in the weeks that followed, but every inch soon became a notch in my learning path. Often I felt inadequate knowing that my lessons were mediocre and sometimes inappropriate. I tried to remember what Mrs. Barron had done in my favorite classes. How did she touch my life so profoundly through the development of my public speaking skills? How could I pass on this great gift of communication to these young people in my charge? I wanted so badly to help them overcome their shyness. I wanted them to speak up, improve their voices and diction, and polish their words so they could command respect and attention. That was the challenge that brought me bright- eyed and eager to my tasks each day. Though I was miserable when I knew I had failed to deliver my message for that day, I could see the signs of success little by little as my young charges stepped out of the cloaks of their timidity and used the power of their presence to make themselves heard.

Our first call for enrollment had brought 400 children to the summer program. By the following week, the center was filled to capacity with children who had become bored with their perpetual vacation-like existence. As the newness of camp life wore off, they preferred to spend their days in school. Enrollment rose to 1200 with a total of 30 teachers. Only a month after our arrival in the center, school was in full swing.

With the help of Senior Girl Scouts, a nursery school began its operation. The girls who participated did so as part of their leadership training. They were instructed by capable Nisei who had been Girl Scouts themselves; now they supervised and organized the activities.

Elderly Issei went to school too. They took a variety of classes from flower arranging to beginning English. There was something for anyone who wanted to learn.

In addition to my public speaking classes, I taught basic English to Issei who never dreamed they would be able to speak the English language. More than 250 enrolled, their wrinkled faces radiant, their eyes bright. Technically, they were classified as enemy aliens, but this did not deter them; they were so eager to learn English. For the first time in their lives, they had time to go to school after laboring 30-40 years in America.

My students listened attentively to my every word. How exciting it was to teach them and to be involved in their profound experience. Long ago, they had sacrificed their personal longings so that their children might be able to be educated, but now it was their turn. They sat on the edges of their seats, eager not to miss a thing. Their bodies were weary, for they had raised large families and worked in the fields from dawn to dusk. Their shoulders ached; their backs were bent from working daily in soil that was so shallow it had to be dynamited in order to plant crops. They had fought the tule in delta lands and battled desert land in the San Joaquin Valley. Now they were ready to take their places as students in our humble school.

Many wore thick glasses and had to sit near the front so they could see. Others could not hear or they had gnarled, worn hands that could barely hold pencils. But, they learned to speak and write their names. They beamed at the prospect of having the freedom of writing their own checks so they would not be dependent on their children.

I was humbled among these venerable pupils. One was my dear aunt, Mrs. Nobu Dakuzaku. She came to learn English from me, but it was Aunty who had been my very first teacher. She introduced me to the excitement of Japanese fairy tales and the rich cultural heritage of my ancestors that captured my imagination so long ago. Now she was here to learn from me.

Though it was late in life for these Issei, they were not discouraged. "Better late than never," said Aunty. It seemed to sum up their spirit and attitude toward learning. I loved their faces and can see them still so highly motivated to catch every drop of learning in the room.

Mrs. Sato smilingly told me why they were so anxious. "If I could only learn to write my own letter to my son in the Army, I would be satisfied. I want to tell him not to worry about us in this place they call Assembly Center. I want him to work hard to be a fine soldier for our America. I know he would be pleased and proud if I wrote the letter myself instead of asking my neighbor to write it for me."

When you have a goal, you can accomplish almost anything. That, of course, is the motivation for all education.

At the end of July we celebrated the successful two months of the session. In the open air stadium, we displayed the student work. More than 1600 students, from the ages of 6 to 76, presented their accomplishments. Even our impressive program of drama, public speaking, and music was accomplished as a tribute to perseverance and dedication.

My public speaking students were scheduled to perform on the giant new stage. I was breathless and weak, hoping I had taught them properly so they could bring their message to their parents and the audience. I knew I had to keep them together so their voices would blend, and they would have to pause, slow down and lift their voices for emphasis in the right places.

I wanted to give a clear interpretation to the meaning Lincoln intended in this brief but masterful address. I prayed that the huge audience would truly listen to these fervent words, spoken through our tears. Most of all, however, I wanted my students to share in this memorable experience and realize that there was hope for all of us. Henry Sugimoto, the distinguished artist in our center, had sketched for us a portrait of Abraham Lincoln large enough to tower over the giant painting of our American flag. My twenty students seemed lost in the middle of the enormous stage, but they spoke courageously:

Four score and seven years ago, our fathers brought forth upon this continent a new nation, conceived in liberty and dedicated to the proposition that all men are created equal.

They were the words first heard at Gettysburg at a dark time in our nation's young history. We, who were trapped in this camp, needed to remember Lincoln's great words as we searched for some bright thread of hope for our future.

It is for the living to here dedicate our lives that these honored dead should not have died in vain. That the government of the people, by the people and for the people should not perish from the earth.

Beneath the shadow of the watch tower, my students spoke out with every pulse beat of their bodies. They tried to express the deep faith born of Lincoln's heart-cry 77 years before. It was an ironic moment in our tragic lives. I so wanted them to understand that they were the people of America of which Lincoln spoke.

There were those who were openly critical of our selection. I was ridiculed for presenting such a message at this time.

"Liberty is a joke in this place," they scorned. "How can we think that government is concerned about us. There is no government representing us."

Others were greatly moved by the stirring words. It was our heritage—our only life line and a tiny ray of hope for our future. We had to believe that "we the people" meant us too.

Our dreams were lost, and now we cried out to the indomitable spirit of our nation expressed so eloquently by Lincoln at that sorrowful burial ground. I dared to hope it would spill over and give us some sense of hope and assurance that America could keep the golden dream for people with Japanese faces.

As a people we were becoming useless to our nation at war. We were ashamed to be the unwilling wards of our United States government. Our children needed meaningful activities to keep them from becoming lazy and shiftless. The thought of a generation of children who might end up as permanent welfare cases was frightening to many of us.

Parents could be heard saying, "We can't let them get lazy." "They are learning how easy it is to be fed and do as they please all day. This is not good." "Children need discipline." The school was vital to us; education was our only hope.

Chapter 8

Life Goes On

"We have to take care of ourselves too—and make sure our intellectual and spiritual needs are being met."

The Issei, pioneers from Japan, ranged in age from about 35 to those who neared 80. The Exclusion Act had eliminated immigration from Japan after 1924. A few younger Issei were called "Yobi Yose" because they had been born in Japan and had come to America as children or teenagers. Yobi means "call" in Japanese; their parents or relatives "called" them to America.

Most Issei had already raised their families and were grandparents. They had labored in the fields or factories of the west coast states until they were sent away to camp.

Al and I were Nisei, the children of Issei immigrants. We were among the older of the Nisei for most were children and teenagers. Some had finished college; but for many reasons, depression or discriminatory attitudes, many of us had returned to the farms or businesses of our parents. A number of us were married and had small children. We began to emerge from these confused times as the leaders for someone had to take charge and make decisions on a daily basis.

Nisei who had been sent to visit relatives in Japan or to be educated there were called Kibei. Some had stayed in Japan only for a short time; others were there for longer periods of time. Their American educations were delayed until their return. Later, some

Kibei became valuable members of the U. S. military intelligence because they fluently spoke and understood Japanese.

Marielle and others like her were Sansei or third generation. Most spoke no Japanese at all though they understood their grandparents. The ones who were old enough to go to school were quite Americanized and much like other children. They loved hot dogs, ice cream, radio programs and Shirley Temple.

Before long all of us—doctors, dentists, lawyers, lab technicians, nurses, accountants, bankers, insurance salesmen, engineers, musicians, bakers, farmers—*everyone* was involved in the daily needs of the center. There were those who were rich, prominent members of their communities, and there were the poor, unskilled laborers, the uneducated ordinary people. It did not matter if you were a common worker or an influential businessman—in the Assembly Center we were all equal. No one was excluded from the mass round-up, and in here, we were all the same.

Anyone who wanted a job could work. Wages were paid ranging from $12 per month for waitresses and latrine cleaners to $19 for doctors and recreation directors. These wages were not enough, though, to pay for mortgages back home.

The majority of our residents were children. Those who were old enough to attend school had missed their final days and graduation from elementary, high school and college. They were understandably upset that they had been excluded from their important year-end and commencement events.

Administration officials were concerned with the morale of people brought together under such unusual circumstances. Attempts were made to bring people together, rallying them for the common good. Cooperation was necessary even though we lived in this temporary place.

An adult forum was established to stimulate our minds to think and plan for the unknown future that loomed ahead. Hurt, bitterness and disappointment engulfed many young adults. Some needed intellectual exercise to bring them out of their private retreats and the deadly sense of lethargy.

We kept up on the news at home and in the nation as best we could. Al subscribed to the *Sacramento Bee* and *Time* magazine which we read regularly.

Weekly forums became regular events at the center. The first topic was on the constructive use of leisure time. A panel of speakers represented a variety of fields: Henry Sugimoto, neo- naturalist; Eizo Nakayama, artist; Mary Kasai, song leader and choir director; Rayko Mano, U. C. literature student; Isasuke Kawaii, student of religious philosophy; Dr. Joseph Sasaki, Boy Scout master; Inez Nagai, teacher; Takeo Kunishige, sumo champion; and Thomas Tanabe, student of philosophy.

The forums were designed to stimulate ideas and discussion. We wanted to provide a sense of moral support and fill our plentiful leisure time with constructive pursuits.

Other forums followed each week with provocative topics and speakers. For a small but serious group of evacuees, the forums provided us with a way to develop courage and bring about wisdom.

I was one of the panelists on the second forum. The topic was "What Are We Becoming?" Frantically, I tried to collect my thoughts so I could present meaningful ideas of social awareness to the audience. I wanted them to know that what we do, think and experience now, and the habits we form while living here, could affect the kind of persons we become.

Never had we had so much free time. As inmates all our daily needs were provided. The food procurement crew ordered and purchased all the food and supplies. The warehouse boys kept track of the supplies and delivered them to each mess hall. Kitchen crews toiled daily to get food to the tables on time for the hungry people. Dishwashers and waitresses did the work we had spent many hours doing at home. There were no fields in which to work, no fruit to harvest, no weeds to pull. Such unexpected leisure time was a shock to us for we had never experienced so much time on our hands.

Setting up order and establishing personal goals were urgent. We needed discipline and meaningful purpose in our lives. We could not dangle hopelessly in mid-air, bewildered and confused.

As we rubbed shoulders with strong, wise leaders, we began to feel a great responsibility. Here was a laboratory of life, a miniature society so to speak, that teemed with all sorts of possibilities. Acts of thoughtfulness, kindness, neighborliness, and caring were contagious. We had a rare opportunity to turn this adversity into a positive force in our lives.

As summer went on, we used the forum as a therapeutic place to express our pent-up emotions and the private, fearful pressures each of us harbored. Each day was a step ahead for the future as we wrestled with our thoughts: "Our problems—what to do about them?"; "Our responsibilities as voters;" "Cooperatives;" "Vocational readjustments of the nation;" "Post war reassimilation into American life."

Slowly, our shattered wounds began to heal.

Our official source of communication in the center was the *Fresno Grapevine*, a small internal newspaper that began almost as soon as the first evacuees entered the gates. It was an extraordinary paper, mimeographed and delivered free to all residents of the camp. *Grapevine* reporters were everywhere, tirelessly searching out news to help us understand camp life. Headed by editors Ellen Ayako Noguchi, Howard Renge and Richard Itanaga, the staff of 25 worked cohesively to put out a first rate paper. Twice a week every word of the paper was read with pride and interest. The paper, written by ordinary people just like us, amazed us as did the immensity of what was going on in the center.

The *Grapevine* was news about us! We could hardly wait for each issue to come out. We were proud of our accomplishments and each other's successes and good news. The paper had a tremendous impact on the development of cooperation among us. People of all ages and stations in life became one motivated community.

"JUNE 3—James Imaharas, formerly of Florin, welcomed an eight pound baby boy, their ninth child and the third child to arrive here in the Baby Derby. The Imaharas arrived on May 29th from Florin."

Such news made us rejoice. But it also made us think of the suffering of expectant mothers. What an ordeal to go through in this strange situation!

"JULY 27—FLORIN BALL TEAM WINS! The Florin A's are victors by winning five games in the first round of the

A Baseball League with the Hanford Nine trailing second followed by Fresno, Bowles, Delano and Elk Grove."

How elated Ojiichan and Obaachan were that their favorite team had won again. I was happy to learn from the *Grapevine* that children and the elderly could find such enjoyment in their long, leisure hours. As the paper reported the array of sports and recreational activities available, more became involved as participants and spectators. Sumo and boxing rings were prepared, a wading pool and shady playgrounds were built for the little ones, and the entire camp seemed to wrinkle up in a giant smile. People chuckled when they read about the funniest softball game ever. Great fun was enjoyed as older Florin Nisei farmers and businessmen played softball.

It appeared that we were beginning to accept whatever we had to face. We each seemed to be doing our share in creating a time for laughter. Even though it appeared that we were "laughing on the outside and crying on the inside," the humor was healing and provided us with ways to cope with the awesome fears of our lives. We still did not know where we were going nor how long we would be gone. Even greater ordeals awaited us, but for brief moments, our anxiety and pain disappeared while we cheered our softball team and rejoiced at new births.

From the *Grapevine* we kept in touch with the outside world too. Hitler's big offensive of the year took place at the end of July. The battle for Stalingrad took place in Russia. Rommel's forces were still stalled on the approaches to Alexandria in Egypt.

Chungking reported that Japanese columns were plunging southward and had reached Wenchan on the coast. The Navy said that twenty warships were lost by Japan in the Battle of Midway. Congress fought over farm prices, and the OPA (Office of Price Administration) was fighting against inflation.

Closer to home, Mitsue Endo, a young woman from Sacramento, filed suit in federal court to be released from the WRA Center at Tule Lake. She charged that she had been deprived of her property rights and that she was a victim of unjust discrimination. Mitsue had a brother in the Army. She sought a writ of habeas corpus claiming that if she had been of Italian or German descent, she would have been exempted from the exclusion order.

We hardly knew what to think about that. It hadn't occurred to us that we had reason to *sue* the government.

There were farm labor shortages in many parts of the country due to the draft and higher pay in national defense industries. Governor Culbert L. Olson of California planned to release some Japanese from WRA Centers for labor work to meet the shortages. This was met with strong opposition, and people were shocked by the governor's stand. A bitter gubernatorial political campaign ensued; Earl Warren campaigned to keep the Japanese confined and out of California.

Our counterparts at Manzanar amazed us with the announcement that they had successfully propagated seeds from the guayle plant, important for the making of synthetic rubber essential for the war effort. Also at Manzanar, evacuees were helping the food shortage by shipping vegetables they raised to other camps. They also raised hogs, chickens, rabbits and bees. A large group of inmates made garments and camouflage netting to be used by soldiers fighting overseas. I wondered if anyone even knew that things like this were going on.

In Fresno Center we proudly learned that Everett Sasaki, formerly our neighbor in Taishoku, headed the victory garden project. Volunteer farmers had 25 production gardens, and soon our mess halls served fresh vegetables daily. We were very aware that throughout the West Coast, food production had been greatly decreased with all of us in camp. Strong, capable hands were idle here while the country needed our help as it staggered under the weight of this great war. We worried and wondered about our farms and impending food shortages. In the center activities we found token satisfaction in the hobbies and recreation programs, but at the same time we tried desperately to weave purposeful endeavor into our busy work. All the while we wondered, how long will this go on?

As I thought about all these things, I began to feel less hostile toward the Caucasian administration of the center. Milton Eisenhower had told Congress how loyal the Japanese were, and surely, by our actions of the past months, the accurate picture was emerging. Regulations imposed upon us, however, made it clear that we were still prisoners. All magazines and books written in Japanese were confiscated. Only the Japanese Bible and hymnal were allowed.

At night every individual had to be accounted for. Head counts were taken between ten and eleven every night. We all had to be in our barracks rooms with the doors unlocked for the official count. Those who worked on the night shift at the hospital or the security patrol, and people who happened to be in the laundry room or latrine, had to have their whereabouts documented by family members. It seemed so unnecessary. No one ever talked about escaping. There was nowhere to go!

Such regulations were annoying and constant reminders of our plight. We were grateful, however, that we were given the freedom to plan and build an atmosphere conducive to the pleasures of the body, mind and spirit. Life, at least for the present, did not need to be a vacuum or a tragic loss. To some extent these were universal human attributes, but they were also uniquely a part of our heritage from the Pacific islands, so central to the reasons we were in this strange life.

The military officials worked hard to maintain the strange community within the assembly center. As best they could, they established a democratic form of government for us. We elected our own representatives from each block to a center governing council. Hugh Kiino, my brother-in-law, who had been JACL president in Florin, was elected to represent Sections H, I, J, K on the community council. Dr. T. T. Yatabe, highly respected first national JACL president, headed the council.

Evacuees began to assume some of the responsibilities within the camp such as the interior security patrol and food preparation. We handled all the jobs of feeding the population of 5500 for whom more than 15 tons of food were needed daily. These changes made a difference. More rice and vegetables were used, and the food was prepared less expensively than before.

Camp morale improved greatly when the construction of the "Hollywood Bowl" was finished. The first event was a combined high school graduation exercise. The outdoor amphitheater seated 3000 people. It was used for talent shows, variety programs and singing together.

Life began to take on a noticeable measure of pride. We found ourselves referring to "our own Fresno Assembly Center."

One memorable evening, Dr. Allen Hunter, pastor of Mount Hollywood Presbyterian Church, came to speak to us. Dr. Hunter entered into my life at a critical moment. Once again, I had found myself hating my Japanese face. All the noisy, complaining, hateful persons crowded around me every moment of each day were beginning to have an effect on me. Everywhere I went, I was in a crowd. So often, people were bitter and whining. I felt great guilt for being so hateful inside. I needed to be forgiven so I could love and care. No matter how hard I tried, my prayers did not seem to help. God seemed far away and as if He could not come into this place of confusion behind barbed wire fences.

There must have been others who felt like me. We needed Dr. Hunter to teach us how to pray. He smiled confidently and gave me a picture to hold. "Tomorrow morning when you get up, Mary, look at every person you meet and imagine a halo over each head. Know that each one is trying to grow tall enough to fit the halo."

Such simple words, but they brought peace and hope to bless my days. Warm joy enveloped me as I realized that I had forgotten that each of us is part of God. I looked at all the faces and smiled into their eyes, and as I did, I prayed. To my surprise, they stopped looking so anxious and smiled back at me. I decided to practice praying so I could feel the presence of God in my life.

I rose the next day at dawn and crept out from the silent rows of barrack buildings. How strange and quiet it was when 5000 people slept. The brightening sky faced me as I sat on the adobe ledge of the stage. I prayed and felt God's voice, strong and clear in the early hours of the fresh new day. Meeting with others who sought God and together feeling the power of Christ in my life was a great, renewing moment. I felt a surge of joy knowing God was near, even in this desolate Fresno Assembly Center.

"Let me always believe that underneath are the everlasting arms to sustain us." My prayer came from the depths of my soul. I knelt there for a long time letting each precious moment fill me with joy. I needed to know that God had not forgotten some of His people.

Smoke began to curl from the mess halls, and I heard voices from the kitchens. The peace and serenity of the sleeping camp disappeared with the noisy clatter of breakfast being readied. Soon the banging of dishpans and the sound of the bugle could be heard in the distance. It was another day at Fresno camp.

FRESNO

VOL. 1 No. 3   Fresno Assembly Center, California   May 30, 1942

1,210 MORE EVACUEES ARRIVE
HUGE IMPROVEMENT WORK STARTED

SKILLED MEN BUSY MAKING EQUIPMENT

Working with their crews of skilled men, the Works division is busy making improvements throughout the Center, according to C. H. Morrill, who is in charge.

In the various new lighting tables...

...pla...
for...
lets...
K...
the S...
noun...
for t...
Section... ...in...
pleted ... that it will be opened soon. Additions are also being made to the kitchen at hospital #2 for a special formula room.

PRESENTING OUR NEW FRIENDS

Leaving their homes in the peak of the strawberry season and bringing a sample of their good weather, the last of the newcomers from the eastern half of ...amento county arri...ay. They represent ...icts of Florin...and Taishoku... northerners' ar...t part stra... with some ...and truck ...them. ...a choice ...Center ...h Owen ...Fresno ...larit...and agric... resented here.

Florin and ...A. C. L. pres... Kiino and No... respectively, ... Nishi, Y. B... among the ne...

(cont'd on p...)

NEW CITIZENS FILL CENTER TO CAPACITY

...the... ...work ...Elk ...ixty- ...Fri- ...trict ...ope- ...le man ...he num- ...in family

...Property ...Officer ...be no more ...into our ...rson wishing ...ings must r- ...s office and ...ose place he...

This is Not the Baby's Place in the Community

NO LAUNDRY MON-TUES-W...

...IN MEMORY...

...To be used only for washing clothes. ...the laundry tubs are...

Library of Congress Collection

Chapter 9

Links With the Outside World

"I was always a letter writer, but there is such urgency now to write to my high school and college friends and teachers."

After the middle of June, government regulations changed to allow visitors in the Center. Caucasian friends and neighbors of the internees could enter the gate and visit families in designated places near the entrance. Fifty visitors were permitted for 30 minute periods. With gas rationing, it was difficult for friends to keep up these visits, but many did. They brought us gifts and news of what was happening back home. They came bravely knowing that many people frowned upon such patronization. They knew they could themselves be victims of overzealous investigators and bigoted politicians. But they came, and with them they brought gifts of friendship that became essential bonds for all of us.

The U. S. Mail was also an important link between us and the communities we had left behind. Letters brought us news from home, and in turn we provided descriptions of center life to friends who cared enough to keep track of us. I wrote this letter to my friend Clara who lived in our house.

Fresno, California
September 4, 1942

Dear Clara,

This is Wednesday—already three lazy days of this wonderful vacation week have slipped by. Vacation? At the Center? Goodness knows how the school teachers have longed for a rest. But finally, by a unanimous vote by the teachers and through the sanction of the Center administrators, a one week so-called vacation was called for the school of this Center. The most important reason for this moment of rest was to make plans for an earnest session of study especially for the elementary grades. Rumor has it that we are certain of being here till the middle of October and perhaps even into November.

Since our children will miss much of school with the pathetic group of untrained but earnest young people as teachers, a regular compulsory elementary program is being planned.

More rooms, equipment and teachers are needed to carry out any sort of a proper program, but something must be done until we are relocated. I have my doubts as to our chances of having any high school classes. If all the grammar age group attended school, there wouldn't be enough teachers and rooms to take care of high school. Fate has it—that I too must drop out of the school system besides a few other valuable teachers. One of our high school teachers has been given a permit on this Student Relocation Program (so vigorously supported by the American churches and Fair Play Committee) and has left the center to attend the University of Colorado. My how we all wish we were students again! Good students too! (Just everybody isn't given this splendid chance!)

I am finally forced to do nothing but sit and rest. My arthritis isn't any better—and the doctor is experimenting. So my left arm is in a cast to keep my elbow from moving. I really have a good excuse now to get my reading caught up. The emotional stress of the past six months has concentrated in my elbow causing me excruciating, inflamed pain.

My sister, God bless her, does my typing for me, otherwise, I don't think the letters I send you would be at all legible.

It has been very cool these last few days. It is almost quite cold in the mornings. It is quite chilly to see the movies that we are privileged to see now which are held in the amphitheater. Most of us take our coats. All the families chipped in to buy our movies. One resident, formerly owner of several movie houses, donated the use of his machine. So we buy films. We have been having two pictures a week—but feel it is too frequent—so from next week we are going to see one movie a week. It takes 3 nights for everyone here to see the show. Our admission is our colored meal ticket so that there will be enough seats for everyone. (The meals are in 3 shifts and so are the movies shown, thus giving everyone a fair chance.)

We saw Deanna Durbin in "It Started With Eve," then "North of the Klondike," then "Keep 'Em Flying"—Bud Abbott and Lou Costello and then Gloria Jean in "What's Cookin'?"

This week-end a most unforgettable exhibit was presented under the sponsorship of the education department. The Hobby Day Exhibit was planned for Friday and Saturday. So great was the interest to attend the exhibit and so superior the quality of things exhibited that, by great difficulty, church programs for Sunday were changed to extend the exhibit a day longer. (We only have 3 halls which we use as a church, school room and gathering place, so to extend the exhibit another day interfered with the Sunday church program.)

The hundreds of beautifully knitted sweaters of all sizes, colors, weights and styles were so neatly done! Then we saw the daintiest baby clothes, a lovely baby cap done in tatting, the tiniest little mittens and booties for a newborn babe. The doilies, the exquisite embroidery work—the beautiful bedspreads, tablecloths, runners—how lovely they seemed! Many of us saw—not just what appeared on the surface—but felt the living spirit of patience, devotion and artistic expression that must have grown in these tired people all those years and were finally given this opportunity for splendid expression.

Delicate paper flowers seemed to grow before our eyes. There was a lovely orchid colored iris that was too beautiful for words. There were wood carvings of unusual pieces from trees that were carved and polished into ash trays, vases and gorgeous decorations. Then there were the tiniest of airplanes, miniature carved fishes, and polished baseball bats and caps, little monkeys from peach stones, tiny crocheted sandals, little wooden clogs, about 1-1/4 inches long. In contrast, there were giant clogs, about 12 inches long—huge model planes, a great big model of a ship about 3 feet long made of whatever possible lumber available—skillfully built! There were lovely paintings, sketches in oil, pastel, pencil and water color.

There were toys (wooden wheels and all), wooden shrines, jewel cases made of popsicle sticks (Imagine?), almost alive fluffy pooches out of white yarn, black and brown! (With no pets to love and care for here, we create pets in their images.)

The entire exhibit seemed to vibrate with life—so significant were these creations. We deeply sensed the manifestations of an inborn gift of beauty. We found new releases into expression here in this assembly center where all of these three months everyone seemed outwardly so idle and bored, but almost like a miracle, these beautiful things came into reality.

This exhibit gave inspiration to the public as well as to those who exhibited their art. We could not help noticing the ambitious ones with notebooks in hand studying the work in an effort to learn. Many took down the names and barrack numbers of the makers so that they too may learn to make these lovely things.

September has come and our pulse beats of grape season and all its accompanying activity of harvest. Every day we hear pleas for men, women and children to sacrifice their every leisure hour to help in the vineyards. Fresno needs help immediately, all California will need help steadily and so does the entire nation. We pray as you enter these busy weeks more than we have ever prayed before for the health, strength, and good luck that surely you deserve for the good work of months passed. We are grateful and will stand by you. As long as your expenses and your labors are rewarded, we will feel deeply thankful.

We cannot help but marvel at your sacrifice of vacation and leisure for this great cause. We should be the ones to send you courage and strength and cheer as you undertake this great struggle. And yet in every letter you have been the smile and gladness of our hearts. Sometimes it is hard to write a cheerful letter because we get so self-centered here. But it isn't very bad. Much depends on our attitudes. I think we are strong enough to take it and should do our part to cheer and support the real soldiers behind the front lines now working in the vineyards and farms everywhere.

How wonderful to have a fine father and seventy years of age! He must be a grand old fellow to have such a fine daughter. I hope you can visit him soon after the peak of the season is over. Al had a friend of his carve Patty a pin. I hope she'll like it. I bet she had a wonderful time at her relatives' and grandpa's. Marielle is a very good girl now. I hope she continues behaving. I think she's beginning to adjust herself more. She isn't as irritable.

Clara, Al feels that his watch isn't worth all that repair and cleaning expense. I don't think he paid much for it so he wishes to have just Nami's wrist watch fixed.

When you have time to go shopping, could you get Marielle three pairs of panties, size 6? I ordered them from Montgomery Ward, but they are out of panties. I prefer the kind that has elastic all around and cotton panties, but I realize things are getting scarce and whatever you can find at whatever price would be all right with us. Nami would like 4 balls of crocheting thread—J and P Coats, size 30, white, and 2 dozen plain handkerchiefs, nickel ones will do if available.

We are enclosing $5. I hope it will take care of the expense. We realize you're right in the middle of a very busy season, so please do not feel that this must be tended to right away. We're not in a hurry. Thank you a million for your gracious help. Good luck to you both and Patty.

Best regards from all,
              Mary

GOODBY FRESNO — OCT. 12

ARKANSAS HERE WE COME

IN ANTICIPATION OF OUR NEW HOME IN JEROME

Many of us were relieved upon hearing from Bishop C. S. Reifsnider last Sunday that Jerome Center is one of the best among all Relocation Projects.

Jerome will be our home for the "duration." What we'll make of it will depend largely on ourselves—whether we work together for the common good or fail to do so because of our selfish motives.

It is one of the fundamental policies of the War Relocation Authority to build the Center into a co-operative community organized for the good of the entire population. The community store, which will be operated temporarily by the Administration, will, as soon as possible, be converted into a genuine consumers' cooperative store. There will be no private business. The stores in Manzanar, Tule Lake and Poston are now in this process of being changed into a store owned and operated democratically by the people.

This is one of the concrete means of community cooperation. This spirit of cooperation must permeate throughout the Center in whatever activity the residents undertake. We must go to Jerome with the determination that no sectionalism or selfishness will disrupt the harmonious community life designed for the common good. —Hideo Hashimoto

Published every Wednesday and Saturday. Distributed without charge to every unit.

EDITORIAL STAFF   ADVISORY BOARD
Editor------

CENTERS ELSEWHERE

MANZANAR

There is an increasing need by the Army for camouflage nets and Manzanar's success or failure will determine in large measure the industrial policy in other Centers, it was disclosed.

Hope was expressed that production schedule could be stepped up. A review of the local record indicated a drop of more than 50 per cent for September. In August, production was up to 15,354 nets. September's total was 7,512. This loss was largely due to loss of workers through the furlough and education program opening.

Hungry jackrabbits and cottontails which have already destroyed three acres of guayule planted in the farm area will meet their nemesis in three lean greyhounds being imported from the Los Angeles racetracks to hunt down the long-eared pests. Now the guayule experimental project is looking for an expert kennel man who can care for the dogs. It will be a fully paid job.

SANTA ANITA

The "honeymoon train" to Jerome, Arkansas, which left two days ago included newlyweds Mr. and Mrs. Joe Oyama. The new Mrs. Oyama was Women's Editor Asami Kawachi, writer of "Feminine ___"

October 10, 1942

Chapter 10

Goodbye to California

"Al and I had only been out of California once before. I wonder if we will ever return to our home in Florin. "

"Evacuation" was a new word for us in the summer of 1942. Nothing in our previous lives had prepared us for our new status as evacuees. Our private existences were assaulted, and like puppets we were told where to go, when to go and how to go. For the second time in a few months, we prepared for another evacuation. The two hour train trip that brought us to the assembly center paled to nothing in comparison to the trauma of moving out of California across the country to a strange place.

Something else new was the War Relocation Authority which we eventually referred to as the WRA. It had been created by yet another executive order for the establishment of permanent inland facilities. Milton Eisenhower (whose brother was to gain fame first as a general and later as president of the U. S.) was named as the first director of WRA. After only three months, Dillon Meyer took on the task of caring for us, the Japanese civilian prisoners, as we were shifted from military command to civilian authority.

We, who were from Florin, had originally been sent to four different assembly centers; now we were dispersed to four permanent camps, scattered across the nation.

Those who had lived south of Florin Road went to Manzanar in Inyo County, California, the only assembly center that became a permanent internment camp.

At least the Manzanar inmates, such as the Uchidas, Senos, Sakakiharas and Matsumotos, were spared a second move. Florinites who had lived in Mayhew went first to Pinedale near Merced and then to Poston, Arizona. Some of the people who lived around Walsh Station also went to Poston, but everyone who lived west of the railroad tracks ended up in Tule Lake. Some had gone to Arboga first, near Marysville, and then were sent on to Tule Lake. Others from Sacramento County, including us, were sent to Fresno Assembly Center first, then later scheduled to go to Jerome Relocation Camp near the town of McGehee in southeastern Arkansas.

Manzanar had been a deserted and abandoned place, reverted to its desert conditions. It consisted of about 600 acres of land leased from the City of Los Angeles, acquired by the city when it built the Owens Valley Aqueduct.

The Poston Relocation Camp had been part of the Colorado River Indian Reservation. It was located at Poston, Arizona, 17 miles south of Parker, the railhead, and near the California-Arizona boundary. The camp consisted of 71,600 acres of land, most of which was highly impregnated with salt and alkali making it impossible to cultivate. Tule Lake Relocation Project was located on Bureau of Reclamation controlled land in northern California's Modoc County, 40 miles south of Klamath Falls, Oregon. Tule Lake had once been a large lake; layers of shells could still be found within the soil.

The Jerome camp was a lowland heavily studded with forest. Military publications claimed it had "excellent bottom soil...neither marshy nor unhealthy, good for growing cotton and vegetables." We were assured not to worry about mosquitoes, malaria or snakes. There seemed to be a continual need to quiet rumors which should have given us a clue as to the reliability of military information.

The military, of course, had never experienced the wholesale removal of an entire population, but they were entrusted with this unprecedented evacuation. It was quite different from moving single males. Old people, the sick and infirm, children of all ages, farmers, women, and once important businessmen and doctors, as we evacuees were, had far different needs than what the army had been accustomed to dealing with.

The entire process was done in record time without the general public hardly being aware that it had happened. Many of us who experienced it could hardly believe it happened either. We walked through the nightmare in a collective trance of obedience coupled with a desire to show our loyalty and citizenship.

"If it needs to be done, we will do it." That reflected our general attitude toward what was taking place, but we felt we had been cut from the only roots we knew and were being tossed out across the face of the nation, uprooted again. We were national discards; our government didn't know where to throw us.

Ten trainloads were scheduled to leave Fresno and go to Jerome in October of 1942. We had been at the assembly center since the end of May, and it was just getting to feel like home. Freight was crated and sent separately as only minimum necessities were allowed on the train. Lumber from shelves, chairs, and tables was converted into crates for our belongings. The entire camp was caught up in moving fever as we had only a few days to prepare for moving across the country. After we had everything packed and ready to go, we spent many idle days waiting and waiting for word of our departure date. The pattern was beginning to establish itself. First there was the incredible frantic rush to get ready and then such long, long hours to wait. Nothing made sense any more.

We were up at dawn on the day of our departure for we could not sleep. Our little room was bare except for blankets, bedding, and the few suitcases we were allowed to carry. Our belongings had been crated days ago. We were surprised at how much we had accumulated during the five months in camp. Montgomery Ward and Sears Roebuck catalogs had become booming businesses in taking care of our many needs. We were informed by the WRA that Montgomery Ward in Kansas City would handle evacuee needs from Jerome, Arkansas.

Butterflies floated around inside me as I anticipated the move ahead. Our tiny makeshift Fresno "town" had become a haven for the six of us. What could we expect in the strange land far from our beloved California? We had never been around strangers before, and we had not even been out of California.

Beyond our private little room, we heard the voices of friends who had become dear to us as we suffered together through this deprivation. We endured and as we did, we knew and understood each other's private thoughts. We had experienced pain together. We sat with the family in the next barrack when the mother tried to drown herself one night by jumping into a barrel of water reserved for fire emergencies. We consoled the young woman whose baby died at birth as she tried to conceal its existence. We counseled our neighbor's niece, the victim of sexual abuse and rape.

We wept with those who lost loved ones, those who buried grandparents and tiny babes without the comfort of familiar churches and known graveyards. Death, a natural occurrence in ordinary lives, seemed far more tragic in this un-ordinary place.

There had been many deaths. Toyoki Kurima was the first, the retarded child whose mother was forced to leave him in an institution only a few weeks before! Our eyes were swollen and red for days as we shed tears for this grieving family and their unnecessary tragedy.

We wept together to lessen the pain. Yutaro Tominago, aged 70, died from fear and weariness; Sagoro Watanabe at 54, too young, but dead anyway. One followed another and left behind bewildered families to grieve and carry on alone. Each time we felt our hearts could not absorb any more pain, but somehow we endured together, deeply scarred, but survivors all.

In like manner, we rejoiced together for the most ordinary events as if they were milestones in our lives. Births were proclaimed loudly with great happiness. Sons were born to the James Imaharas and Hiro Taharas, daughters to the Sam Tsukamotos and the Oyamas. Weddings took place. Instead of honeymoon trips, the newlyweds were given rooms in Barrack D for brief interludes before being assigned to their parents or other relatives who made room for them.

There were other celebrations we shared together. We rejoiced with talented Kazue Sekiya, a piano instructor and student at Fresno State, when she was accepted to study at Duke University. This meant she was free to leave camp. We admired her bravery in moving out into the hostile world.

We joyfully attended a mass graduation ceremony for the young people who had missed their school functions. There were 142 of them from 42 different high schools, and many teachers and principals came to camp to present their diplomas. Beyond the stage I saw the MP on duty at the watch tower, alert and at attention against the night sky. Again, I was deeply pained and bewildered, but on the outside I proudly took part in an activity that was dignified and symbolic of normal lives.

As I packed to leave, I thought about how we had so quickly adjusted to camp life. Determination and perseverance had prevailed at least until now.

Even in such a place, in traditional family councils, we met to pool the wisest thinking and to give moral support to each other when difficult decisions had to be made. There were no private places, only the humiliating indignity of having to discuss personal situations in the middle of an open thoroughfare or in the midst of bustling people all around.

Such a family council had taken place when my sister Isabel and her husband were faced with the possibility of Isabel's hysterectomy. Her condition worsened, and we had to decide what to do. We stood under the hot Fresno sun and agreed to risk her life by trying medication so that her hope for a family would not be destroyed. As we later found out, it was a wise decision.*

Memories of the summer months haunted me as I waited to leave the only home I now had—our dismal barracks in a camp rapidly emptying itself of its occupants. Our Nisei boys in service had come here to visit their families. We wished them well and treated them with the highest dignity and respect. Many were in limbo waiting for confused army officials to decide what to do with them. Others were demoted or not given promotions they had earned. Still others had been shamefully mustered out.

Although they were as confused as we were, we were proud of them and the uniforms they wore. Our patriotism somehow remained untouched. I had even voted. Seriously, I sent for my absentee ballot and had it notarized so that I could vote in the primary election. As

---

* The two children who eventually were born to them were joys beyond their belief: one a concert violinist, Neil Oshiro who went to Annapolis and became a commander in the U. S. Navy; the other an artistic, creative dancer and a notable choreographer, Judy Oshiro Dehont showed these talents while still a child to the delight of her amazed parents.

a citizen, I felt I had both the privilege and responsibility to take part in my country's election.

It was here at Fresno that our dearly beloved Grandpa, Al's father, had almost slipped away from us. Ojiisan had almost died after surgery for his varicose veins and a nearly fatal reaction from penicillin. His eyes swelled and closed, and his entire body was covered with red welts and swellings. The itching and pain were more than he could bear as he perspired greatly from the intense heat of the hospital ward at Fresno in mid-July. Not one to complain after his many years of hardship, Grandpa whispered weakly to us, "No more. I want to die. this is unbearable." But he did not die, and we nursed him back to health.

All these memories rolled up into one as I prepared to leave Fresno. Behind me were five months of hard work, pride and tears, but I was thankful my family and I had survived this first ordeal. I only hoped and prayed that we could do the same as we met the next challenge of our internment.

The truck rumbled out of Fresno Center. What a change from the sight that had greeted us five months ago. Black tar-paper buildings, covered with a layer of brown dust last May, now bloomed with a profusion of morning glory vines. Intense shades of purple and every shade of violet and white imaginable transformed the ugly barracks into things of beauty. We farmers, who had made California the most productive agricultural spot in the nation, had magnificently changed even this barren desert city of barracks.

Issei farmers in their twilight years had used their time wisely doing the one thing they loved and did so well. They planted seeds and enjoyed the thrill of watching their gardens grow. Our departure was brightened by the knowledge of what we were leaving behind.

An advance crew had left for Jerome in early October. My brother George, a high school student, was among the volunteers; so was Dr. Kikuo Taira, a respected evacuee leader from Fresno and a distinguished physician in his other life. Their task was to construct living quarters for the 9,000 evacuees who would soon be there.

We eagerly read Dr. Taira's letters as they appeared in the *Grapevine*. The considerate doctor made suggestions for babies, mothers and the elderly as they prepared for the long trip. We were warned that it would be cold at night and we should take pillows and blankets for the long train ride. Old, vintage railroad cars had been gathered to transport us, with the trip expected to take four to five days. For the 2000 mile journey, we would need toilet articles, cups, towels, food, snacks and Kleenex. Dutifully, we prepared for this next journey.

A family of 5000 souls, we journeyed together to Jerome with about 500 on each train. In spite of many misgivings and our continuing sorrow at the loss of our freedom, we shared a strange but warm sense of camaraderie. We had been diverse peoples abruptly dragged from our homes and placed here together, but we had come to love one another in our adversity, and our earlier quarrels, divisions and conflicts were laid at rest.

At 4:00 p. m. on the 14th of October, our train, loaded with California evacuees, left Fresno Assembly Center enroute for Jerome, Arkansas.

As the train headed south, we internees witnessed our last California sunset from the dry desert of Bakersfield. The shades were pulled down as we passed through towns and cities, but we watched the sun sink through the spaces between the shade and window.

Al kept a little notebook as a record of the trip. He wrote on his first page: "We know it is the last California sunset we will see for the duration. This makes it even more impressive and beautiful. We will remember it for a long time."

Our seats were our beds, and we tossed back and forth trying to get some sleep. My back was sore from the hard seat, but I tried to wedge my body into place with some measure of comfort. It was mostly without success, but somehow, the night faded into dawn.

Early the next morning we saw an army tank in the desert near the Arizona border. We passed Needles, and a voice called out, "Look down below. There's a river. It must be the Colorado." And it was the great river—winding its way like a long, thin, ribbon snake in the desert. At 8:53 a.m., according to Al's notes, we sadly crossed the border and left our dear California. Breakfast went uneaten as we said good-bye to all we knew.

It was a time of sadness and we were lonely, but we found ourselves experiencing some shreds of excitement at the same time. The train ride itself was exciting, for many of us had never been on such a long trip. We were impressed with the black waiters wearing white jackets who served us meals. They treated us with warmth and understanding and seemed to have a special sensitivity to our unjust treatment.

At times I felt as if I were on a glorious adventure. I sat back and enjoyed the beautiful scenery. The desert never ceased to amaze me with its scenic views. The monotonous terrain of sand and sagebrush was broken periodically by the brown, rippling, ribbon of water that weaved its way across the desert. I could see how vital the Colorado River was to Arizona livelihood.

As I contemplated the beauty of the scenery, my pleasant thoughts were jolted as I realized I was just a prisoner being transported to another camp. There was no beauty in that thought.

Kingman, Arizona, 11:45 p.m. I peeked out through the closed blinds about a mile past a little mining community. To my surprise, there were hundreds of barracks visible in the faint light. I looked at them suspiciously. They looked like the ones we had just left in Fresno, but without the morning glories. I realized it was the relocation camp of Poston. We passed there in the night, and how I wished I could shout out to everyone who we were. We were so close to friends we loved, yet really so far, far away.

Frequently, our train sat on side rails while priority troop trains rushed by. Their national mission was of great importance compared to our useless lot. I felt shame and despair at being such a burden to my country. How much rather I would have been on the other train eagerly serving my country in its need. Instead, I was being escorted to camp under armed guard like a criminal.

On the day we passed the halfway mark to Jerome, I was strangely moody and sad as I contemplated how our smiling, jolly faces masked the dejected usefulness of our lives. Innocently, many of us were accepting this rare train ride like an unexpected privilege in our lives. All through the cars, people played card games and Chinese checkers with colored marbles moving to and fro. Children napped when they were tired, and they too were able to enjoy simple games as long as they stayed quiet. At times, we put them all into a huddle and sang with them using song sheets provided in each car. It seemed so unpatriotic to be enjoying ourselves at a time of national tragedy.

Hours ticked away slowly as the train made its way eastward. The gentle rhythm lulled us into complacency. Ever onward, we covered the miles. The shrill sound of the lonely whistle punctuated our quiet moments. Clouds of black smoke drifted past the windows as we heard the giant beast make its presence known. The pistons clanged and the train rolled along. Soon there was a sameness to the sounds, and we began to feel we were one and the same with this huffing, puffing monster that hauled us farther and farther from our homes.

When something happened to break the boredom, it was usually some kind of crisis we could have done without. Lightning, they say, does not strike twice in the same place, but it did with Al's sister, Edith. On the day we left Elk Grove her son, Sonny, was found to have the chicken pox, and the family had been quarantined for the trip to Fresno. On our third day on the train to Jerome, Lester, the next youngest Ouchida, found his body covered with measles. We could hardly believe that patient, caring Edith could have such misfortune strike her twice.

The Ouchidas were quickly placed in quarantine again, but this time instead of being hastily locked up in the ladies' bathroom, they had an entire compartment for their isolation. Poor Lester—now it was his turn to be sick. We were not able to see any of the eight of them for days.

We passed through unfamiliar states and saw many things we had never seen before. By the 16th of October, we had covered miles and miles of New Mexico sagebrush. I sketched a map of the U.S. from memory and was amazed at the route we seemed to be taking. For some reason we were weaving in and out of the state and going up into Colorado. My sister, Isabel, and neighbor, Bill Okimoto, kept notes. With Al's journal and mine, we had a clear record of our historic train ride to Jerome. Only once in the 2000 mile journey did we set foot on land. In a desolate part of the New Mexico desert, we were surprised one day when we were told to get off and walk to stretch our legs. It was strange to step down from the rhythmic clattering of the rails to firm ground when it seemed like the earth was still moving under our feet.

How good it felt to breathe the warm air and sense the freedom in the breeze even though it was only for such brief moments. The

Military Police were more visible now than they had been on the train; we had no idea there were so many of them. They stood guarding us as if we were going to escape. How could we? There was no place to go, and if we even harbored such thoughts, what could we possibly have accomplished by doing so? They needn't have worried; all we wanted to do was greet old friends and relatives we had not seen for days.

Dodge City...Newton, Kansas...we were exhausted from long, sleepless nights. Though physically tired, we could not sleep. In desperation, we played cards to keep our minds occupied.

On Saturday morning, we stopped in a jungle of railroad cars in Wichita. Four long hours passed until finally, the breakfast call was heard. How grateful we were that a dining car had been rounded up. We crossed into Missouri, and by late that evening, we viewed the great Mississippi River we had studied in our geography books in grade school. I never thought I would see it on a train ride like this.

Before we knew it, we were in Tennessee. I had no idea how we had gotten there or why we were going in that direction. Dinner wasn't served that day until midnight, but by then we were too tired to eat. The next day we headed back, retracing our route until we crossed the Mississippi again. It did not make sense, but we were getting used to things not making any sense.

We moved southward. I pulled up the blinds to get my first view of the South. We were in Missouri, moving into Arkansas. Along the railroad tracks were pathetic, unpainted shacks surrounded by weeds and dead trees. People stood idly in their yards and watched our train go by. Their clothes were old and ragged, the expressions on their faces tired and forlorn. I had never seen such poverty before. How can humans live in such wretched conditions as these, I wondered. In Florin we had been poor, but nothing had ever looked like this.

As I looked out the window, I saw a tall black fellow walking along the road. He wore a bright blue, broad-shouldered, zoot suit and carried a Bible under his arm. On his head was a smart straw hat, but I chuckled when I saw his hands, for he carried his shiny, polished shoes. How wise he was, for the path along the yellow weeds was full of slippery mud holes. Only in his bare feet could he have hoped to get to his destination.

All day we rode, but the call to eat never came. The children began to fuss and cry. The snacks we had packed long ago in Fresno were all gone, so there was nothing for the hungry, whimpering children. The sultry, oppressive heat we would get to know well in Jerome was already making itself known to us. Everyone was thirsty, but there was no water to quench our thirsts.

The sun had set, but still the train moved on. We strained our necks trying to get our first glimpse of Jerome. They said Jerome was in the Mississippi River Delta—there was nothing but swamplands covered with shrubs, cypress, white oak, persimmon and all kinds of trees on either side of our train. I envisioned terrible snakes and giant mosquitoes and who knows what sort of crocodiles and other creatures lurking in the dark. All the rumors I had heard came rushing into my consciousness. Could this really be the site of our new home?

After what seemed like hours, the train came to a stop and we all got off. In the darkness we had no idea where we were. Grandpa sat on his suitcase and stared straight ahead, the picture of forlorn humanity in his crushed coat and hat. Grandma's look of confusion brought tears to my eyes. Nami was silent, waiting patiently for someone to tell her what to do.

My baby, Marielle, sat on a crate fighting sleep. She had eaten nothing since the previous day. I saw her falter and start to slip, but before I could reach her, she fell to the ground. She cried out angrily, frightening the other children. Soon their loud protests added to our fatigue. An ugly, purple bump blossomed on Marielle's forehead. Such was our introduction to Jerome, our new home.

Nothing was ready. The grumbling kitchen staff pulled out a little bread and leftovers they had for our first meal. No one had told them we would need meals when we arrived. We were told to sleep in Block 9, but we had to use the latrine and mess hall in another block. There were 472 new arrivals, but it seemed as if no one was expecting us to arrive this day.

It was an unforgettable night—October 18, 1942, and we were in Jerome, Arkansas.

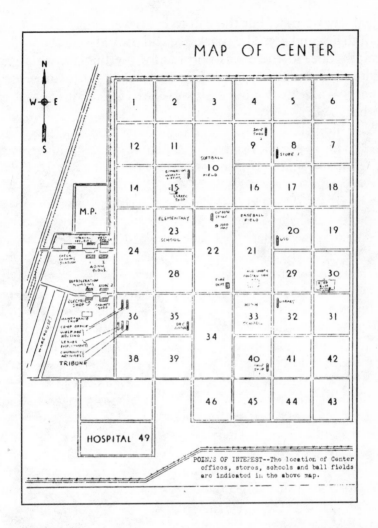

MAP OF CENTER

POINTS OF INTEREST--The location of Center offices, stores, schools and ball fields are indicated in the above map.

COMMUNIQUÉ   No. 2

Jerome Relocation Center, Denson, Arkansas   October 27, 1942

Dance
Get Acquainted

A Get Acquainted dance
will be held at 7 o'clock
tomorrow night at Recrea-
tion hall 4.

Sponsored by ex-Fresno
nans, dancers from Santa
Anita are especially in-
vited to meet the newcomers.

Admittance will be for
couples only.

Local Girl

In the first
featuring a Ce
dent, Clara T
was married t
Kerry I. Se
Villa

DIARRHEA NOT INFECTIOUS

The prevalent cases of
gastro-enteritis (diarrhea)
are apparently of chemical
and not infectious nature
and last about three days,
Dr. Donnell W. Boardman,
acting Chief medical officer, reported.

Cases of enteritis are
reported as far as fifty
miles from the Center and
their cause is being investigated by the State Public
Health officials.

Dr. Boardman also re-
quested that residents note
the signs posted in the
local Pos lavatories by the
staff. It should also be
everybody's concern to keep
quarantined children within
their respective homes, he
added.

Deliver e
to your bloc
cetain receipt,
be delivered to
ier who will
manager a recei
will be secured s to
ered to payee wit
ified ti e.

Mail Order Service Set Up In Canteen; New Items on Sale

...ter's first mail order service bureau has
... in Canteen 8. Arrangements were com-
..., manager of the Kansas City
... and Company.

... actions are now a-
... with sales
all residents an equal opportunity in obtaining jobs
regardless of date of their
arrival, Love added.
Job applications should
be made in the Placement
office, Recreation hall 5,
from 8 a.m. to 5 p.m.

New items on sale are
cosmetics, drugs, pastries
and magazines. Beginning
tomorrow the magazine rack
will have Colliers, Look,
Life, Readers Digest, Time,
Detective Stories, Western
Stories, Ladies Home Jour-
...man's Companion, Cosmo-
...comics. The
...crat is now sold at
A full line of cosmetics
will be on sale soon.

Men Needed To Clear Land

One hundred men are
needed by the Engineering
section to clear land,
build roads and for drain-
work. The using of
and heavy equip-
will be required on
this job according to William C. Love, placement
officer.

An additional 150 men
are needed by the Agricul-
tion for logging,
and for clear-
farming.
rs are wanted
and sharpen

Cut Rugs to Local Jive Band

...ST CONDUCTED
AME SCHOOLS
...two grammar
...school
...contest

Interested in Scouting?

Do you know what to do
for a snake bite? or for
poison ivy or oak? Do you
know the plants and animals
here? Do you want
camping in the area?
tween 12 and 15
who want to say

This is just the place for
All boys interested should
contact Eddie Sakanishi,
7-D, or Paul Caito, 6-B-F.
Leaders also are wanted.

BLOCK MANAGERS

...ting block managers
...newly occupied
...oro Yamasaki,
... and Fred H.
...Nobuto,
...o,41.

FIRST CENTER BABIES WEIGHED ON FISH SCALE

The honor of being the farmers. They have a two- of Dr. and Mrs. Y. Fred

Governme
be cashed in
manner:

with the moving of e-
quipment into one of the Center buildings of the Cen-
ter hospital yesterday,
the medical staff expects
to hospitalize patients
...arters section
next week.
Although some families
may find housing facilities
cramped for the present,
persons, he sai...

127

Chapter 11

Internment at Jerome, Arkansas

"It is a strange Christmas in 1942—locked up in the swamplands of Arkansas."

Wearily, we dragged our tired bodies to our new home—an "apartment" in Block 9, Barrack 8, Room E, 20 feet by 16 feet. It was smaller than our Fresno room, but what heaven! Al, Marielle and I had a room for ourselves! Grandma, Grandpa and Nami had the room adjoining ours. My parents, brother and sisters were near by, and the Ouchidas were also in our barrack. Nearly 350 of our Florin friends were near us in Block 9 including my sisters and their families. For this pleasure, we were very, very grateful.

Our room even had a wooden floor unlike the soft asphalt of Fresno's barrack. The walls and ceilings were well constructed of good wood. They were solidly built and did not have knotholes such as we had known in Fresno. We basked in the privacy, such as we had not known since leaving our Florin home five months ago.

The next morning we discovered the error of Jerome's excellent construction. Everything in the camp had been constructed for tiny people. We had wondered about the strange closet in our room; it was so close to the ground that Marielle could almost reach the rod. In the latrines, little, low toilets were set in rows. Laundry tubs were placed on stands as if they were built for kindergarten children. Our mess hall picnic tables were much too small.

A construction worker provided the answer in response to our puzzled looks. "Are you the people we are building this camp for?" he asked in surprise. He looked in amazement at young, Nisei teenagers who stood almost six feet tall.

"They told us little, brown people would be coming here," he said. "We were thinking they were like pygmies."

It was a silly mistake and an inconvenient one, but it provided us with a touch of humor that helped to brighten our arrival. Of course they had to adjust everything to fit our big bodies, and until this was done weeks later, most adults could not sit anywhere in comfort. But, it was still much better than Fresno.

In many ways our arrival, 17,000 of us at the two camps of Jerome and Rohwer (20 miles apart), was quite a cultural shock to the people who lived near the swamplands of southern Arkansas. Most residents of Arkansas had never seen people of Japanese ancestry before. No wonder there were those who were alarmed and appeared to be on the verge of panic. Rumors circulated through the small towns of an enemy invasion, which seemed strange for the "invaders" were locked up in concentration camps under armed guard. Our arrival, however, definitely altered life in the state of Arkansas, culturally as well as economically.

The sister states of Mississippi, Missouri, Louisiana, Oklahoma, and Texas were affected too. When 20,000 people come into an isolated area practically overnight, it is bound to affect almost everything. The same thing happened in all the areas where War Relocation Authority (WRA) camps were established. There were ten in all, and all were established in dismal, abandoned places far from the West Coast. Their colorful names disguise the sorrowful memories that are part of their story: Minidoka in Idaho; Amache Granada in Colorado; Heart Mountain, Wyoming; Topaz, Utah; Gila and Poston in Arizona; Manzanar and Tule Lake in California; and Rohwer and Jerome in Arkansas. Eventually 120,000 men, women, and children were confined behind the barbed wire fences of these ten camps.

We wondered how our loved ones in other camps were getting along and whether the problems we had were similar to theirs. There was little communication from camp to camp, so when letters were received, we eagerly gathered around to hear the news.

We waited many days for our freight to reach us at Jerome. There was a war going on, and we knew we were not a top priority, but it seemed to take such a long time. We were desperate for our bedding and clothing, especially when we started getting sick, one by one, many before the first day was over. A wave of dysentery hit the camp just as we were trying to get settled.

The sickness had disastrous effects because the camp facilities were not completed. I searched block after block to find a latrine ready for use and walked long distances to find hooked-up showers. The few working latrines and showers had incredibly long lines. The people queuing up were just as upset and embarrassed as I was.

"If only the freight would get here," Al implored to the great spirit of slow trains. It was our chamber pot we needed so desperately!

By the time our crates arrived, our critical need was nearly over. Our illness was found to be gastroenteritis diarrhea caused by the water supply which had been exposed to contamination when new plumbing was installed. When they identified the source of the problem, we were warned not to drink the water unless it was boiled.

Our water source was 700-900 feet underground, and it was good safe drinking water except for this incident. It was strange water, very soft, and its sudsing factor was extremely high. The soapy feeling was impossible to rinse off. I had never seen so many suds; they just wouldn't go away.

Our bathrooms were such a big improvement over those at the assembly center. We were pleased with the gleaming white, porcelain, flush toilets. The only thing we didn't like was the long, open wall of toilets with no partitions. Some women took huge paper bags and wore them over their heads as they sat there so exposed. Their loud protesting finally convinced the camp directors to correct the situation. We scrounged for curtains to provide privacy, and finally, the bathrooms met the approval of the mothers and daughters among us.

Dreary, tiresome days fell into place week after week. We recovered from the stressful train ride and the attack of diarrhea that weakened so many of us. Al and I sat in our little room one afternoon and talked about the health of each of our loved ones. Though we worried about each of them, they all seemed to be better than they had been for weeks. Cautiously, we hoped that our lives might be free from worries for a while.

"Why do you perspire so?" my husband asked, and I noticed at the same time that his brow was moist as well. The temperature was not high; we were accustomed to hotter days than this in California's valley. As we talked, we realized that the climate in Jerome was vastly different from what we had previously known. Gone were the cool, invigorating breezes of the Sacramento Delta. In their place were humid days and nights, a great difference to Californians who knew only dry desert-like air.

I noticed that people were reacting to the new climate in subtle ways. Their energy seemed sapped, and they were getting listless and lethargic. Many of us hoped that things would change as fall turned into winter, but we worried about the purposeless lives, feelings of drifting and lives without dreams. As Al and I talked about this, we knew we would have to work to make this place worth living in, a place where human potential could grow and children could develop as normally as possible.

One evening shortly after our conversation, I walked home from visiting my cousin, and as I crossed a wooded area, I came upon a pile of scrap lumber left by workers. I found a beautiful, square piece of hardwood that had been finely sanded. Though it was heavy, my sister helped me carry it home to our apartment. Al was mighty pleased and made it into a nice table. I used it as my writing desk all the time we were in Jerome.

Al made our little room pleasant by partitioning space with wire and a bedspread so that we had a "living room" and a "bedroom." From scraps of wood he made shelves, a table and chairs for Marielle, and a kidney-shaped dresser and vanity for me. I covered the vanity with a pretty flowered print I ordered from Montgomery Ward's catalog and made little curtains to match. I had enough left over to make a bed cover for Marielle's cot. With a mirror, also ordered by mail, I felt quite special to have such classy furniture in my new room.

Many rooms were thus altered to fit individual tastes and the creativity of both men and women. Some men complained because their wives kept after them to make improvements. For those unaccustomed to carpentry it was hard, tedious work, and the wood was so hard that hammering and sawing were difficult. It was just amazing to see how scrap lumber could take on such new looks, and with colorful fabrics, stitched according to each owner's ingenuity, we had quite attractive apartments in our tiny family spaces.

Life was certainly better than it had been at Fresno, but the barbed wire was still there to separate us from the outside world. Once inside the gate, no one could leave without a properly authorized pass. Sentries with guns were on the watch towers and always alert.

There was more privacy, but we still ate at picnic tables in large mess halls. Our buildings were farther apart, better constructed and much better insulated. That provided us with a sense of quiet that was good for body and soul.

Gradually as Al and I assessed our strengths, we realized how fortunate we were to have among us many who were so very talented. When I heard George Seno sing "Thanks Be To God," I felt as if the barrack's roof would lift off, as if God Himself had touched us and held us close, even though we felt so far from him in this strange camp city.

We were crowded into this concentration camp from which we could not escape. It was a time of humiliation and despair, but when I was asked to speak to the Christian Youth Fellowship, I pondered what to say. We hungered for spiritual food and we did not want to be here, but as Christians in search of God, we needed to come face to face with our Master, Lord Jesus the Christ. I decided to focus my presentation on living eternity day by day.

I spoke about pain, disappointment and degradation, and how they could be overcome with steadfast faith. Christ indeed could turn despair into triumphant joy. Hope and faith, edged with courage, could help us model His indomitable spirit day by day. This was my message to our youth, and I realized that first, I had to believe it myself. I needed to be the model they could see to live eternity here by taking one day at a time. What an awesome humbling responsibility. I faltered. But there could be hope even in this internment camp.

In December we began to celebrate Christmas. It marked a full year of trauma and anxiety for our future. Most of the former community of Florin, California, was incarcerated in American concentration camps. Though we had lost Florin, hope doggedly stayed with us.

Our Christmas spirit transformed the camp as we sought to create a magical time for everyone from the tiniest Sansei child to the most elderly Issei. Even though we were far from home, we were determined no one would miss Christmas. For a few hours we would forget these cold swamplands so that Christmas would be a merry and cheerful time.

However, just as Christmas planning began, a pressing emergency superseded all other thoughts and plans. It was discovered suddenly that there was not enough fuel for the camp. All regular work ceased, and the men and boys were sent out to the woods to chop firewood. If enough wood was not gathered, we would freeze to death in the cold days of winter about to come.

Women were sent to the kitchens to take the jobs of men so they could cut wood. At each block, women sawed the heavy logs into wood as the trucks and horse drawn sleds brought them from the forest. The task required everyone's cooperation for the danger was real. Somehow, no one had realized how much wood was needed for the winter's needs. Every barrack room had a potbellied stove insulated with brick to retain heat. This was our only heating system, and we needed wood to keep our fires going.

The fuel shortage frightened us, but Christmas plans kept popping into our minds. Al and I organized a caroling group and practiced in the evenings when the work for the day was done.

One cold night as I walked out into the clear darkness after practice, I saw a bright star in the sky. Smoke curled up from each chimney in our strange city of barracks, row upon row. Suddenly, I was reminded of Reverend Sasaki's words in Florin a full year ago, and how he had insisted that we should keep our faith and courage alive by believing that all the darkness in the world cannot blot out the light of one little candle.

As I looked at the star I realized that Reverend Sasaki's words meant much more to me now than they had a year ago. We had survived a year of war and half a year of imprisonment. I tried to understand the meaning of my existence in this camp. I was thousands of miles from home, but I tried not to think about the ugly hate and greed stirred up by war hysteria. It didn't matter that we were

133

American citizens; they still said, "We can't trust them."

We had been deprived of our freedom, our liberty and our property, and no criminal charges had been filed against us. There had been no trials. Though the U.S. was at war with both Germany and Italy, only we citizens of Japanese ancestry had been subjected to this cruelty by our own government. Our only guilt was that we were of the Japanese race. Our Constitutional rights had been terribly violated, and there was nothing we could do about it.

Even the WRA was becoming the target of zealous racists as they attacked the program and claimed the government was pampering us;

"It is a waste of money."

"The government is too lenient with the evacuees."

"They are coddling to their wishes."

"The Japs are disloyal and dangerous."

"They should be kept confined."

Word reached us of this kind of talk, and I trembled as I wondered what else they could do to us.

The frenzy of injustice increased when a bill was introduced in the California legislature to deprive us Nisei of our citizenship. There were those who demanded our immediate departure out of the country. They wanted to send us all to Japan and make sure we would never be able to come back to California. Imagine! It was bad enough that we had been forced from our homes; now they wanted to send us even farther than Arkansas. Al and I just didn't know what to think.

In spite of all this talk, the administrators of the relocation camp and WRA officials showed sensitivity to our massive travail. They personally became involved to show their care and good will during our first Christmas away from home.

Huge Arkansas pine trees were delivered to each mess hall as gifts from the project administrators. The freshly cut giant trees reached up to the ceilings and filled the halls with the pungent fragrance of pine. The Arkansas pines reminded our Issei of the venerable pine tree of Japan, a classic symbol of enduring strength and noble dignity. Their eyes were bright as they enjoyed the nostalgia and stood a bit taller, determined to be noble and enduring themselves.

My eyes glistened with gratitude as I gazed at the symbols of hope brought into this barren place where Christmas joy seemed thousands of miles away. The life-giving green made my body bubble with the spirit of the Yuletide as I forgot for a while my weary soul.

Block residents were encouraged to think of ways to decorate the trees in the mess hall. Each day when we walked in, we saw new evidence of holiday decorations being placed about. There was such ingenuity displayed! Fruits and vegetables were turned into Santa Clauses with cotton whiskers. On the trees were festooned chains of jam jar rings, decorated cans and tiny boxes, berry chains, popcorn strings and dried fruit hung in interesting patterns. Paper wreaths, homemade bells, tinsels, crepe paper flowers and streamers were used as garlands to convert the mess halls into magic places fit for grand Christmas celebrations.

Mr. Wheat, the sawmill superintendent, reported that there were holly and mistletoe in the woods. Before long the entire camp was bright with holly berries tied with red ribbon on barrack windows and in the mess halls.

Block 28 had a surprise giant Santa created by someone with a good sense of humor. A pile of red sand had been delivered to the block, and some creative passer-by had stuck wooden eyes, a nose, mouth, pipe and shoes onto it. I chuckled when I saw it. The arrangement generated quite a bit of excitement until the crew arrived to spread the sand on the path between the barracks.

Mail arrived at an astounding rate. Every day there were cards and packages for someone in the block. The Denson post office that served our camp reported 28,760 pieces of mail during the Christmas season. There were 5,727 packages, almost one for every inmate.

We held a church program with musical talent from many churches. Violinists, trumpeters and vocalists flanked the many-voiced choir made up of musicians who had spent previous Christmases all over California from San Pedro to Florin. It was our first Christmas away from our homes—one that we could not have imagined a year ago.

The banging of the dishpan sounded especially merry on this special day. Whispers had been heard for days of the holiday dinner that was being prepared. From our Block 9 Mess Hall, we smelled delicious smells all day. They kept us guessing joyously as we waited to be called.

Al and I gathered Marielle, Nami and our two old ones and together as a family we entered the Christmas dining hall. Before us were hundreds of colorful decorations that camouflaged the crude rafters overhead. Children were wide-eyed and smiling as they looked with wonder upon the transformed hall.

Marielle's eyes were filled with the wonderment of Christmas. I was grateful that my child could enjoy these simple pleasures. The smiling faces of the hard-working kitchen crew—cooks, waiters, dishwashers—gave away their big secret. Their smiles were bigger than we had ever seen as they anticipated our astonishment.

Their surprise for us was a complete chicken dinner with all the trimmings. Our crew had scrimped and saved to make this dinner extra special, and that's exactly what it was for all of us. Fat chickens had been roasted for our table, chickens that had been raised by our fellow evacuees in Tule Lake. The variety of vegetables was from our own Victory Gardens. Tasty stuffing, cranberries and candied yams met our surprised gazes. For a few moments we forgot our loneliness and separation as we enjoyed this marvelous feast. We rejoiced, determined to bring the Christmas spirit to our miserable existence.

Each child under the age of fifteen had a gift. Some came with the names and addresses of their senders and messages of love and concern. They had been donated by sympathetic Caucasians from 30 states, gifts of friendship and gestures of the true Christmas spirit. Many were from Sunday Schools and churches.

We were comforted to know that we had not been forgotten and that so many people had sent greetings to us at this time. The Quakers of the American Friends' Church were on the top of the list of churches who remembered us and were foremost in their concerns and generous gifts. Christians and Buddhists alike, we celebrated together at this strange holiday time.

Messages such as this from an eight year old in Pennsylvania cheered us immeasurably:

"To a girl I have never met, but I know the receiver of this gift loves America just as much as I do, and I know you are true to the land both you and I love."

Gifts had also been purchased by camp officials. They had helped facilitate a grand shopping trip for the camp council representatives.

Seichi Mikami headed a group of shoppers on a two-day buying spree to Little Rock. WRA Regional Director E.B. Whitake had authorized the expenditure of $1000 for gifts to supplement those sent from outside so that all the children would have gifts. The group also bought small gifts for the elderly Issei. The people the shoppers met in Little Rock were friendly and concerned. It made us feel happy about the good will in the spirit of the 1942 Christmas in Arkansas.

Dec. 24 1942

COMMUNIQUÉ No. 21

Official Bulletin of Jerome Relocation Center, Denson, Arkansas

Greetings

RESIDENTS

Paul A. Taylor

A CAPPELLA CHOIR SERENADES TONIGHT

Starting at 6:30 o'clock tonight, the Center a cappella choir will make the rounds of the Center singing Christmas carols.

Under the direction of Pauline Austin, Center music teacher, the choral group will appear at scheduled dining halls, the only change being use of Dining Hall 43 for Blocks 31, 42

Chapter 12

Trouble in Camp

"Yes-yes and no-no . . . these two questions are destroying more families than we can believe. How can our government officials be so insensitive. None of this is necessary!

During the Christmas season, I renewed my letter writing with vigor and enthusiasm. I wrote hundreds of letters to everyone I knew as I reached out to the outside world in my anguish and hurt.

My typists were my sisters, Isabel, Julia, and Jean, and my cousins, Yeiko and Shizu. Willingly, they typed pages and pages of my letters with many carbon copies. I wrote about camp life and my concerns and included these paragraphs with my personal letters. Our friends were anxious to hear how we were being treated and what was happening to us. Though it appeared dark and hopeless, I tried to make sense out of the bewildering circumstances and wrote to those I thought might care.

I continued to keep a diary and wrote the details of every day. When my heart was tight from crying and the pain in my chest and throat made me feel like I was perpetually weeping, I found solace in writing. I tried to capture in words the feelings of our collective existence.

The path I chose, inevitably, seemed to be the Issei sense of accepting fate, no matter how hard it was. Stoically I endured, without spilling the bitterness and disappointments. I remembered the words of my parents:

"Kobosuna." (Don't spill your gripes.)

And, *"Gambare."* (Make a great effort to survive bravely. Endure quietly no matter how hard.)

I sent cards of good will, faith and hope to Caucasian friends all over America. I sent them to former classmates now scattered at Tule Lake, Manzanar and Poston. I wrote to Nisei boys in uniform, a growing number from Florin and Sacramento.

My sister Julia was talented in drawing. She helped me sketch a barracks silhouetted in the night sky, lit by the brightest star and showing a shadowy figure kneeling in prayer. Julia made dozens of these silhouettes for me, and on these pages I wrote my Christmas messages to my friends.

This letter writing began a disciplined habit that has stayed with me for the rest of my life. When answers came addressed to Block 9-8-E from all over the world, I realized what a fragile life line I had to freedom and the sweet breath of liberty. Faith and justice were slowly being woven into strong threads of gold—enough to last me a lifetime. My daring courage with writing letters surprised both my husband and me. I even wrote to Dillon Meyer, the director of the WRA, about his leadership.

I wrote to Dr. Albert Palmer, president of the Chicago Theological Seminary, a dear friend whom I had met ten years before. Dr. Palmer's stirring words of faith, expressed in his "Christian Watchwords," had sustained me through many travails. Printed on a small sheet, they were the most treasured gift ever given to me. I, in turn, gave them as gifts of my own. "Christian Watchwords for Everyday Living" became a part of my life and provided me with sustenance for the struggle I found myself in.

Christian Watchwords for Everyday Living

✚ ✚

AT NIGHT

THE day, with the work God gave me to do, is done and now the night has come, quiet and calm and beautiful from Him. As shadows gather around the earth I will trust myself, body and spirit, into His loving tender care and go to sleep. His love is round about me and as flood tides from the ocean fill each nook and cranny of the bay, so power and love and peace from God can fill my life to overflowing as I rest quietly in Him. These are the great words in the spirit of which I am going to live; bravely, quietly, calmly, patiently, lovingly, trustfully. Amen.

IN THE MORNING

All this day I am going to be a child of God. His love is round about me. Underneath are the everlasting arms. I am going to be honest and true in all events of life, and I believe that to those who love God all things work together for good. I am going to rise above all worry, fretting, fear and hatred, and live in an atmosphere of spiritual serenity. My life is not apart from the life of God and that which is divine within me can never fail nor be defeated. Behind all that comes, God's love and wisdom will be present to strengthen and sustain.

IN DAYLIGHT HOURS

The same God who teaches the trees to grow beautiful and tall, who inspires the birds to build their nests and through the mystery of instinct leads all living things along their way, is also present in my life, calling me to be true, to be honest, to be steadfast and unafraid. My life is not isolated and alone—God's power and wisdom move through it; I will therefore walk bravely as His child. He has said, "I will never leave thee nor forsake thee," and "As thy day is even so shall thy strength be," and I will trust His word.

✚ ✚

"Dwell deep, my soul, dwell deep!" I am not my body, my body is only the physical house in which I live. The essential thing about me is my spiritual life. So long as I am honest and true and trust in God, my soul is beyond the reach of all adversity. No physical illness or financial trouble can touch the essential and eternal "me." Because I am God's child I can meet all that comes in the day's work bravely and serenely. "My life is hid with Christ in God." "In Him I live and move and have my being."

✚ ✚

I will think as little of myself as possible today, fixing my mind upon my work, my friends, those I can help, and God. I will throw off vain regrets and fears for my personal future by trying to serve God worthily this hour and this day. I am not working for men or money but for God, who is the Master of the universe and whose recompense is sure..

ALBERT W. PALMER
President, The Chicago Theological Seminary

WE THE PEOPLE

I had met the imposing Dr. Palmer when I was a girl of seventeen on my father's strawberry farm. He had been commissioned by the Protestant churches to write a book about Orientals in America. Dr. Palmer had heard about me winning the Wakasugi Silver Cup in San Francisco in 1933 for my first place oration when I was in high school, so he interviewed me and included my story in his book under the fictitious name of Martha Matsu to protect my identity in those days of confused racial tenseness. When I was at COP, I was often remembered by Dr. Palmer with gifts for my scholarship.

Dr. Palmer sent us religious books for Marielle and continued his caring communication to us at 9-8-E, Denson, Arkansas. His encouraging letters brightened our dismal days. I often copied parts of the Watchwords to include in my letters, and I quoted these great words of faith in my speeches. All my life they have been gifts to pass on to others.

I even wrote letters to President Franklin Roosevelt and his wife, Eleanor. The mailman delivered a letter to 9-8-E one day, and I wondered why a little parade of curious people accompanied him right up to my door. He handed me a letter, and his eyes were excited as if he were so proud to be delivering such a letter to me. On the envelope were the gold letters that said, THE WHITE HOUSE. Who could possibly be sending a letter to 9-8-E in Jerome, Arkansas' internment camp from the White House?

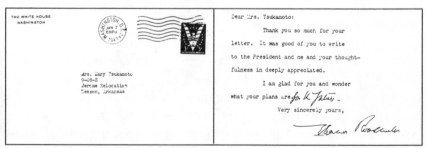

I shook from head to toe as I carefully opened the envelope. Inside was a letter from Eleanor Roosevelt. It was as if the great lady herself had entered my humble, little barrack room! The letter was brief. Eleanor Roosevelt thanked me for the Christmas letter I had sent to the President and the First Lady. She expressed her kindness and concern, and that was it, but I almost felt her presence, her caring, gentle eyes that understood our suffering. I knew she would be deeply touched if she could see how we lived. I held the precious letter in my trembling hands and read it over and over again. Eleanor Roosevelt wrote a letter to me! I walked on air.

Al was excited too. He was so proud of what had happened and went around telling everyone about it. "Mrs. Roosevelt wrote to Mary from the White House."

And my mother—I will never forget what my mother said to me. "This is what I like about America."

Mom's spontaneous comment filled with faith left me deeply impressed. I was surprised that she would feel so positive and affirm her faith in our country in this way. She, who had spent years bending over her big washboard, scrubbing, rubbing, and boiling big tubs of water until her face was flushed and wet from sweat; she who had worked from sun-up to sunset, if not in the kitchen, then in the fields; and now locked away in an armed prison camp, she still had her faith in America. I was overwhelmed with pride.

As the mail kept coming in to me from the outside, I realized how this invisible life line linked us like a golden silk thread to the possibility of a better life tomorrow. Could I dare to hope for such a day when we would be liberated from this stigma of disloyalty? The letter from Eleanor Roosevelt made me believe that such a day would come.

In January of 1943, the government announced that Nisei boys would be allowed to fight in the U.S. Army. A special all-Nisei combat troop was going to be formed, and Uncle Sam wanted our younger boys who were still in camp.

Until then, 5000 soldiers of Japanese descent were in the U.S. Army, but they had been forgotten in scattered posts all over America. Secretary of War, Henry L. Stimson, declared, "It is the inherent right of every faithful citizen regardless of ancestry to bear arms in national battle. When obstacles to a free expression of that right are imposed by emergency considerations, those barriers should be removed as soon as humanly possible."

Our own Jerome camp newspaper put it like this: "Loyalty to

country is a voice that must be heard and I am glad that now I am able to give active proof that this basic American belief is not a casualty of this war."*

Newspapers around the country praised the War Department's decision, but there were those who resented the segregation of the unit. In many ways it did seem like an extension of racism and prejudice.

One unforgettable, cold, March day the Army descended upon us. Not everyone, however, was ready to sign up. There were hundreds of questions that needed answers. We wondered why the Army was seeking volunteers at this time. Many men were nervous as they listened to the recruiters. Such difficult decisions had to be made. Young men had to leave their elderly parents to get along as best they could. The final decision was a personal one, and each family had to make theirs privately—one by one.

In the midst of this confusion over the draft, the WRA announced that there would be a camp wide registration of all evacuees. Everyone over the age of 17 had to fill out a confusing registration supposedly aimed at eventual relocation life on the outside. The two sets of registrations, one for the army, the other for everyone, led to incredible misunderstanding and campwide confusion. This was true not only at Jerome but at all the internment camps. Each questionnaire consisted of long pages that seemed to have been hastily put together by someone who had no understanding of the people who would be filling them out.

There seemed to be no reason for the registration. I wondered at the mentality of those who designed such a procedure for people in our circumstances. I wondered about the timing. If it had been done earlier, wouldn't it have prevented having to take us forcibly from our homes? What purpose did it serve now? We had already been imprisoned for almost a year.

There were two questions on the form that caused an incredible amount of confusion. These two questions, known as Number 27 and Number 28, caused the breakup of many families as family members disagreed on whether their answers should be "yes, yes" or "no, no." Eventually, these two questions tore the camps apart. Bloodshed and violence were their aftermath, all because of bureaucratic stupidity in asking people to submit to questions of loyalty that were subject to such gross misinterpretation.

The two questions read like this:

"27. Are you willing to serve in the armed forces of the United States on combat duty wherever ordered?"

Can you imagine an 80-year-old grandfather or a mother with small children trying to respond to such a question?

"28. Will you swear unqualified allegiance to the United States and faithfully defend the U.S. from any or all attack by foreign or domestic forces and forswear any form of allegiance or obedience to the Japanese emperor or to any other foreign government, power or organization?"

Most of the evacuees simply answered "yes, yes" without thinking of the implications of their responses. When we explained to Ojiisan and Obaasan what must be done, they did not hesitate to reply with their "yes, yes's." Of course they chose America! With tears in his eyes, Ojiisan signed away his private ties with the country of his birth and simply said, "yes, yes". His time had passed when he could even lift his arms against Japan to protect America, but if he was needed, he was ready to go.

I often heard elderly Issei talk as they sat around the camp idling their time away, and so frequently they talked about their appreciation for basic shelter and food. They asked for so little.

"America da kara yo – Kon nani shite kureru no yo." (Only in America would they do all this for us!)

These words came from the lips of brave souls whose days and years of struggle in California had been filled with hardship and insults. They had been denied the rights of citizenship, kept from owning land, and now they had their freedom taken away. But still they expressed their gratitude to the only country they knew, the land they had adopted long ago.

Some of the camp families had children attending school on the outside. Young people in colleges and universities that were not on the West Coast had not been interned even though their families were. Many of us had positive relationships with our former Caucasian neighbors. Our decisions reflected loyalty and faith in America even though the past year had been rife with grief and disappointments. That's the way Al and I felt; there was never any question about that.

Other inmates, however, were insulted by the questions and the way the Loyalty Oath was handled. Some mistrusted its purpose and wondered what would happen to them if they cut their ties with Japan to choose a country that had rejected them and locked them up in armed camps. If they said, "yes, yes," they feared they would be left with no country at all.

Angry Issei in some camps threatened to call the Spanish Counsel (the neutral intermediary that negotiated grievances with Japan about nationals) until the WRA finally agreed to hear their protest. Number 28 was changed to read: "Will you swear to abide by the laws of the U.S. and take no action which would in any way interfere with the war effort of the U.S.?"

The damage, though, was already done. Emotional fury, once released, was difficult to restrain. We who lived through the chaotic days of governmental inquisition were left forever with a sordid taste of the proceedings.

Al and I registered with others like us, but there were strong reactions against the coercion from all over the camp. Several men came into our hall one day and tried to keep others from registering. I was scared to death. It was such a mess. Questions were shouted back and forth:

"Are they trying to force us all to go out?"

"What will happen to our old folks and the little ones?"

"How will families with small children manage on their own?"

"Will the Issei be forced to fight in battle?"

"Is the Nisei combat team wholesale murder?"

"Will we be shipped away to Japan if we don't sign?"

"Will we lose our jobs in camp if we say no?"

We heard about secret groups that met to oppose the registration. People were terrified as a wave of uncontrollable anger swept through the camp. It was the first time we had been in conflict with one another—a stark contrast to what had previously been a pure sense of unity.

One night there was violence! The Reverend John M. Yamasaki, a respected and wise Episcopal minister, and Dr. Thomas Yatabe, past National JACL president, both of whom spoke out and urged internees to stand for America, were attacked by a gang of ten to twenty men. Both men were severely beaten by the hoodlums. I could not believe this was happening to us.

My brother-in-law, Tom Oshiro, was caught up in the strange drama that resulted from this incident. Tom, an ambulance driver who spent many hours helping out with emergencies, was frequently sent to the army dispensary at Rohwer, the other internment camp about twenty miles from Jerome, for medicine. Often it was a matter of life or death. Tom was called to make a midnight ride out of camp; his passenger was Dr. Yatabe who was being whisked out of camp for fear of further violence. Because of the mob attack, Tom was told to keep the whole thing secret.

When Tom got to the main gate, however, a routine check of his identification brought a halt to his involvement. The person on duty noted that Tom had been born in Okinawa. Though he had come to America when he was thirteen, he was not allowed to take part in the secret mission. Always, it seemed, we were at the mercy of the strange quirks of the military and government. They had never been concerned about Tom before. When he couldn't pronounce the names of the unusual sounding medicines he was ordered to bring back on his trips to the dispensary, they wrote them out for him. Until this night he was a trusted courier, but now because he had not been born in America, he could drive no more.

Hugh Kiino, was on a blacklist circulated by the agitators. They objected to his being a council representative and former president of the Florin JACL. Many others were rumored to have been listed too. Block 29 held secret meetings organizing a protest that would lead to repatriation to Japan. I could not believe what was going on. We were tearing ourselves apart from the inside, becoming victims of ourselves.

All activities and club programs came to a stop as we argued and shouted at one another. A sensation of hopelessness came over the entire camp. These powerful issues were destroying us.

The thinking of some of the Kibei leaders shocked me. Though they were American citizens, they had been educated in Japan and did not think like the rest of us. Often the oldest in the family, these young men, the Kibei, had been sent to Japan for their education by their Issei parents. They were usually alienated from both cultures and did not know where to fit in.

Some became the principal agitators regarding the Loyalty Oath. Their actions reflected their lack of acceptance by their peers and their indifference to the American culture.*

One day twenty protestors marched to the front office and gave up their citizenship. Boldly, they renounced their birthrights. It was unbelievable that things had come to this. Though these were the actions of only a few, they jeopardized the future of us all.

The great majority of Nisei were only interested in becoming as American as we could. Our parents had made us attend Japanese language schools, a fact that caused agitators to point out how unassimilable we were and how we would never make good Americans. What they did not know was how difficult it was for our parents to keep us interested in learning Japanese and how fruitless their efforts were. Most Nisei understood spoken Japanese when their parents spoke to them, but they made their replies in English for they could not speak Japanese. Like most immigrant children, we rejected old country values and did not see ourselves as being the bridge between the two generations—our parents and our children. We considered ourselves to be Americans, not Japanese.

On the surface, it did not seem that the Loyalty Oath would have such a devastating effect, but we didn't know it would be taken so seriously by the government either. I could never have imagined the protests and conflicts that surfaced over this issue.

Letters brought us news of trouble in other camps. At Manzanar there had been an ugly riot. The possibility of violence for us in Jerome was magnified by this news. The emotional struggle was a great one. Many of us were on the verge of mental breakdowns. I thought of the fury of the wind that whipped and snapped branches of trees, even the sturdy, enduring bamboo. Certainly, it was the worst time of our lives.

---

* Others, however, became valuable members of the U.S. military because of their language skills.

Chapter 13

Uncle Sam Wants Us

"If only I were a man, I too would volunteer to serve my country in this hour of need."

Winter caught us dashed to the bottom of the deepest well. Our spirits were demoralized. The challenge of life on this "perpetual camping trip" had deteriorated. We had been away from home too long. We were lonely and disillusioned, and our spirits were disintegrating day by day.

I felt the victimization and found myself getting cold and weary, numb and dull to my senses. I was outraged to be corralled in a pen in this southern corner of a state, this God-forsaken piece of swampland. I was tired of armed guards, spotlights, constant surveillance with guns pointed at me from watch towers, and barbed wire fences so tall that no one could possibly climb out. My bottled up submission seemed about to burst like a volcano, bubbling and boiling silently while it readied itself for a big blast.

Battles continued between children and their parents, between supporters of America and Japan, and between those who chose patriotic loyalty to their country rather than filial loyalty to their aged parents. Little apartments were far too small for the battles that waged in almost every room. Young people and old were stunned and dazed from the daily verbal assaults. In our family we were fortunately all in agreement, but many families could not make that claim.

The War Department sent top level men to the camps when they learned of the rebellion there. They were surprised to find that their registration questions had created such a fuss. They had removed 110,000 shocked people from their homes on the West Coast with hardly a voice lifted in protest and had expected the same smoothness with the loyalty registration.

Decision makers in Washington, however, didn't eat each day in crowded, noisy mess halls. They didn't live in makeshift barrack rooms with infants, children and their elderly. They didn't have to watch as family units crumbled away amidst the anxiety. They didn't have to face the freezing weather with shortages of wood, and they didn't have to revert to primitive methods for meeting that crisis— men chopping wood in swampy forests and women sawing logs brought to them on mule-drawn mudsleds.

If we had known that in Germany, Jews were being systematically rounded up, placed in camps and sent to gas chambers, I wonder at the panic that would have taken place in our internment camps over the Loyalty Oath.

The whole issue of the Nisei combat troop continued to be a source of conflicting views both in the camp and in the rest of the nation. Many believed that the troop's only purpose was for use as "cannon fodder." Others passionately wanted an opportunity to prove their loyalty in the greatest way possible.

Colonel William Scobey, representing the War Department, spoke to the block managers and councilmen: "This is no time for equivocation...The combat team is the first step toward rehabilitation...We want to be able to present the combat team to the people as a symbol of your loyalty...If the response is poor, those who do not like the Japanese will say - I told you so. They are not loyal; they won't serve the nation." (Denson Tribune, March 5, 1943)

Words like this only escalated the conflict.

Many Florin boys, however, signed up. Even before we had left Florin in the evacuation, more than fifty Nisei boys were already in the U.S. Army. They had enlisted before Pearl Harbor, but in the spring of 1942, most of them underwent humiliating experiences wearing the uniform of their country. Some had their guns taken away from them by their superiors. Others suddenly had been discharged without explanation and sent home. There were those who spent months wondering what would happen to them, not knowing if they were respected soldiers or prisoners of their own army.

I remembered how I had seen Toshiaki Kawaji in civilian clothes, deeply crushed over his discharge as a reclassified 4C (friendly, alien enemy). Henry Hashimoto of Mayhew also had been discharged and sent home to evacuate his family. Ted Miyata of Florin had come home on a furlough to help his widowed mother pack up to leave. One of the famous pictures taken by a government photographer, Dorothea Lange, showed Private Ted in the strawberry patch with his hard-working mother.*

Much to the dismay of the army recruiting team, the registration took much longer than they had anticipated. We received a memo from Dillon Myer on February 2 that warned us what would happen if we did not hurry and get it done.

"Failure to register is a violation of war regulations and offenders are subject to 90 days of imprisonment."

"It's a joke," Al said. "We are already in prison. If somebody refuses to register, are they going to put them in prison in this prison?" There was of course no answer to his question.

We had other enemies to fear in the winter months of 1943 in addition to the threats of internal violence. Tuberculosis once again loomed its dangerous head. This disease had taken its toll in Florin where sorrow went hand in hand with poverty that haunted our farm families during the depression years. Many frail bodies strained beyond their endurance as they labored unendingly in the berry fields and vineyards where nourishment was often not adequate for growing bodies. Prolonged years of hard work accompanied by a simple, economical diet left many young children vulnerable to tuberculosis. Recovery took many long years, and death was frequently the result. Nami, Al's sister, had been exposed to the lung disease. Frail and thin, she seemed to be slowly recovering in camp. Her months at Jerome were spent in the TB ward of the hospital at the far end of the camp.

We all spent as much time as we could with Nami, hoping to cheer

---

* The photograph is in the National Archives and has been printed many times in various publications. Ted's army uniform is a stark contrast to his helpless appearing mother, labeled an enemy alien and dangerous to her country as she labored in her strawberry patch.

her as best we could. The long walk across the camp was made daily by Ojiisan, her devoted 76 year old father, who lovingly visited his youngest daughter and kept her informed on what was taking place in our barrack lives.

Al had to be careful with his health too. He had already had a bout with pleurisy and his lungs were weakened as a result. I was always watching him to make sure he did not exert himself and get exhausted, for his well-being was essential for our survival.

Al turned 31 on March 21, the first day of spring. I wished I could have baked him his favorite banana cream cake as I had done for the wonderful seven years of my married life. We had been incarcerated for almost a full year by this time.

The leadership of our family had been taken over by Al and gracefully relinquished by the venerable Kuzo, his father, more than ten years ago. In addition to his 64 year old mother and our invalid, Nami, Al worried about me, crippled with rheumatoid arthritis since before we were married. With all this weighing heavily on him, I was amazed when Al confided a secret desire to me after long weeks of anxiety and thinking about it.

"I want to volunteer to fight for America," Al stood in the middle of our little apartment and told me the thoughts he had harbored for weeks. I could hardly believe what I was hearing.

"I have a moral responsibility to stand up for the only country we have, Mary. We need to prove to people of Japanese ancestry and everyone else in the world that there are American citizens with Japanese faces who are loyal and willing to give their lives for our country. If I volunteer, then others who can't make up their minds might follow. We need leaders to prove that this is no time to lose our heads. We've been wrongly accused of disloyalty. We have to show them how wrong they are."

I understood what my husband was saying. I was sad and proud and frightened all at once. I knew how deep the pain was that brought forth his sincere longing and the desire to serve our country. We must cling to our citizenship and stand boldly faithful and loyal to America.

I fervently wished I could go too. If only I would be allowed to join the WACS. If only I were healthy enough that such an honor could be mine! But alas, it was not to be for either of us. Though our hearts were willing, our bodies, wracked with disease and pain, determined our destiny. We would stay in camp.

As the days went by, an increasing number of soldiers came to visit Jerome. They were from the 100th Battalion, volunteers from the island of Hawaii, and the newly established 442nd Nisei Combat Unit from Hawaii and the mainland, trained and stationed at Camp Shelby, Mississippi. The soldiers came with smiles and special treats for us from the outside. They knew they were being used as an experiment, a symbol of loyalty, and they were willing to die for America to prove that Japanese Americans were worthy American citizens. These soldiers had two battles to fight: the nation's war against the Axis powers in Germany and Japan, and then their second battle on the home front where people were obsessed with bigotry, prejudice, and discrimination. They knew they would be mistreated, endlessly tested, and constantly watched perhaps even by military intelligence.

I wondered again about our evacuation as I talked with these Hawaiian-born soldiers. Japanese in Hawaii were 3000 miles closer to the enemy than any of us who were stateside, yet there had not been a wholesale Hawaiian-Japanese evacuation. I pondered this for a long time and wondered about the irony of it all. For their battle cry, the 100th Battalion chose: "Remember Pearl Harbor." We all remembered Pearl Harbor. How could we ever forget?

The Nisei soldier on furlough had no home to go to except that of his family in the internment camp. The young men were concerned about their families and spent as much time as they could with their loved ones if that were possible. Tragically in those times most could not join their families. There were many difficulties for the soldiers and their families in their contacts with people outside the camps.

When Mr. Nishikawa died, his widow wanted to have his remains cremated according to their family custom. Her son, PFC George Nishikawa, was designated to escort his father's body to Memphis, Tennessee, to a crematorium. He was accompanied by his civilian brother-in-law, Hideo Kadokawa.

"When we arrived, I was shocked to see a military policeman confront him, requesting George's identification. The MP checked the papers, and as he did, he accused George of being a spy."

"Where did you steal the U.S. uniform? It must be a fake ID," he muttered disdainfully. The young soldier was humiliated to be so insulted while wearing the uniform of his country with his PFC stripes. Reluctantly, he was cleared, but it was an incident he would never forget. (Nor did Hideo forget, and he still talks about it.)

Other soldiers received similar responses from Caucasians they encountered. In the little town of McGehee, a Nisei soldier was attacked and yelled at. "You dirty Jap!" Such an assault on a U.S. soldier reverberated throughout the internment camps.

Private Louis Furushiro, whose family had been fruit farmers in Clarksburg on the Sacramento River, was shot at when he stopped at a cafe in Dermott, a little town near the camp, for coffee. His assailant was a 72-year-old man who had two sons in the service. He fired at him from just ten feet away; Louis dodged just in time and escaped with only powder burns on his face. The man was arrested, but in the barracks, stories circulated of such unjust treatment.

"It's just not fair," Al protested as we discussed the situation one night. "In every barrack there is at least one family with a son who feels called upon to go. They argue far into the night until the old people agree to let him go. You know them, Mary, and so do I. After the decision is made, they extend their blessings and are proud when their son steps forward to volunteer and sign his name with the brave."

I knew it well for Al had counseled many such young men. They came quietly to speak to us at night in strictest confidence, eager to find an ear they could share in their feelings of jubilation and celebration. It was hard to find words to soothe the worries of these parents. There were dangers out there for our Nisei soldiers that other soldiers didn't have to worry about.

Still, they continued to volunteer and fill the ranks of the newly formed 442nd combat team. A few rebellious ones, however, shouted their rage at them as they left.

"Your parents can't even be citizens here. They don't accept you. Some Americans are trying to pass a law to take away your citizenship! How can you give up Japan, the only country that will have you? Go ahead and be slaughtered in the suicide unit."

The names of volunteers were kept secret until they were ready to be shipped out for fear of their safety in camp from the dissidents. One night at dinner, an animal bone was placed on the table of a family who had voted for America and sent their son as a volunteer. The worst accusation made to someone in the Japanese culture is to be called *"inu"* or dog. The bone was a symbol of such an insult.

I was sick when I heard about this incident. How terrible that our people had been driven to act in such a despicable manner. Tensions got worse as we divided clearly into two factions.

On one side were those who had voted "yes, yes." We quietly stood on the side of America and ached to prove our loyalty in any way we could. Our sons were the volunteers for the special combat team, ready to serve their country and give their lives if needed.

On the other side were the vocal dissidents who claimed that Japan was really winning the war, that there had been secret communications with Japan, and that newspapers were printing lies. They believed that they would be welcomed as heroes in Japan, loyal to her in this time of great trial. Some believed they would be rewarded when they returned to Japan with each person receiving thousands of dollars to make up for the months of imprisonment. A persuasive Buddhist priest filled barrack services to overflowing with such talk, and at this stage, some were easily swayed.

When the "yes, yes's" and "no, no's" were counted, it was found that 85% of the internees voted yes, on the side of America. At our camp 1275 people voted no and turned their backs on us.

The rules and regulations were suddenly relaxed for those of us who were cleared with our "yes, yes" votes. A few at a time were permitted to go shopping in McGehee or Lake Village—with escorts, of course. Each of us who was so fortunate took along a list of items to purchase for others who were not so blessed.

We noticed that the surprise on these visits was to find out what a sleepy, little place Lake Village was. There were only a few stores, but they enjoyed a booming business on days when camp residents came to town. Shelves were often cleaned out completely, especially of popular items like fabrics, sewing materials, soaps, cosmetics, shampoo, trinkets, toys, magazines, and books.

Every time some were allowed out to go to town, little touches of freedom made all of us realize how much we longed for the normal and ordinary pleasures of living free.

Al and I kept track of the soldiers and their training with the 442nd and the 100th. Shortly after the establishment of the all-Nisei combat team, Camp Shelby was selected as their training camp. Carefully chosen Nisei soldiers from 32 army posts in 19 states were reassigned there. Cadremen from the 100th Battallion of Hawaii and a few mainland boys were chosen to train the volunteers.

Of the 5000 Nisei draftees and volunteers, only a small number were called to Shelby. From Hawaii, 10,000 had stepped forward to volunteer, but only 2500 were accepted. These men, plus 2000 volunteers from the WRA centers, made up the special team desired by the War Department.

Relationships between the Hawaiians and the Japanese Americans were strained at first. After their shocking visits to the Arkansas internment camps, the Hawaiian soldiers understood how the background of anti-Oriental agitation for decades had affected what was at stake for their counterparts who had grown up on the West Coast.

Camp Shelby was only a 15-hour bus ride to Jerome and Rohwer, so visits there were easy to arrange. The island visitors spent many weekend furloughs as guests of the internees along with soldier sons and relatives of camp families. Soldiers who had families in Tule Lake and Manzanar couldn't visit them at all because no Japanese were permitted to enter California even if they were wearing U.S. Army uniforms.

In February we were surprised to learn that two trainloads of internees had arrived at Jerome from Hawaii. They were families and relatives of Japanese school teachers, ministers and community leaders that the FBI had rounded up and interned in North Dakota, New Mexico and Texas. These people had been confined to an island in Hawaii, but they wanted to be nearer their loved ones who were incarcerated on the mainland, so they were sent to Jerome. The evacuees from Hawaii occupied two blocks; the soldiers from Hawaii felt closer to home when they visited those blocks. The Hawaiians enriched our cultural contacts as we became friends. Many outstanding community leaders and dedicated workers came from the group of Hawaiians.

Those from Hawaii had great adventures with us. They enjoyed hunting rattlesnakes because they had never seen snakes before. Our swamps had all kinds of snakes, not only rattlesnakes, but poisonous water moccasins and copperheads as well. Curiosity prompted many a hunting trip. Once a huge, eight foot rattlesnake was on exhibit for a number of days until the officials heard about it. Alarmed, they hauled it down. Barbecued teriyaki rattlesnake, a most delicious treat, was the talk of the camp. Soon after the evacuees from Hawaii came to Jerome, we noted snakes became scarce around the camp.

As winter drew to a close, our health became an increasing source of concern. Even healthy people seemed to be getting very ill. Exhaustion of mind and body was taking its toll.

Al's sister, Margaret, had an attack of appendicitis. It was a time of great anxiety for the mother of seven children. We rushed her to the hospital just in time to have her appendix removed. Herb Kurima, our baseball hero from Florin, gave us a scare and was gravely ill for days. We always feared the worst, as we had little confidence in the meager hospital facilities and the quality of medical care even with fine Nisei doctors and nurses—who were always working under the strain of being short handed.

There seemed to be too many fatal illnesses and accidents. Everyone was jittery. Some felt that when you went to the hospital, it was time to prepare for a funeral.

Illness and death had followed us from Florin to Fresno, and now to Jerome. It was hard to cope with grief in this strange atmosphere. We had to make decisions of whether to bury our loved ones in these swamplands or opt for cremation, only possible if there was someone free who could accompany the body to Memphis.

Block 9 was saddened by the death of Shozu Suyeda who became ill at the age of 52 and died from internal surgery in Rohwer Hospital. Mr. Nishikawa, the father-in-law of Al's cousin, Hideo Kadokawa, died from cancer discovered on his long train ride to Rohwer in October. Mr. Nishikawa had been hospitalized for three months at Rohwer and died in February.

Sorrow and tragedy came in rapid succession. Mrs. Sankichi Takemoto, who had raised strawberries in Florin, died on the same day as Mr. Yukichi Iwatsuru, a respected religious man who inspired others and challenged them not to abandon their dreams. Both were in their 80s. Their surviving spouses, relatives, and friends mourned their losses in the loneliness of our concentration camp.

I worried about all my loved ones especially Marielle. Sometimes I just could not believe that this was the life my child had to live. I worried about being too busy and not having enough time for my little girl, but Al consoled me.

"Don't worry about her, Mary. She is six years old already so she is not a baby any more. Grandpa, Grandma, and my sisters and all the cousins are around all the time. They help Marielle feel that she is a part of their lives too. We are always together at meal time, and when you have to go to meetings and places, I will read to Marielle and tuck her to sleep."

It was so like Al—always kind and gentle. How fortunate I was to have such an understanding husband. I talked over everything with him and sought his advice. He respected me and recognized my ability to lead and serve. He seemed so proud of me and what I did and never opposed anything I felt was important.

We shared our worries and anxieties and hardly kept any secrets from each other. Together we cared for our family members who endured each day with great courage.

At about this time in our camp life, I became greatly concerned about the arthritis in my back and joints which was worse than it had ever been. I was in pain all the time, but I didn't want anyone to know—even Al. I was afraid my entire body would become solidified and remembered reading a tale long ago about a prince who was turned to stone. When my rib cage ached as I breathed, the pains were so sharp I thought surely I was going to have a heart attack!

Finally, I spilled out my fears to Al one night.

"What if I were to die here? What if such a catastrophe fell upon all of you? Marielle, my darling, would be left motherless. Who would take care of you, Al? You would be a widower, and if something happened to you, Marielle would be an orphan."

I almost convinced Al that I would not live long. We cried together and wished with all our might that I would last long enough to see our daughter grow up. Al insisted that I go to a doctor, so I had my first ride to the hospital (on a truck which served as the camp

157

ambulance) with great fear and trepidation.

My fears were for naught. My heart was fine. It was the arthritis that caused the pain and the difficulty in the beat of my heart. Dr. Taira prescribed Vitamin D and rest and told me not to work. I was okay except for the arthritis for which there was no medicine and no cure. Greatly relieved, I decided that perhaps I did have a few more years to live.

Painting by Henry Sugimoto

Painting by Henry Sugimoto

Chapter 14

Taking Care of Each Other

"We seem to be turning into a real community at last. We have already been through so much together."

Life went on in the camp. There were births, weddings, and deaths, and we adjusted to each accordingly. Happy couples were united before the justice in the little town of Lake Village. The newlyweds were given a few hours of leave to be married. Even in this time of emergency far from home, old traditional customs from Japan were observed whenever possible. We continued to use the marriage go-betweens called "Baishakunin," who were asked by each family to represent them formally in the engagement and wedding plans. They were usually well-respected couples, best family friends or relatives, who were asked to perform this important function.

Newlyweds had no honeymoon, but tiny rooms called apartments were provided for them. Many soldiers decided to marry, knowing that their futures were uncertain but bravely taking the step to launch forth into married life.

Day-to-day camp living began to take on a pattern as we tended to the jobs of basic living. The women adjusted to the drudgery of primitive scrubbing boards for washing clothes, quite a blow for those who had enjoyed the luxury of modern washing machines at home. This back-breaking job was the only way to keep bedding and clothes clean. The army provided a huge supply of washboards, and every day, the internees scrubbed their clothes. All except me; this was one job I could not handle with my crippled arms. Al's sister, Edith, took over my family's wash along with hers. She did her own private washing for the eight in her family and then took the washing for the six in my family as well! Through the oppressive heat of the long, Arkansas summers and through the iciness of its winters, Edith scrubbed and washed for me. I don't know how she did it, but she washed clothes every day. I loved my angelic sister-in-law even more as she labored over my washboard.

Keeping our bedding and clothing clean was a major preoccupation for women and girls at camp. We could only wash four days during the week, Wednesday through Saturday. The hospital's enormous linen wash was done on Monday and Tuesday so they needed all the available hot water.

Sharing of resources was a necessity and one that imposed a high amount of discipline. People could be found washing late at night or very early in the morning so they could get their clothes and sheets washed without interfering with the smooth operation of the camp.

We took part in unique projects such as making our own soap. Katsuji Oyama realized that waste fat from the kitchens could be utilized to manufacture soap. All it needed was the addition of lye and water to the grease. In two months, Mr. Oyama, assisted by his wife and three others, produced nearly five tons of laundry soap for us to use in the kitchens, laundry, and hospital. Their equipment consisted of a few washtubs, pans, cans, knives, a sink, and the washstands in the laundry room. They were able to produce 600 pounds of soap a day.

Mutton tallow, which was not edible, was the best grease to use for general use soap. Grease from chickens made excellent, fine-textured toilet soap. The soap crew collected grease from each kitchen and cleaned it through a boiling process. After clarification the grease was cooled to lukewarm, and diluted lye was mixed expertly into it. Next the mixture was poured into large molds. This process was developed as a result of Mr. Oyama's careful research into soap making, but it shows the determination people had in not letting things get them down. Mr. Oyama had 20 years of experience in the cosmetic field. He had headed a company of his own in Los Angeles. His wife demonstrated beauty care in Sacramento, and they both sold cosmetics. With the use of their creative talents and ingenuity, they found satisfaction in their new tasks.

We had some light moments that spring too. Spud Tamura brought home a bold raccoon he had captured while he was out chopping wood. Somehow, he had managed to trap it and brought it back to us in a barrel. It was quite a prize for Block 9. We had it on display for everyone to enjoy. It was a mini-zoo of sorts, a captured animal on display for captured humans. Camp officials eventually found out about it and ordered it returned to the woods where it could not bite anyone and possibly contaminate them with rabies.

We also had an adventure with flying squirrels. Al had read about them but had never seen one. It was exciting when one was spotted— everybody wanted to catch it, but it was almost impossible to do. The young people tried so hard. When a squirrel lit on a branch, they would rush to chop it down, but the squirrel would then glide to another tree as the first one trembled before its fall. Many trees were chopped down, which was all right for we needed the firewood, but usually there was no capturing of the lithe fellow. I did see one taken though; the frightened little thing sat huddled in a corner of a box. I was so disappointed because it looked like a very drenched rat, his fur wet and matted from his fright. His magnificent glory was there only when he was free to glide triumphantly from tree to tree. I wondered if it was the same with us.

Like Edith, there were unheralded heroes and heroines in many places. They went about their tasks quietly, unknown to most of the people in the camp. Some mothers had large families of 12-13 children to care for, but somehow they managed and I never heard a complaint.

Community activities kept many of us occupied and our restless hours filled with meaningful pursuits. Al was one of the energetic internees who worked with the development of community activities. This was of great importance in our strange camp for there were many who had mental health problems. There was an urgent need for building morale, especially after our internal conflicts over the registration.

Good Caucasian leaders were found even though wartime emergency conditions existed. Often these people left promising positions

162

behind to come into our camps to work with us, victims of trauma from our forced uprooting. One of these leaders was Dr. Runo E. Arne, Director of Community Services. Dr. Arne was familiar with the Nisei, having taught an extension course in social welfare at the University of California at Berkeley for five years. He understood some of the problems we faced.

Al worked for G.F. Castelberry who was the director of community and recreational activities under Dr. Arne's supervision. As new ideas broadened the scope of activities for people of all ages, hundreds of internees were recruited to work in the community activities section. Al organized people into groups of like interests and had them meet regularly. They played card and board games and were the first organized groups to fill the long hours for both adults and youth. Eventually the activities were expanded to include hobbies, interests, and talents of the internees. As instructors were found, we set up classes for cultural pursuits, as well as arts and crafts.

Henry Murayama, director of the boys' clubs under the recreation department, installed the first club for boys in the camp—the 6-10 Toppers. Many of us believed that success or failure in life would depend upon one's personality and attitude, thus the need for strength in these areas. Goals of sports, fun, and community service were chosen with Joe Oyama as the advisor. Once these were launched, other clubs were started in the various blocks.

The Densonitas was the first girls' club. Its goals were similar to those of the boys, but socials were included to help youth become better acquainted and to develop friendships. Adult leaders inspired young people to think and work cooperatively with one another for the betterment of themselves as well as for the improvement of life in the camp.

An organized plan emerged with four categories of activity: athletics, entertainment, indoor recreation, clubs and organizations. The types of groups were as varied as the talents and interests of the people who joined them.

Al found and introduced activities intended to interest the diverse groups among us. For those who were interested in athletics we had baseball, basketball, boxing, judo, sumo, softball, volleyball, track, and weight lifting. For the women there were basketball, softball, tennis, horseshoes, and ping pong.

The list of clubs and organizations was varied and suitable for anyone: boys' clubs, YMCA, YMBA, YMWA, social clubs, hobby clubs, Boy Scouts, girls' clubs, Camp Fire Girls, Red Cross, PTA, mothers, and sewing clubs.

Those interested in indoor recreation could choose from Chess and Checkers, Bridge, Shogi, Goh, hobby exhibits, art exhibits, poetry clubs, Shigin, Ping Pong, lectures, debates, forum, panel discussions, oratorical contests, and carnivals.

For entertainment we had dances, community sings, recitals, glee clubs, music appreciation, plays, pageants, talent shows, operetta, and Issei entertainment programs.

I was the coordinator of the girls' clubs. These included YWCA, Girl Reserve Club, Business and Professional Girls and Students, College Y Coeds, Junior Matrons, Y Mothers, USO Mothers, and USO Hostesses.

Treasured friendships grew there as exciting, warm human beings began to surface through the establishment of the YWCA and later the USO.

One very special person was Amy Murayama, an extremely intelligent social worker, a sensitive and caring person. One day in a discussion she said, "I'm so afraid we will all be wrapped up in a deadly lethargy if we are here too long." Amy worked tirelessly and was an inspiring leader in our organization of the YWCA, but I never forgot her words. Al and I worried that her prediction might come true. We vowed to do our best to keep our people active and involved. Amy left the camp and went to Chicago where we later learned that she died of consumption. What a tragic loss for her family and for all of us, an inconsolable sorrow, but her creative spirit touched our lives forever.

It was slow at first, but we had to make people realize that they could make something worthwhile out of this boring existence. Some blocks were harder to organize than others because they had more children or more adults. Block 1 was mostly bachelors so it had to be handled quite differently.

Block 43 was an example of cooperative planning. They had a lot of young people and children, so a five club installation was held at one time. I set up an inspiring candlelight ceremony to install the new officers. It was a cherished moment in the midst of our dismal existence.

I chuckled at the cleverness of the names of the new clubs—Happy Hour Club, Six Forty Hi Teens, Jovial Peppers, Eleveners, V-12 Zepherettes, Southern Belles, Blue Wave Clippers, Bronco Babes, Zorro's Boys, Gremlins, Shamrocks, Lotus Club, Eight Elites, and Twinklers.

The topics of their programs reflected their ordinary teen concerns as well as their brave thoughts for the future:

Boy Meets Girl
Mess Hall Manners
Neat Appearance
Earnest in Our Aims
Starters Never Quit
Quitters Never Start
Victory Through Service
Growth Through Service and Fellowship

These were our young Nisei and Sansei, refusing to accept defeat during their turbulent internment years.

The Densoneers, a seven piece band, was a big hit with young and old and a tremendous asset to the camp's morale. Frank Tashima was the outstanding leader; the band played for dances twice a week and provided enjoyment for us all.

The Vargettes were also a big hit with their flag waving Miss Liberty, a Nisei beauty who led the patriotic grand finale of a wonderful show put on by a group of entertainers. Violet Ogata, my niece, was one of the dancers who showed us skills we didn't even know she had. So it was with others who needed these groups to bring out hidden talents to be developed.

This happened all over the camp. How exciting it was to see people involved in such worthwhile activities. They reached out and touched others in so many ways. One of the most exciting groups was the Florin Champion Baseball team. Both players and fans became emotionally involved during Jerome's baseball season. This was the same team that had been victorious when we were back at the assembly center in Fresno. They continued to play together, cheered by their many fans. They provided thrills for everyone with their exploits on the playing fields, and for a little while, people forgot where they were. We were grateful to these athletes for their dedication to the sport that entertained us so well: Herb, Mac, Dick and Ernie Kurima; Yosh, Bill and Sam Tsukamoto; Hiro and Shiro Tahara; Hats Omachi; Ichiro Miyagawa; Jim Tanigawa, Ted Taniguchi—they made us proud to be from Florin.

There were all sorts of occasions chosen by club members to help and recognize others. Issei over the age of 60 were honored, newcomers were welcomed to Jerome, invalids were helped with their washing, apartments were cleaned, and food was brought to the sick from mess halls. Toys were painted and gifts wrapped for Christmas and Valentine's Day. Birthday and farewell parties were planned. A popular project was to surprise the people on the mess crew by giving them a Sunday off. Club members, all scrubbed and clean, took their places waiting tables. Some of the members had to get up at 4:30 a.m. to cook the meals for the day. The Zephyrettes from Block 12 honored their mothers for Mother's Day by taking their places in their jobs on that day. They did the same for their fathers for Father's Day. Such thoughtfulness inspired all of us and helped create better relationships between parents and their children.

Our Boy Scout activities involved many boys and men. A new campground four miles east of the camp was opened for Boy Scout training in camping and recreation. A trail was planned east of the sewage plant across the Big Bayou. More than 2000 young boys were involved in these activities that developed into a rewarding and healing process.

One by one our college-aged students began to leave the camps. Proudly, we internees sent off the "cream of our crop." Outside churches joined in assisting these young people to continue the education that had been so abruptly interrupted in the spring of 1942. Education, however, continued to be our main priority in spite of constant delays due to lack of textbooks and equipment. The schools were opened a few months after we arrived in Jerome, and even though the children had a semester gap in their schooling in 1942, education went on.

Our camp was divided into north and south for the two divisions

166

in the school—we had the North Side School and the South Side School. Caucasian civil service teachers were hired along with internee volunteer teachers who worked for $16 a month. We had elementary school, high school, and a kindergarten-nursery.

I read the notices carefully to find out where to take my Marielle when the school began. She and other children had already missed almost a half year of their precious education. I had awaited anxiously for her first day of school, never dreaming it would take place in a prison camp like this.

George, my brother, had to finish his last year of high school. All the students were to meet at 8:30 on a Monday morning in Dining Hall 33. Marielle seemed very happy to be going to her first day of school, but I wondered if the strange memory would be forever imprinted upon her. I hoped her bubbling joy would overcome any negative thoughts. At an early age, she had caught the stoicism of the five adults in her family, and though we tried hard to hide our emotional strains from her, she often picked up adult-like reactions to difficult experiences.

Marielle held my hand tightly. I knew she was scared and unsure of what was to come. Memories of my own first day of school tingled through my head. I thought of the many Septembers I had marched happily off to school even though I had butterflies in my stomach at the same time.

Marielle and her two cousins, Lester Ouchida and Yone Ogata, and I stepped carefully along the muddy road so we would not stumble and fall. The cold rain stung my nose like tiny needles, but it felt good to be bundled up from head to toe. Our red noses peeked out along with our eyes from tiny spaces between our scarves. We made our careful way to Block 23, Barrack 5, for the first grade classroom.

The room was like all others I had known since our arrival at Jerome. I should have expected that, but in my wishful mind, I wanted to see a nice, brick building with windows and long corridors for my little girl. The wooden floor was bare; a pot belly stove in the middle of the room was surrounded by benches, and that was all there was. I could hardly hide my disappointment. Cheerfully, though, I smiled for the sake of the children and met the teachers. They looked confident and capable, and they were smiling. That was a good sign.

I felt relieved as Marielle took a seat with her cousins, and I slipped out of the room. With a heavy heart, I struggled back to our room. The silence of our sanctuary at 9-8-E was what I needed at this time.

It was a discouraging time of weakness for me; I felt compelled to commune with God in prayer. My tears filled to the brim and overflowed as I felt the need to surrender myself to the only One left for me to turn to. I wanted so much for the children of our camp to sit quietly in their classrooms and gain the skills they needed for their growth and development. They ran so loose and undisciplined. Their lives were filled with games, sports, and activities. They loved it, but as parents we were concerned that the dismal environment would have serious consequences for their spiritual, moral and cultural values, and most importantly, their academic development. We anxiously awaited the school to begin, yet we harbored great concerns about the quality of education that would be provided.

Now I had seen the school, and my worst fears were rushing to the front of my thoughts. Out of this meager environment, how could our children receive a decent education that would help them build the kind of world they so desperately needed? I was also concerned about all the mothers of the world and the need for world peace so we could put a stop to the terrible fighting, hatred, and killing. Out of all this destruction and desolation, what kind of children were we raising? What would they need to know in order to be able to build a lasting world of brotherhood, good will and harmony?

I turned once again to Dr. Palmer's "Christian Watchwords" and spent hours wrestling to feel the nearness of my personal God, to feel the vitality of Jesus as my friend. What would God do if Jesus had a Japanese face? How could I make my life show I believed in His teachings?

I read once again the letter from Reverend Hideo Hashimoto, my sister's college friend from Berkeley. He was looking for an article about a Japanese American mother writing about life in a relocation center and the problems of both material and spiritual needs. I felt a story rise within me and began to write.

My article was published in the April 1943, *Christian Advocate* entitled, "'Til We Are Home Again." It was my first published story, and the biggest surprise was the check for $10 that came in the mail.

A month's work in camp was worth $16; I had received a fortune for my first story! Marielle's childish prayer was how I ended the article:

"And dear God, bless my little doggie until we get home. Bless and watch our house so we CAN go home again...Amen." She was soon fast asleep. I knelt beside her bed for a long time. My heart wept to discover the deep ache that clung to her childish innocence as even my five year old longed for the privacy of her own home.

Denson Magnet, April 1943, p. 11.

Spring Night
By J.D.

Last night I took a walk around the camp. It was a very beautiful moonlight night and just right for romance, but I found myself wondering if this was my home. I saw spotlights in the towerhouse shining up and down, the police car prowling with no lights, the outline of the barbed wire fence across the ditch, the lights in the Adm. building, the cars going in and out.

I heard the sentinel on duty walk back and forth, back and forth; I heard the frog crying in the creek and then heard the wild geese flying overhead; I heard the dog bark in the distance and the sound of the runaway horse. I heard the squealing of the pigs in their pen, and the baby crying in some barrack. I heard the slam of the door in the wind, and someone singing down the road, and another playing a harmonica. I heard the radio softly playing into the night. I heard laughter of a girl, then a voice of the man. I saw lights slowly go out, and the camp settle down to its slumber.

Chapter 15

A Time of Growth

"We are developing skills we didn't even know we had. It seems as if everyone is doing something. I am perfecting my speaking skills. My arthritic hands aren't good for much so I may as well talk."

Of all the camp activities, one of the most successful was the arts and crafts program. Though most adults had not considered themselves artists, their work was so beautiful we could hardly believe they had created everything out of scraps of wood, waste items and bits from nature. Al organized a one week show of their work, and there was talk about nothing else in the camp for days. We were simply amazed when we saw the beautiful sculptures and treasured art pieces. Working quietly at home, men and women had discovered talents they didn't know they had. They made their own tools from nails, needles, and common household items, melted down, pounded, scraped, and filed to make just the right tool for each job. Even brushes and paints had to be ingeniously created.

There were beautiful dolls, exquisitely sewn with every fashion detail in their clothes. One Issei woman had learned how to make Sakura ningyos as they were made in Japan during the 1920s. (They were dolls clothed in the style of dancers of the day.) She taught others in the old craft, creatively substituting for the materials she needed.

Intricate silk Tsumami art was turned into crepe paper art as bright and colorful as the pieces were intended to be. Some objects

170

were functional such as pin cushion stands, toothpick holders, ash trays and plaques. Many were fantastic creations from the artists' talented minds.

Most fascinating was the wood work. On display were wood carvings and sculptures made with such intense detail that it was hard to believe they had been fashioned with farmers' hands. There were tiny wooden birds, painted to perfection to look exactly like the birds we had known back home as well as those that flew around the camp. They looked so real, it seemed they might just fly away. Cute little lapel pins were made in the shapes of squirrels and other animals. There were rings and pins made from toothbrush handles, miniature wooden panda and teddy bears, and all sorts of good luck mascots made of yarn for our servicemen. I chuckled at the Carmen Miranda pins with their pecan heads.

What caught our attention the most, however, were the cypress burls or "knees". The ugly Arkansas swamps were things of beauty to our Issei who had grown up in Japan. They were pulled as if entranced into the woods. Instinctively, their keen eyes were drawn to the natural beauty of the strange growths on the trunks and roots of some trees, especially the cypress. They found special pieces that intrigued them, and then with native ingenuity they transformed the ugly clumps into beautiful works of art.

I watched Fukuju Sasaki hard at work, quietly delighted with what he had found for himself, a special piece growing under swampy water. He wrapped it in a wet gunny sack and buried it deep in the moist earth. In this way the bark was allowed to deteriorate naturally. Mr. Sasaki spent many months polishing and polishing his piece. He gently rubbed it with a variety of materials—rough sponge, heavy cloth, soft cotton, and eventually a piece of raw silk. He rubbed it with a hard piece of marble to bring out the ultimate in luster. With the right touch and eye (and a bit of magic it seemed to me), Mr. Sasaki envisioned the hidden beauty of that piece of cypress "knee" which he had taken from the slimy mud of the Arkansas swampland. It was simply an outstanding feat.

Quietly, our Issei found their hours transformed as they went "kobu" hunting. A kobu, literally translated, was a bump on the head that might arise from a severe knocking. That's what the Issei called the strange lumps on the cypress trees. Even dear Ojiisan, with eyes bright and hopeful, worked patiently over his. Some were ordinary, others quite lovely and almost of museum quality, but they all provided great feelings of self-worth sorely needed for all. These were their once-in-a-lifetime treasures—gnarled, old hickory roots; smooth, white persimmon roots entwined in spiral form; and rough, moire-patterned oak tree roots. They were multicolored marvels, wonderful examples of nature's jewels.

I found something fine and admirable about these things of infinite beauty, these objects so totally Japanese in their interpreta-tions.* How I had despised and rejected that which was Japanese as I tried so hard to be an American and because the shame of being Japanese caused me such pain. For the first time in my life there was no need to cast off my ancestral culture when so many openly loved and respected it and created such beauty because of it. We demon-strated this common joy and pride, and slowly for a brief time, I began to appreciate the values inherent in being Japanese.

Life went on in the internment camp, however, and before long, summer turned into fall. As internees we sadly celebrated a full year of camp life. Much had happened since the previous October's train trip that moved us from Fresno to Jerome plunging us into cultural and geographical shock. We survived our first bout with dysentery, the fuel shortage emergency, our overwhelming fears and illnesses, the death of our loved ones, the organization of the special Nisei Combat Unit, and the question that we still wrestled with—the loyalty registration for army and relocation clearance. From this turmoil and the anger, resistance, and beatings, there were still positive threads of action as we did what needed to be done and volunteered willingly as caring, sensitive souls.

---

*Who could have anticipated that many years later a growing awareness of "camp art" would bring these dusty, old subjects out of closets, garages, and barns? How could we have ever expected that they would be displayed at historical exhibits and even at the prestigious Smithsonian Institution? The same emotions that were with the artists when they created these wondrous art pieces stayed with them and kept them from tossing out what seemed to be insignificant pieces, junk left over from camp. Fortunately, the camp art of the 1940s, Issei art born of the interment camp, was finally recognized for its real worth in the 1980s.

WE THE PEOPLE

One of these caring people was a young woman, still a teenager, who was the leader of a group of girls called the Crusaders. She was Mary Nakahara, organizer of a mammoth writing campaign for more than 700 Nisei servicemen. A bundle of energy, Mary scurried around the camp with a bag full of papers, notes, and stationery. She seemed too busy to fuss over herself though she was neat in appearance, but she spent her time dedicated to the feelings and needs of our Nisei soldiers in uniform. Skilled in communication, Mary's brief, touching notes were sent to many—a touch of caring from one human being to another, a touch of warmth when needed the most—a birthday card, a thank you note, or a Mother's Day message.

Mary's amazing letter writing campaign inspired others to follow her lead. Her father had been taken away by the FBI in the early days of the war, so Mary wrote to him regularly too, but it was the men in uniform that benefitted the most from her tireless energy. When soldiers came to Jerome because they had no other place to go on their furloughs (usually their parents were incarcerated in faraway camps and travel was often impossible to such isolated places), it was Mary who met them at the gate long past midnight, welcomed them and arranged places for them to stay.

The Crusaders were too young to take on the task of entertaining soldiers, so block clubs began to invite the young men to attend their dances and parties. They were invited to play in ball games and eat at different mess halls.

This one woman USO, Mary Nakahara, inspired many with her deep spiritual message and her compulsion to teach. She invoked a spirit of gladness and appreciation. A sense of values accompanied her cheery smile and her creative attempts to bring joy into the lives of so many.

Another inspiration to us was Beryl Henry, director of curriculum in the Education Department who worked under the Denson School superintendent, Amon G. Thompson. Miss Henry was a strong, constant supporter of education and served as a model of support and guidance to us. She worked quietly with a group of us—potential leaders of internee women—and brought to us the message of the changing world outside. She believed in the concept of permanent relocation outside the camps as proposed by YWCA.

We met in a pouring rainstorm—a tiny nucleus of twelve women at that historic meeting held in Midori Kasai's little room in Block 15- 11-C. Mrs. Henry Tucker of Little Rock and Mrs. J.K. Chestnut had driven 115 miles in the rain to meet with us. They represented the National YWCA. Their encouraging words rang with great possibilities, not only for girls and women, but for all Jerome intern-ees.

That night we said "yes" to organizing a chapter within the camp, an awesome responsibility. We were officially chartered as the Denson YWCA. The link with outside groups, we felt, would give our lives a greater purpose based on deep spiritual values.

We were excited about the contact with the outside. We might be able to attend conferences and exchange ideas as we sought to bring about better understanding among people of different races. We wanted to bring about harmony, fellowship, and closer community feelings among the camp girls and women.

I was elected president, and my chartered board of directors agreed that we would serve everyone in a non-sectarian manner. Beryl Henry was to be our advisor.

One day Mrs. Frank Ono, who had worked with us in preparing the Y Hospitality House, surprised us with her exciting news: "We are leaving the camp. Our long-awaited clearance has arrived. My husband has accepted an offer of employment in Chicago. We will be leaving soon."

It was what we all hoped to achieve, but we didn't really expect it to happen. Somewhere out there on the outside, we each prayed there might be a place for us and our families so we could leave this place and be free again and on our own!

The strongest, most capable leaders were the ones who first found the courage and opportunities to leave camp. They paved the way for others to follow, but when they left, it was a blow for the rest of us who remained. We moved into the positions they vacated, however, and in this way new leaders continually moved into the void.

As early as the spring of 1943, WRA relocation and resettlement regional offices had begun to open in key cities to assist evacuees as they ventured out of the internment centers. The job offers were checked out to see if they were accurate and honest. With this protection and assurance, people began to move out by late spring and early summer. Most went to cities such as Denver, Chicago, Salt Lake City, Cleveland, Kansas City, and New York.

We could not foresee what would happen in the uncertain days ahead. Our camp experience was a collective one; we were part of a large group, but now we faced taking individual steps into communities. We had to take jobs without knowing much about them. We never knew for sure what the job applications that came pouring into camp in such large numbers really meant. We had to make decisions without advance interviews, relying entirely upon the good faith of the employers as verified by government officials.

Aunty and Uncle, my father's only brother and his wife, were among the first Issei to leave camp and work out on their own. Their son, Hide Dakuzaku, was completing his education at the University of Washington in St. Louis, Missouri. Aunt and Uncle were so pleased that their eldest son was able to go on with his dream of becoming a dentist.*

Though we had been together in camp, it became time to part with these dear, sweet relatives. Yeiko was one of the first to leave; she went to Chicago to work for a church related to the Commission for World Peace. Wise Auntie and Uncle thought they should also prepare to leave. As difficult as it was, it was preferable to the distasteful situation of being wards of the government. So they sent Shizu out to Chicago to pave the way for them. I cried until my eyes were swollen to see them leave. I came away feeling sad and lonely,

---

*Ruth and I had lived with Auntie and Uncle at various times during our growing up years. The bond between our families was so strong that Al borrowed California Farm Company's truck and moved Uncle's family all the way from Oakland to Florin just before we were all taken away. We thought at the time, March, 1942, that Florin was safe from evacuation. The truck was piled high with all of Aunty and Uncle's worldly goods, even their piano, for they knew that if they stayed near the coast, they would be forced to go to camp. We brought those city folks to Dad's strawberry farm where they picked berries with us hoping that Florin was far enough inland and if we were busy producing food for our country, we would be allowed to stay. It was a false hope, of course, but when we evacuated, at least Auntie and Uncle were with us.

In 1936 when Shige, the youngest child, was twelve, he and his sister Yeiko, had

realizing that parting and sorrow would go on and on.

Al and I began to talk about how it would be for our family. There were many loved ones to think about—his parents and Nami; my parents, sisters and George; Edith, Margaret and their families; and of course, our darling Marielle. We talked long into the night and thought about how it would be out there on the outside.

So many things had changed in our lives here in camp. Neither I, my mother nor Al's mother had cooked or planned meals for our families since the day we left home in May of 1942. This right to provide for our families was a big part of our responsibility as mothers and wives. The tables had been turned in camp. It was the men who presided in the mess hall kitchens.

The cooks' jobs were thankless ones at best—seven days a week for $12 a month, and they were always under constant pressure to make sure food was ready to feed thousands of people three times a day. Whatever the Quartermaster's warehouse delivered, their task was to creatively stretch the food and make it tasty at the same time.

My father had been recruited as chief cook after a period of conflict in our mess hall kitchen. Father had once worked as cook for the Southern Pacific Railroad when he first landed in America at the age of seventeen. Everyone on the block affectionately called him "Chief," and he worked successfully with his workers to get the job done each day.

Out in the outside world, we women hoped we could once again take over our wifely chores of cooking, baking, and keeping our homes. We wondered what it would be like to have that freedom again.

My first trip out of the camp was to the National YWCA leadership training conference in Jackson, Mississippi. Amy Mu-

---

been sent to Okinawa to care for our grandmother. This was a great responsibility Uncle felt as the eldest Dakuzaku.

Yeiko did not like Okinawa and returned home to Oakland in 1937. Shige then took on the job of caring for Grandma while he studied in Japan. He stayed in Japan where he works for the famous Mikimoto Pearl Company.

During the war, all communication with the Shige was cut off. We were all concerned about his safety and Grandma's as well. Father and Uncle both worried about this constantly.

rayama and I were chosen as delegates to represent Denson YWCA at this conference. What an eye opening experience it was for us, victims of racial discrimination, to travel far into the deep South. We learned first hand about two centuries of degradation of blacks that was still taking place in wartime America of 1943. The bus ride was shocking. We could not believe the bus driver's tone of voice as he ordered black passengers to stand at the back of the bus, even though there were many unoccupied seats in the front. We wondered what he would do with us, but he smiled and told us to sit in the seat behind him. We were relieved but had strange feelings; apparently we were not "colored."

The National YWCA leaders were triumphant that we could all meet together. This was a historic step forward for black and white YWCA leaders to meet. But, never once did we eat together at a luncheon or banquet because the black delegates could not eat with us! My heart was heavy and sad to know the deep shame of hatred and prejudice in America.

I spent another week away from camp among college-aged Christian students at the beautiful, Ozark Mountain conference grounds. I took Marielle with me and managed somehow to get through the week as a seminar leader. I had never led a seminar before, but I learned from the challenging experiences and was inspired as well.

In May the Disciples of Christ Church of America sent Jessie Trout, their missionary who had served in Japan for more than 20 years, to preach to the Issei in internment camps. Jessie pled with church superiors to give her a chance to do something special for the internees. Out of her zeal came the idea for a "Mission to Indiana," a three member internee team to do public relations work in Indiana. Jessie was in charge of the itinerary, and Al and I were persuaded to take on the challenge. We went with the goal of winning friends for the internees who were determined to be loyal and eligible for relocation in July of 1943.

Our Mission to Indiana provided us with ample opportunities to tell people about the internees who needed to be welcomed out of the camps. Paul Sato, a farmer of 6000 acres in Stockton, accompanied us. We looked for farm employment for internees who had known nothing but farm work for most of their lives. We met with interested groups of people, and I gave speech after speech. It was a personal spiritual pilgrimage and religiously, a growing time for Al and me.*

WAR RELOCATION AUTHORITY

IN REPLY, PLEASE REFER TO:

November 17, 1943

To Whom it May Concern:

Mrs. Mary Tsukamoto has lived in our Center
for one year and during that time has been the most
outstanding worker in the Center. Her efforts in
behalf of the welfare of the people have been tireless and selfless. She has shown herself absolutely
trustworthy, deeply loyal, and dependable.

She is a consecrated Christian woman with
unusual ability to organize groups.

It is with the deepest regret on the part
of the people of the Center that she is leaving for
the outside, and we know it is the keenest loss to
the Center that she goes. She goes with the blessings of many, many groups with which she has worked.

Yours very truly,

Beryl Henry,
Curriculum Adviser
Denson High School

---

*Years later Al, Marielle and I visited the amazing Jessie Trout, retired in a lovely place in Owen Sound, Canada. She had been honored by her friends in Miyazaki, Japan where she had taught kindergarten for 20 years. She still spoke Japanese, and we loved talking about our many fond memories.

GIRLS!
LET'S DO OUR PART!

100 GIRLS INVITED TO
CAMP SHELBY, MISS.
JUNE 19 & 20
ALL EXPENSES PD.

All girls 18 years of age and over,
get your application from Mary Sato
at 36-12-B, Community Activity Office.

3 buses to be provided. One Caucasian
Personnel and one Evacuee Mother will
chaperone each bus.

DEADLINE SAT. JUNE 12

Chapter 16

Leaving Camp

"The more I get out of camp, the more I realize how important it is to be out."

My next time out of camp was to visit Camp Shelby with a bus load of USO girls. Lt. Norman Gilbert had invited us to the base—100 Denson "Lasses" as two day guests of the base. Several matrons and I went along as chaperones.

When we finally arrived at Camp Shelby after an all night bus ride, a joyous welcome awaited us. The picnic, dinner and dance were filled with laughter and appreciation.

I danced with a young soldier from Hawaii who told me he had lied about his age so he could volunteer. He was a young kid of 17 who talked continually about his mother. She had taught him to make a bed and would inspect it, and now he was proud that he knew how to make his bed properly. He thought of his mother whenever his bed was inspected, knowing she would approve of how well he had done. He told me how he missed Hawaii and the blue ocean and spectacular sunsets. These young men were to be sent overseas any day. This was their last chance to have a little fun and relax a while thinking about home—but mostly they thought about their moms.

A personable young man, busy with pencil and notepad, stopped to talk to me. I recognized him as Mike Masaoka, Executive Secretary of the National JACL. He was the author of the Japanese American Creed. How often had I read and reread his stirring words of faith and love for America! And now confined under the guarded watch tower, I struggled to deepen my faith and set roots deep in my American heritage.

WE THE PEOPLE

THE JAPANESE AMERICAN CREED

I am proud that I am an American citizen of Japanese ancestry, for my very background makes me appreciate more fully the wonderful advantages of this nation. I believe in her institutions, ideals, and traditions; I glory in her heritage; I boast of her history; I trust in her future. She has granted me liberties and opportunities such as no individual enjoys in this world today. She has given me an education befitting kings. She has entrusted me with the responsibilities of the franchise. She has permitted me to build a home, to earn a livelihood, to worship, think, speak, and act as I please—as a free man equal to every other man.

Although some individuals may discriminate against me, I shall never become bitter or lose faith, for I know that such persons are not representative of the majority of the American people. True, I shall do all in my power to discourage such practices, but I shall do it in the American way: above-board, in the open, through courts of law, by education, by proving myself to be worthy of equal treatment and consideration. I am firm in my belief that American sportsmanship and attitude of fair play will judge citizenship and patriotism on the basis of action and achievement, and not on the basis of physical characteristics.

Because I believe in America, and I trust she believes in me, and because I have received innumerable benefits from her, I pledge myself to do honor to her at all times and in all places; to support her Constitution; to obey her laws; to respect her flag; to defend her against all enemies, foreign or domestic; to actively assume my duties and obligations as a citizen, cheerfully and without any reservations whatsoever, in the hope that I may become a better American in a greater America.

–Mike M. Masaoka

I had often read about Mike Masaoka in the Pacific Citizen. He had been the first to volunteer for the 442nd and had worked for the Army's approval of the all Nisei combat team. He and his four brothers all served in army uniforms.

Nisei boys were often heartsick for they missed their families and homes. Proudly we opened a hospitality shelter for them at Jerome so they could come there on furlough. There were so few Japanese families outside of the camps that most had nowhere to go. We considered it our patriotic duty to boost the morale of our boys who were preparing to fight for our country. They claimed that our internment camp was the next best thing to home, poignant words from young men who had no home other than the one provided by Uncle Sam. The hospitality center was Mary Nakahara's dream come true, a place to entertain our Nisei boys and a place where they could visit with young people, talk to Issei grandparents ,and get a taste of home while longing for their families who were locked up in some other internment camp.

There were those, however, who ridiculed our efforts. They accused us of using innocent young girls as "call girls" at our USO dances. We enlisted the aid of Issei mothers of G.I.s to help us in our patriotic gestures. With the blessing of WRA administration and block managers, we had simple parties with food like "Mom" would have made, but we could only serve cold rice and Japanese pickles, leftovers from the mess hall. The Nisei soldiers loved these "*Ochazuke*" parties. Little by little, our detractors quieted down as they saw the good accomplished by our efforts.

In September we witnessed the arrival of a new group to Jerome. They were internees from Tule Lake who arrived by train. They were the "yes, yes" registrants, encouraged to leave Tule Lake and resettle in other camps to make room for the "no, no's" from all the other camps. This was the government's plan for following up the horren-dous registration process.

The "yes, yes" internees were eligible for employment and their freedom if they found jobs. When they arrived at Jerome, the date for the departure of our dissidents was announced: September 15, 1943.

A great chasm had developed in many families who were now being forced to separate, perhaps forever. Some of this was due to the difficulty of communication between parents and their children, a so-called generation gap. These bitter resentments were harbored for many years, some until death.

Though only 1275 people refused to sign "yes, yes" on the loyalty oaths, 1564 were sent to Tule Lake from Jerome. The difference was family members who wanted to keep their families intact and young children who had to go with their parents.

Individual hearings were given to each person to clarify feelings of loyalty to the U.S. or loyalty to Japan. One group of dissidents marched to the head office and demanded repatriation. They announced a 6:00 a.m. military calisthenic call for all loyal Japanese to stand by their country. Why not abandon a country that refused to give citizenship rights to those from Japan? Why become a person without a country?

Al and I had heard these arguments before, but once again, we were confronted with furious arguments and the pain of seeing families ripped apart.

I watched silently as young sons and daughters, not yet old enough to sign for themselves, were forced to accept the decisions of their parents who had turned their backs upon America. Their anguish at leaving their friends and their country was tragic and bitter to see. Weeping, they were dragged away from their friends and teachers and were pushed onto trucks that carried them away. We watched, demeaned and shamed, and wept for them and for their parents.

On the night before the "disloyals" departed for Tule Lake, Al and I helped a young couple in their attempt to circumvent the decision of her parents. She was to go to Tule Lake as she was not yet 21 and was under her parents' guardianship. Though she argued and begged to stay with the young man she intended to marry, her parents would not relent. She cried for two weeks at the thought of going to Japan as her father planned to do. Finally after great consideration, and in complete secrecy, Al and I agreed to help the two of them. We hid them with some friends until the train left, and we never doubted that it was the right thing to do.

Our last months in Jerome in 1943 were an endless parade of weeping as family after family of our nearest relatives left the camp. First my younger sister, Isabel, and her husband, Tom, who had been domestics in San Francisco were attracted by an offer from the Upjohn family in Kalamazoo, Michigan. They accepted, and early in March they said good-bye. Then in May, it was my sister Ruth's turn. She and Hugh Kiino, her husband, and their son, Carl, were ready to make the big step. Their job too was for domestic help. With a three year old child, it was a sensible thing to do. They went to Jackson, Michigan.

Our barrack rooms were being emptied one by one, and this affected those of us who were left behind. The sadness of being left was increased by the foreboding and fear that gripped us as we knew that our turn would come soon.

A letter came from Auntie and Uncle from Chicago. They had found employment at the Eleanor Club, similar to the YWCA but a place for business girls. They wanted my mother and father to join them because help was needed, and although the pay was not the best, a place to stay and board were provided. There were also the possibilities of jobs for George and Julia.

It was good news for my father who missed his only brother. The two of them had been close ever since they had left Okinawa long ago to "seek their fortunes" in America. The risk of going out for Issei was greater than it was for those of us who were native born, but it was encouraging to know that Auntie and Uncle, both nearing their 60s and aliens, had taken such a monumental step and done so well.

The WRA had become the target of criticism once again as voices sharply accused the government of wrongdoing. This time they were not complaining that we were being mollycoddled, but they talked of constitutional abuse in how American citizens had been handled. More than 75,000 of the internees were citizens, so the U.S. was sensitive to such charges. The furor over the loyalty oath had caught WRA officials off guard; now with that over, they didn't want another problem. They began to urge the Nisei to move out of the camps. They assured us that we didn't have to go if we didn't want to; we would not be forced out, but it was just a matter of time before the camps would be closed.

Newspaper advertisements sent us clear messages of future employment. "The country needs your laboring force," they claimed. "You *can* help instead of being idle in the camps." Well, that's what we were saying ever since they took us away a year and a half ago.

Before we knew it, Al and I found that our turn had arrived, and it was time to leave Jerome Wartime Internment Camp. Al had gone to Kalamazoo and found employment. A telegram was sent by Paul Taylor, Project Director, from Jerome to Al in Kalamazoo:

MARY TSUKAMOTO AND DAUGHTER MARI-
ELLE LEAVING JEROME 754 PM NOVEMBER 17
SCHEDULED TO ARRIVE IN KALAMAZOO 1258
PM NOVEMBER 19 VIA NEW YORK CENTRAL

As exciting as it was, it was unbearably hard to leave the camp and the dear families and friends with whom we had endured so much. Our entire block had become like a big family of 300 people, so the moment of parting was one of great pain. We had shared meals together three times a day for more than a year, shared the laundry room, shower and latrines, wept together at funerals in the mess hall, and thrilled with pride over our victorious Florin baseball club, champions of Jerome.

The predominant factor in our leaving, though, was the future of our daughter, Marielle. As responsible parents of a school age child, we could not risk the camp atmosphere which was so destructive to family life. It was essential that we get into some kind of normal living.

My greatest concern in leaving was the forsaking of my responsibilities as the Tsukamoto bride, wife of the only son, Alfred. It was Al's filial duty to care for his parents; he would always do this, and as his wife it was my moral obligation to assist him. I felt deep remorse at leaving them and violating this strong tradition. They were 76 and 64. Then too there was frail Nami who had been hospitalized for six months with tuberculosis.

Michigan was too far away to come back for an emergency. But, both of Al's wonderful sisters, Edith and Margaret, had always been close to their parents' concerns and both were towers of strength. They assured me they would look after Grandma, Grandpa, and Nami, and I knew they would and could do better than I. But, the guilt stayed with me for a long time.

Moving into an unknown America seemed threateningly unfriendly even though it meant walking away from barbed wire fences, watchtowers, and the oppressiveness of camp. The newspaper head-lines were filled with the harsh language of war and propaganda, and frightening thoughts filled my head. I tried my best to set these aside for I was going into a free America to join Al, so I took our daughter and boarded the truck that would carry us away.

The day was gloomy and overcast. Marielle and I were dressed for a long journey. The driver called, "It's time to leave if we are going to catch the train."

Obaachan wouldn't let go of Marielle. They had never been far from each other, and Grandma's tear-stained eyes followed us as she tried to say good-bye. All I could manage was, "*Genki de gambatte.*" (Stay well with all your might.)

My clearance papers were for an indefinite leave, but I knew I would never live here again. The endless nightmare was behind me, and there was only hope for our future. A new life on the outside was written on the master plan of my life. I was destined to follow.

For Marielle, though, it was a sad day, perhaps the saddest day of her life. Parting with Grandma and Grandpa was hard for her to do. They had always been there for her ever since she was born. Their generous, loving arms, and the special, unfailing love and affection that only grandparents can give were hers. Now she was losing them, and it was hard to explain to my little girl what it was all about.

My last look at the barrack city brought me anguish mixed with exultation. Each chimney with smoke reaching to the sky meant that someone still lived there. I stood there for a moment taking one last look, a tired, 28-year-old Nisei mother with her child, taking this big step onto the train at the gate. Only a few officials and two internees at the gate waved a last Jerome good-bye.

Marielle and I made our way down the crowded train aisle. I was surprised to find the coach filled with servicemen and only a handful of people in civilian clothes. There was hardly room for our suitcase, it was so crowded. I also had a bulging totebag filled with gifts from loving hands that were thrust at us as we left. Marielle would not lack for snacks to appease her on this long journey to Chicago.

We sat on our suitcase at the end of the car, but before long, a handsome, sandy-haired soldier came up and helped us to his seat. I smiled and thanked him with deep appreciation. Marielle was tired and drowsy.

My heart quickened at the thought of seeing my Dakuzaku family soon in Chicago. I filled my mind with lively thoughts of what the future would bring. The hours were soon gone, and we were approaching our first destination.

Suddenly, Marielle vomited all over herself and me and the beautiful suit of the woman who sat next to her. I was so embarrassed I could have died. I was angry at myself for I should have realized that the child was not feeling well, that the ride was long and tiresome, and that the coach was stuffy. But I hadn't, and now I had a mess facing me.

It was so hard to squeeze down the crowded aisle to the washroom so we could clean up. Everyone looked at us and my face stayed beet-red. I apologized all the way to Chicago.

Dad and my cousin were there to greet us at the station. How good to see them again. But how noisy and frightening this gigantic, cold Chicago was from anything I had ever seen before. There was loud clattering all around; trains whizzed over and under us and alongside. I could hardly keep my wits about me; for a tiny moment, I longed for my quiet sanctuary in Jerome.

Auntie and Uncle, Mother and Father—they were all there, and it was wonderfully good to see them and hug them and, suddenly, I realized I was free! I breathed deeply and a wave of peace came over me. No matter that Marielle and I both smelled from a child's upset stomach; no matter that there was deafening noise and we were in the midst of more traffic than I had ever seen. I was in the real world, and I was free at last! My parents and Auntie and Uncle were happy to be safely employed and protected at Eleanor House, but Mother and Dad were ready to join us in Kalamazoo as soon as we got settled in a house. Farmers all their lives, they found the hectic city overwhelming, and they longed for a quieter place.

My brief visit was a whirlwind tour to see special friends. I visited Dr. and Mrs. Albert Palmer at the President's House at Chicago Theological Seminary. We had a brief chat midst hugs and expressions of gratitude for the many loving gifts, letters and encouragement during our internment.

A quick cup of tea and Marielle and I were on our way again. This

187

time the train was taking us to Kalamazoo in the last part of our wonderful, but frightening, journey. We would soon be on our own again with Al. Our young Tsukamoto family would begin a new life as free Americans in a free America.

We got off the train, and Al came running to meet us. Happiness sometimes defies description. Our new life in Kalamazoo began with this kind of happiness.

DEAR DADDY

THANK YOU FOR THE Big pumpkin. It came just in time. WE HAD REAL PUMPKINS To play with too, so we made JACK-O'LANTerns. Today, I saw a fur around the inside of his nose. Mummy said we have to throw the pumpkin away because HE is getting ~~too old~~

I HAD A good time at the block party Saturday nite. ~~THE~~ WE ALL wore funny costume. Lucy got 1st PRIZE. She was dressed like an old witch.

It's getting too cold for Butchy. ~~So~~ we will HAVE THE police come and take Him away. WHEN we go outside Mummy says ~~she~~ we will get a ~~so~~ cute Dog for me.

HAVE you found me a good school? Please find me ~~a school~~, one. When Mummy comes back from Indiana I am coming up to be with you Daddy. When we go outside I want to go to the restaurant. And go to the park.

EVERY NITE I am going To pray for you.

GOOD BYE

Chapter 17

Freedom at Last in Kalamazoo

"I had almost forgotten what it is like to be free— free to walk down the street, free to shop for groceries in a store, free to take my child to school, free to go to church..."

Kalamazoo was like a dream. We stayed in my sister Ruth's huge house on Lovell Street for a few weeks. It was filled with members of the Kiino family: Ruth and Hugh and their son; Hugh's 70 year old mother, and his sister's family of six. They were already crowded with the ten of them, but they made room for us and Al's YMCA roommate, Howard Miyoshi. Fourteen of us ate together, almost like a mini camp mess hall. We laughed and reminisced about everything. We got caught up on who was working and who was in the service, and we talked about those who were ill.

Far into the night, there were tales of sadness and gladness, tears and laughter at the same time. We talked about old friends in Florin, and on that cold, wintry night in Kalamazoo, we tried to establish some semblance of roots. It was November, 1943. We had left our berry farms in Florin a year and a half ago. Nothing until that night had even resembled home.

Far from our strawberry fields, we recalled stories of long gone days. We remembered old Mr. Ozato who always tried to sneak green berries into the bottom of his baskets. He was caught by an agricultural inspector one season as he tried to make a record breaking shipment. We chuckled at the names of the growers who were on special lists and had to be watched for such trickery.

We talked about Mother Kiino, widowed with six children, and how she had labored until late one November picking her berries when it was far too cold. Still she continued filling up crates with tiny berries, too small for sale, until she had ten crates piled up. Dick Ito, the Nojiri produce driver had warned her that her berries were too green and tiny and could not be sold, but she stubbornly went on with her picking. One day, she came out to the fields and found the stack of green berries scattered far and wide. She was so angry she never forgave Dick, even though green berries were worthless and could not be sold.*

We laughed that night in Kalamazoo remembering incidents of frantic harvest days in long-gone Florin. We had no idea then that the strawberry days of Florin might be forever gone. We couldn't even imagine what it would be like if we never returned to Florin again. We expected that the day would come when strawberries and grapes would once again dominate our lives and occupy our time.

Kalamazoo was a warm, healing experience for all of us. The church, PTA, and our YWCA friends were wonderful to us. Our life there was one of seclusion and those who worked at outside jobs did so at night when their Japanese faces were not so visible; the rest of us stayed indoors as much as we could. This night time life was highly preferable to life in camp. The trade-off meant that we kept quiet and went about our business without being noticed. We relied totally upon the tolerance, rational thinking, and calm actions of the majority populace. Usually, those strategies worked.

We were in Kalamazoo because Al had found work there. The proprietor of the Peter Pan Bakery was recruited by camp officials to hire internees. The nature of bakery work, necessitating night time employment, provided us with a good way to get started in an independent existence. It didn't matter that our Florin farmers did not have training in the baking of bread and other bakery products; they were quick learners and hard workers, and they were dedicated

---

*Years later as we sat talking about long ago Florin, Al's cousin, Hideo, who had been a neighbor kid of the Kiinos, "confessed" to the crime committed in Mother Kiino's field so long ago. It was Hideo who had dumped the berries in the field, and all this time we had thought Dick Ito had done the deed for which he had received the tongue lashing of his life. No wonder Dick had protested so!

to employers who were willing to make a commitment to them by giving them a chance.

In camp I had forgotten how to smile. My face had become a mask of unemotional response. In this new place, it became my job to venture out of the house daily to do the marketing for the household as they slept during the day and worked at night. It was hard for me to face strangers on the street and in the store. I was frightened and did not know how to act toward them. They didn't know how to act toward me either, but little by little, as I learned once again how to smile and be myself, I became braver and more comfortable in this new role.

As Al worked at Peter Pan and I took care of household chores, our healing process began to make its mark and a new life emerged. It was most important, however, for Marielle. Kalamazoo was a happy, innocent time of learning during which she made school friends and began to build a solid base of her academic skills.

In the early spring of 1944, Father, Mother, Julia, and George joined us in Kalamazoo. George, Father, and Julia all got jobs at the bakery with Al. We found a house of our own at 817 Lay Boulevard.

They all slept during the day and worked at night. Mother helped me cook, wash, iron, and keep house. Marielle's job each day was to walk to school across the street. Although we were alone, there were still seven of us that lived together in the house.

Grocery shopping was the most difficult thing for me. It was hard to carry the clumsy bags home with my crippled arms. One day we found a wooden cart with four wooden wheels, and when Al fixed it up for me, I could manage it just fine, even in the snow. We had wartime ration stamps for meat and other items. There were stamps for the seven of us, but no one knew there were that many of us living in the house. People wondered about the huge amounts of food I carried home on my cart, and I worried about what they thought. I was so self-conscious! I felt eyes peering at me from behind curtained windows. Did they think perhaps that I had stolen precious stamps or that I was secretly selling food I had obtained illegally? Each time I went to the store my head was filled with such paranoid thoughts. I tried so hard to come and go quietly, but the wooden wheels on my cart creaked loudly through the snow. No matter how hard Al tried to oil them, the loud creaks continued to accompany me on my shopping trips.

One day on a school holiday, Marielle went with me to do the daily marketing. In her cute snow outfit, she ran ahead of me and around me. To my surprise, people who had never smiled at me smiled at my child. My mask of terror broke into a timid smile, and suddenly I realized how tense the muscles of my face had been and how my body had struggled to prepare for some assault in this new community. Unconsciously, I had been drawn into that guilt. But on this day, I learned that I was stared at with such frightening faces because I appeared to them as one stricken with fear. Marielle, my innocent child, had broken the masks. I learned that I needed to try harder and that I must be brave even though I was frightened. From then on I forced myself to smile and found, to my pleasure, that it worked.

Al worked at the bakery at night with the rest of the family. Night after night they made loaves and loaves of bread, rolls, cakes, and cookies. Al's job was to tend to the baking of hundreds of round cakes. The giant ferris-like wheel in the oven, fourteen feet in length, took one hour to make its rounds. Al had to have folded flour sacks on his hands. There were slits in them and five were strapped together. If the glove slipped, the fingers would be burned. It took quick moves to keep things moving to the rhythm of the mechanized oven.

Supplies were hard to get because of the war, so the workers had to make do with what they had. Hugh Kiino was the mixer of bread dough, operating the huge mixer that was something like the kind that mixed concrete. There were many opportunities to make mistakes, but the employee who made them did not last long. Training consisted of a few simple directions; the rest was experience. There were many things to watch out for. Pans filled with oil were quick to burn. Workers had to guess when the cakes were done. When something was wrong, there was little time to correct it. Accidents happened in split seconds. My father had the tip of his finger cut off one night while he was feeding dough into a cutting machine. He was paid $500 for the accident, but many times in the years to come I heard my father say, *"Soredemo jibun no yubi ga hoshii"* (even so, one's own finger is best). All the money in the world couldn't pay him for the pain he felt from the absence of his finger tip.

193

At the bakery, the workers made sweet rolls by mixing 50 pounds of flour with several five pound chunks of lard and dozens of eggs. One night they were out of raisins, so a case was brought up from the basement. When they opened it, they found the contents alive and wriggling. My father, who was in charge, frantically called the supervisor, "Red" Umloff, a Russian American who was quite the character. Red saw no problem with the raisins. He just picked up the box and with his strong arms, dumped the contents into a large washtub and filled it with water. All the white wriggling creatures came up to the top. He swished them off several times, and then said to Dad, "They're okay now. Go ahead and mix them into the batter."

For a long time, none of us could eat sweet rolls, raisin bread, or anything with raisins in any shape or form.

Another night, molasses was dumped into the batter instead of food coloring. They had to throw 800 pounds out.

And so our lives went on. We began to hear that the camps were going to close. Jerome was one of the first; the people were to be sent to other camps. Al and I talked about it, and he decided to send his parents and Nami to Gila in Arizona. The desert climate would be better for Nami. We reasoned that Gila was a large camp that would probably last the longest, and they would be closer to home too. The Ouchida family went with them. Margaret and Charlie Ogata had found work in Benton Harbor, Michigan. Violet, their daughter, joined us in Kalamazoo. In this way many families became separated as they decided what was best for old ones, young ones, and those in between who had to find jobs in strange places where it was not easy to be Japanese and find employment. Headlines about Japanese war atrocities daily pointed accusing fingers at us. This kept us fearful and our work situations tense, but we could not go home and had nowhere to hide, so we had to do something.

Before the camp at Jerome closed in June 1944, Al and I went back one more time to attend Grandpa Ouchida's funeral. It was our last event in Block 9. How strange and wonderful at the same time to visit old friends and relatives. I was pleased to see how well the USO was continuing in its brave work. I was even more pleased to walk away knowing I would never return to the existence I had known there.

In July we moved to a big house at 410 West Dutton Street. We were only a block from Marielle's new school and in a nice neighborhood close to stores and our church.

In August George was drafted into the 442nd. On a furlough he went back to California to get Harold Ouchida's Dodge which was left in Florin when we went to camp. Although George wore the uniform of the U.S. Army, he was denied permission to enter California to get the car. Bob Fletcher, who lived on our farm, drove the Dodge to Reno, Nevada, where George waited for it. All the new tires had been stolen from the car, a serious problem for us with tires rationed and new ones almost impossible to get. George drove it back however, and we had a car to ride around Kalamazoo and to drive back to California when it was time to go home.

All the internment camps were scheduled to be closed in the coming year, 1945. This caught people by surprise. Suddenly they had to find whatever work they could. The best jobs were domestic work for there was a built-in protection by the employer. People had a place to live and did not have to be out in public much. It was still frightening to be around other people because you never knew how they would react.

Suddenly, also, hundreds of men of draft age were called up by their local draft boards back home. How strange that those who had contrived for our removal and arranged to have us placed in camps, now sought to fill their draft quotas with the Japanese American boys they had sent to internment camps. Many wondered if this allowed them to keep their own boys at home.

Julia was still living with us. We worried about her though because she so wanted to live a normal life like other young people. She worked at the bakery at night, but she got tired of that schedule and asked if she could work during the day. They agreed to try her on the daytime shift. When the customers saw her Japanese face on the line however, they became alarmed and began to boycott the bakery. The personnel officer had to handle the situation. He attended our church and we counted him as our very special friend, but he had to ask Julia to go back on nights. There were tears in his eyes as he made the request.

"Julia," he implored. "You've got to work at night. People are afraid. It's not *you* they are protesting against. Japan is responsible for their sons being killed and all the terrible things of this war. It's not *you*, Julia, it's the war!"

Julia wouldn't do it, and they had to fire her because of her refusal. The church minister walked the streets with her to help her find another job, but there were none for a young girl of Japanese ancestry!

Poor Julia. She could not find another job, so she went back to Peter Pan at night. How disappointing to find that although we were employable, our work had to be done secretly at night. Julia found this impossible to accept, and eventually she quit. I worried about her and her attitude. She was stubborn but also vulnerable to depression and despair. She sat around the house and moped, and there wasn't much any of us could do to make her feel better. I took her to see our minister, Dr. Dwight Large of First Methodist Church, for counseling.

Then one day Julia joined the WACS and was sent to Pasco, Washington. She was proud and happy, and we were glad. Maybe Julia finally found herself.

Al and I worried about Marielle too, but she appeared to be adjusting to this strange life. Our lives had been in various stages of disruption since she was five. Marielle celebrated her seventh and eighth birthdays in Kalamazoo, and though somewhat shy, she seemed to do well. We took great pride in watching her grow and develop.

One night Marielle listened as Al told about his wild motorcycle ride on the way home from work that morning. Red Umloff, the floor supervisor who lived in a little town outside the city, commuted to work on a shiny motorcycle. The sun was about to come up that morning when Red offered Al a ride on his big motorcycle. He was on his way to have a beer.

"I'll be glad to drop you off," he said. "You'll like riding on this big machine."

With his lunch basket in his hand, Al climbed on.

"Before I got settled, the big Russian took off with a roar. I grabbed my hat with one hand and clung to my lunch basket with the other, but I lost my grip on Red. My legs flew upward and knocked me off balance. I managed to get my legs caught under Red's arms. That's the only thing that kept me from falling off. Red pushed my legs down and

I jerked into an upright position. I hung on for dear life until I was safely home!"

Al acted out the reckless ride. It was his first experience on a motorcycle and the way he talked, it would probably be his last. We marveled that he had escaped unhurt.

We forgot about the incident until we went to the next PTA meeting. Marielle's teacher laughingly told us how little, shy Marielle had come to the front of the class to tell the children about her father's crazy motorcycle ride. She had even acted it out just as Al had done for us. The teacher was surprised, and so were we. I felt warmed and grateful that our daughter was so happy at school and was so at ease in sharing family experiences with other children. As long as her education was challenging and helping her to develop so well, we could endure the little discomforts and problems of our lives.

Rays of hope entered our lives as news of the war brought hope that the fighting all over the world might be ended. The longings for a real home were becoming unbearable in our third year away from Florin. We began to hear that legal issues related to the internment might be settled and we would be allowed to go home. It was almost too much to hope for.

All during 1943 and 1944, we had read about the all-Nisei fighting combat unit, the 442nd, with its inspirational motto, "Go For Broke." They blazed a trail of victories across Europe. Wounded and maimed Nisei soldiers were at the Veteran's Hospital in Battle Creek, Michigan.

One spring day in 1945, a handsome young Nisei came looking for a Japanese American family he had heard lived in Kalamazoo. His looks and slight "Pidgin English" immediately gave away the fact that he was from Hawaii. Lenny Ishihara was a veteran of the famed 100th Battalion; his heroic deeds in the European battle front had left him severely wounded. He had lost his leg, and he limped as he walked with an artificial leg.

Lenny was working with the Veteran's Hospital helping wounded soldiers learn how to adjust to the shock of their injuries and trying to build their morale before they were returned to their families. He was looking for families, particularly Japanese Americans, that soldiers could visit and asked if we would help.

Of course we were delighted. We invited a car full of wounded soldiers who were able to make the 30 minute trip to Kalamazoo and venture forth to visit and have a Japanese meal with us. Mom and I were happy as we busily prepared Japanese salad, rice and sukiyaki. Another time we fixed chow mein, chicken teriyaki and other foods they missed. The boys were very appreciative.

In this small way, we let them know how proud we were of their contributions to America. Some were too shocked and injured to return toHawaii; others were from families who were by nowscattered all over the U.S. after their dismissal from internment camps. So many of them had no one to visit them. We went as often as we could and invited them to our homes.

We learned that Joe, who had a severe head injury and a metal plate over his wound, was reluctant to go home. Many of these wounded boys were deeply concerned about facing their loved ones back home. We ached for the suffering they had endured for their country and realized how great a price was paid to win the war in Europe and help preserve our precious liberties.

On December 18, 1944, the U.S. Supreme Court ruled on the Mitsuye Endo case claiming that the government did *not* have the right to detain a citizen without due process and without a cause. That's what we had been saying all along. Though the decision was several years too late, it was clear now that the ban on persons of Japanese ancestry could no longer be enforced. The very next day, December 19, President Roosevelt lifted the ban excluding us from the West Coast. Finally, we could think seriously about going home.

The return to California was not as easy to plan as it was to talk about. The first homecomings had not been successful at all. We heard of families who had bravely tried to go home. They hoped to get their vines pruned and readied so they could look forward to a 1945 crop. But the public was not ready for their return. Going home turned into a frightening mistake.

People were beaten by hoodlums in their California home towns. Houses and buildings were burned. We were sick as we heard about these incidents. Going home, which we had so eagerly anticipated for so many months, was turning out to be something different from the joyous occasion we thought it would be. For many it turned into disaster, and now they wondered where they would go and what they would do to survive.

For those of us who waited anxiously to hear of safe travel, we just did not know what to think. Such unrest and confusion! First we had been taken from our homes, then the government was found to have been wrong to have detained us, and now we were not allowed to go back home because of those who took the law into their own hands. They apparently felt they had the right to do this since the government had boldly driven us out. It was a strange series of events, and we seemed to be the victims once again.

The war in Europe ended in May. Hitler was dead and the Allies had won the war. Al and I decided it was time to go home.

Before we began our plans, however, Al suggested that we take a trip to Washington D.C. to see our nation's capital. It was potentially a dangerous trip for us as we were still at war with Japan, but we so wanted to walk in the footsteps of our country's founders and experience first hand the workings of democracy. It was our patriotic duty to go there if we could.

We decided to take both our fathers with us. We knew it would be the last opportunity for these two elderly Issei to make such a trip.

Ojiisan, Al's father, was still at Gila Internment Camp in Arizona, but he was given permission to visit us for one month. The West Coast Exclusion Order had been lifted at the beginning of 1945, so technically we were free to travel as we wished.

Ojiisan came to Kalamazoo by train, and together the four of us traveled to Washington D.C. We were afraid, but we went anyway. We thought we would be questioned by angry people who would wonder why we were enjoying America's historical sites when the country was still at war with Japan. Feeling apprehensive and apologetic, we nevertheless made plans. We knew it was something we had to do for the sake of our parents as well as for ourselves. And so we went—Al and his father, and my father and I. At the hotels we must have looked impressive. They thought we were a delegation from China! We didn't know what to think of that!

When we walked up those white, marble steps and stood awed and silent by the magnificence of the Lincoln statue, all my anxieties disappeared. I was breathlessly inspired, my heart filled with longings that reached back into my childhood. Now that I had miraculously come to the spot that commemorated this great man's accomplishments for a free nation, I was awed by the immensity of what I felt. We looked up, dwarfed by the size of the Great Emancipator, a giant among men, and we literally fell to our knees.

Here was my father, Taro Dakuzaku, Florin strawberry farmer, Jerome camp cook, Kalamazoo baker—this man who had told his children all about Abraham Lincoln and how he had read about him when he was a boy in Okinawa. Father had always believed that anything was possible in America, and on that spring day we were witness to that fact by our very presence in that place.

Al's father was equally moved. Ojiisan had lived life so immensely and had worked so hard in spite of having been labeled an alien and not allowed citizenship. Nevertheless he had developed a great love and faith in America's goodness. These two Issei had labored honestly all their lives and had implicitly believed in the America of Lincoln in spite of all.

Our fathers felt great pride in their adopted country. My father was especially proud of his son and daughter—George who was with the U.S. Army in Europe and Julia who was in the WACS.

I prayed there at Lincoln's tomb that as our American boys returned home from battlefields all over the world, the work of cleaning up our land would begin. I prayed that the fight for freedom from prejudice and hate would continue until all people were free to stand tall with dignity and pride.

I recalled the day that my students had recited the Gettysburg Address when we were at camp in Fresno and how so many had laughed at the irony of it. Now I realized that there had been truth in what I had done. It proved to me what a wonderful future could be anyone's in America.

I didn't ask my father what he was thinking of as we knelt at Lincoln's memorial. Later I wished I had, but the moment was such a private one, and thoughts were difficult to share.

Our trip to Washington included side trips to New York and then to Sea Brooks, Birdseye's New Jersey farm. We visited Al's brother George (a nephew adopted by Al's parents before Al was born to carry on the Tsukamoto name as there were only girls in the family before

200

Al was born). We also visited Harold Ouchida who was a big businessman there. Harold was a recruiter for Birdseye Company, a frozen food company in Bridgeton. This company needed good handlers of vegetables, and since Japanese Americans were experienced with that, Birdseye was anxious to hire them. Many Florinites had settled in Bridgeton as a result of Harold's recruitment.

We also made a trip to New York. After an exhausting day of sightseeing around Times Square, Radio City, the Empire State Building, and the Statue of Liberty, Al and I said, "Tonight you two old fellows go to bed. We are going to see a famous play on Broadway." But we knew they both wanted to go too and would enjoy the movies more. Ojiisan and Dad hurriedly dressed and off to the movies we went!

The trip was a totally memorable experience. We were frequently mistaken for Chinese diplomats; people assumed we could not speak English. This astounded us, and we did not know how to act in these cases of mistaken identity. However, such thinking provided us with a measure of safety, so we let it be. On the entire trip, we did not encounter one unpleasant incident.

When we returned to Kalamazoo, we decided it was time to go home to California and Florin. We prayed that our trip west would be as free of problems as our tourist trip east had been. Somehow, though, we knew we would not be mistaken for Chinese visitors.

We steeled ourselves for epithets of "dirty Jap," and being spat upon, and what else we could not even imagine, but we placed such thoughts in the backs of our minds and said good-bye to Kalamazoo.

Chapter 18

Home to Florin

*"For more than three years I had wondered what it would be like
to come back home again. Some parts of homecoming are sweet and
incredibly joyful. Other parts leave my body drained and my
heart with gaping holes through and through."*

Across America in the summer of 1945, former residents of the
internment camps longed to return to their West Coast homes.
Symbolically, we tested the winds to see if there would be favorable
conditions for us if we returned. Al and I wondered if we should make
our future home in Kalamazoo or some other place where we could
find employment. These were hard decisions to make— and they
could not be made lightly, for whatever we decided now would affect
us for the rest of our lives.

Nor could such choices be made without considering the needs of
our parents, our children, and other family members. All were inex-
plicably bound together in choosing the direction for our future.

For those of us who decided to risk returning to our former homes,
the WRA agreed to pay the cost of shipping our belongings. Since we
had left our homes with only what we could carry and had lived in
temporary situations for more than three years, the cost of freight was
a small problem to consider, but we greatly appreciated this tiny
gesture.

The big problem was traveling across the country at a time when
automobiles were not available. Gas and tires were rationed, and we
didn't have much money to finance our traveling.

We Tsukamotos were· more fortunate than most because Bob

Fletcher had cared for our farm during our long absence. Our house was intact, and we knew there was something there to go home to. This was not the case with most people. Some had literally nothing left. Everything had been lost in the three long years they had been gone.

In Kalamazoo, farewell parties were held for us by church friends, Marielle's schoolmates, and family members who had decided to stay in Michigan. My sisters, Isabel and Ruth, and their families decided not to return to California. Margaret and Charlie Ogata and their seven children stayed in Eau Claire, harvesting fruit. Eventually, they made Benton Harbor their home. Ruth and Hugh Kiino stayed in Kalamazoo; Isabel and Tom Oshiro and their little son, Neal, also decided to stay. For all of these and many more, Florin would never again be their home.

My parents and Jean headed for Sacramento by train. We decided to drive. Harold Ouchida's 1942 green Dodge that we borrowed was filled with our family. Ojiisan, Marielle, and her little, black Scottie, "Inky," crowded into the back seat. Al and I were in the front seat with snacks and things. The little car was piled high and packed full with the last necessary household possessions we could not ship by freight.

The tires on the Dodge were bad. We had seven flats along the way. Each time we had to unload the entire car to change the tire. One tire became completely useless. We had to beg for another ration stamp to buy a new tire. Over the high mountains, along dangerous cliffs, we drove with those terrible tires in a car overloaded with people and their belongings. Someone must surely have been looking after us!

All along the way, we picked up servicemen and gave them rides. Somehow, we squeezed closer together so we could do our patriotic duty as good American citizens.

We tried to make the trip an educational one for Marielle and Ojiisan. We studied geography and calculated the mileage from one place to another. We pointed out the wildlife along the highway so they could learn what the country was like. One morning, we found a little turtle for Marielle and took it along for a pet.

Our first destination was Gila, the scorching hot desert city in

Arizona. Our friends and relatives had turned dark with deep sun tans. We hardly recognized them. In Gila we celebrated Ojiisan's 78th birthday with a party. It was so good to be together again with more of our loved ones.

Al took our nieces and nephews who had lived like hermits for three years to Phoenix for a day. In a candy shop, we enjoyed little, five-year-old Sonny as he gazed at cases filled with more candy than he had seen in his entire life. His sparkling boyish eyes were wide open, and there was nothing he could say at the wondrous sight before him. When children were treated to a movie, they were surprised. "You mean we go inside a house to see a movie?" Lester remarked. They had only known outdoor movies in camp. How we enjoyed being back with our family once again!

Then it was time to leave. There were seven of us brave souls ready to travel in the cool morning hours of July 9, 1945: Al, Marielle and I; Harold, Edith, little Sonny and Hitoshi, Harold's younger brother. We said good-bye and headed the Dodge toward California and our Florin homes.

With our faces looking toward Florin, we drove off. We had decided to take the shortest route to California, but that decision turned out to be a mistake for we found ourselves traveling on terrible roads. However, it was necessary to stay off the main roads and to be as inconspicuous as possible. Traveling was safer like that and with two families together, it was even safer because there was safety in numbers. In this secret way, we sneaked home toward Florin.

Every time we stopped for gas, our hearts pounded as we feared the reception we might have. We were too frightened to try to spend the night anywhere. We didn't even have the nerve to stop to rest or eat. We drove on bone tired and anxious; yet, we were afraid to reach our destination for we didn't know what to expect when we got there. We knew, however, that Bob Fletcher, our faithful friend, would be waiting for us, and we would be safe from harm in our home.

As we slowly covered mile after mile of central California, we talked about the news reports of harsh welcomes given to other returning Japanese Americans. Hatred had been agitated toward the return of Nisei soldiers to Florin earlier in the year and homes set on fire. If heroic veterans in uniform had been treated like that, what

204

would happen to us? How could we ever expect to live as free Americans again?

Our friend, Mike Umeda, had returned to Taishoku early in January. He wanted to prune his vineyard for the fall grape harvest. Next door his neighbor's place, the Mukai's, had been burned to the ground. Churches and halls where people had stored their goods had been ransacked and precious possessions were destroyed and taken. We wondered and worried about what we would find in Florin, so near to Taishoku and Mayhew.

Prepared for bad news, we finally drove down Stockton Boulevard. We passed Seven Mile House and turned onto Florin Road. We were heading for our dear town of Florin at last. It was early in the morning, much before sunrise. All the homes were dark. No one stirred or noticed our homecoming. We were relieved to find it so.

We had been gone for three years and 42 days. On the unforgettable day of July 10, 1945, after almost 24 hours of non-stop driving, we came home to Florin at last.

But where was the bustling economic center we had left? We were totally unprepared for the devastating appearance of our town. Akiyama's Store, Nishii's Basket Factory–they were all gone. Fire had destroyed them all during our absence. We were returning to a town that no longer existed. Florin was gone.

None of us spoke. What was there to say? Quietly, we hurried down Florin-Perkins Road and turned into our own Tsukamoto driveway. How good to see our familiar buildings and our own place. The old barn was still leaning against the big walnut trees. The two old cabins by the bath house and the one on the other side of the main house were still there. Our humble little house stood bravely under the big walnut trees. We ran happily here and there touching everything to make sure it was real, feasting our eyes on the dear place we had missed so much.

Best of all, the Fletchers were there to welcome us home. They had already moved out into the one-room cabin by the water pump so we could have the house we had left in their care.

Very few returning Florin residents were as lucky as we were. Many came back to find that they had nothing left. They wondered how they would be able to start all over again.

Home to Florin

People crowded into the basement of the Japanese community hall after the crates stored there were removed. Empty buildings were turned into temporary hostels. Some families managed under these emergency conditions for several years.

Those who were elderly had a very difficult time, especially if they did not have children to help them out. Often, children of the Issei were scattered all over the United States or they were in the military service, so there was no one to help them get started again.*

The days and weeks that followed our return to Florin are blurred in our memories. It was a busy, difficult time. Our house was filled with people. Arrangements had to be made for renters to find other places to live so that people could return to their own homes. Families that were still at Gila Relocation Center had to be brought home. As people wandered back, many needed temporary housing — a night or two or even longer. They came to stay with us. We slept all over the floors, packed like sardines, as there were not enough beds. It didn't matter though—we were home, and our unusual boarding house provided assistance for people who had a lot of adjustments yet to make. We painted and cleaned, remodeled our house, and just enjoyed being back home again. With food and gas rationing, it was hard to keep everything going, but it had to be done.

We could not help all the families. Many had to double up with neighbors or friends until they could find permanent places. Some found wonderful Caucasian friends who opened their hearts and homes to them in this strange emergency. Heart-warming stories were told of special kindnesses. Many of these, however, we knew nothing about until many years later.*

Al's parents were released from Gila camp in August. They too finally came home to Florin where they had lived most of their lives.

---

*At the Commission hearings forty years later, neighbors told for the first time of the hardships they encountered when they came home to Florin. Until then no one had known of their humiliating situations. Each family was so busy taking care of their own immediate needs that they didn't have time to share experiences and problems. Many wanted to forget what had taken place. We needed to put that part of our lives behind us and move ahead for we had been taught to make the best of whatever was our lot.

Physically fit at 66 and 78, Ojiisan and Obaachan had survived the ordeal of their evacuation. Now they were prepared to spend the rest of their lives in Florin.

A few days after their arrival home, however, these two old ones found themselves enduring yet another painful experience. Word reached us of the ending of World War II and the bombing of Hiroshima. What should have been a day of gladness for our two old, gentle Issei was instead a day of insurmountable grief. The atomic bomb had been dropped on their home city of Hiroshima, filled with relatives and friends they would never see again.

It was tragic news to Al's parents that the city had been completely destroyed. They worried about the agonies their dear relatives must have suffered.

"War is a terrible thing," they said. Their pride in America winning the war was saddened by the knowledge that they were the only survivors of their families and that in Hiroshima, everything was gone.

My parents and Jean had arrived in Florin earlier than we had. They had taken a train from Kalamazoo and had been met by long time, wonderful friends, the Jenkins family, upon their arrival. They were already settled on their Gerber Road farm by the time we arrived.

Harold Ouchida, Al's brother-in-law, was determined to get the strawberry business started again in Florin. It was almost apparent from the beginning, however, that it could not be done. It was such a formidable undertaking to tackle alone.

---

*Nellie Sakakihara (Seno) spoke at the Commission hearings at Golden Gate University in 1981 and told how horrified and ashamed she had been when she found her elderly parents living in a chicken coop in Florin. Their farm had been sold for a pitiful sum when they were in camp because they could not keep up the payments on their debt. The older children had left camp to work in cities in the East and Midwest, so the parents returned to Florin alone. Alvin, their only son, was in the service. The Senos were grateful that their neighbors, the Bonucellis, were kind enough to find a place for them to stay for they had nowhere to go. After a while they moved to the community hall with many other families. As limited as the facility was, it was far better than the chicken coop.

Issei farmers were older and many were not physically well enough to start over again, but they tried valiantly. For ten years they grew berries, but the famous, delectable Florin strawberries would never be what they once were. Strawberry time was over for Florin. Other parts of the state had taken over berry production and sales during our absence. Nisei men and women were forced to turn to other employment. Florin's strawberry days were over.

In early September our family had another blow as we discovered that Julia had fallen victim to incarceration and war. A WAC, stationed in Pasco, Washington, Julia became a casualty of World War II at the beautiful age of 22. My independent sister, who had refused to work nights at the Peter Pan Bakery in Kalamazoo, who had joined the WACS in a desperate attempt to find something rational in her life, was dead.

The telegram came to my parents at their farm on Gerber Road.

> *We regret to inform you that Pvt Julia Dakuzaku died today. Her body will be shipped to Sacramento. It is due to arrive tomorrow, September 10, at 11 A.M. at the Southern Pacific Railway Station*

We could not believe it! How could this happen to our family? The telegram only said she had died; there were a thousand unanswered questions in our hearts. The shock and pain were too much for us to bear.

Al and I met the tall, attractive, blonde lieutenant, who escorted Julia's flag-covered coffin to Sacramento. We took her to meet Mom and Dad. She was the Army's sad messenger to tell us in person the words that could not be written down. Quietly, she tried to explain to us how Julia had died. We were stunned. We could not believe it. Not one of us could put voice to the tragic truth.

I tried to explain in Japanese to Mom and Dad. I could hardly get the words out, and when I did, they would not hear them. Deep down, the painful truth settled to become a silent secret for us all. (Some of my sisters didn't even know until many, many years later.)

This heart-breaking news froze the homecoming joy that was in our hearts. Julia came home to Florin in her flag-draped pine box just six weeks after my parents' return. The youngest girl in our family had become the first to leave us. This shocking end to our long ordeal devastated us. We had been taken across the nation, tossed around for three long years, and now we were home, but for Julia there was no joy in coming home.

Mom sensed what had happened. She told me how Julia had confided in her during her growing up years about her difficulties in coping with life. I recall Mom trying to tell me about something that had happened in Kalamazoo which I did not pay much attention to at the time. The shocking fact of what Mom knew and what Julia had tried to do finally made sense to me. I should have been alarmed at Julia's private struggle to overcome the shame, confusion and frustration that piled up around her during our hectic years of internment. Truth like this is deep and painful and filled with guilt and regret.

The shock of suddenly leaving her sheltered, rural farm life and being thrust into the emergency community of internment had done Julia irreparable harm. She had been the artistic and sensitive one in our family. I have been told that it is the shy, gentle ones who weaken under stress that is too severe. This is how it must have had been with her.

Julia had huddled in our cold barrack room on wintry days in Jerome and made pastel drawings for us. I cherish to this day the two cute puppies she sketched for Marielle. Julia loved to dance and was graceful on stage in talent and variety shows. She harmonized with us when the Dakuzaku sisters were asked to sing. She worked with the USO and wrote letters to lonely Nisei soldiers far from home.

The incident at Peter Pan Bakery was more than Julia could bear. She had tried to work days, but found that because of hysteria and bigotry, she had to work at night or not work at all. After brooding several months, she had joined the Army to gain some measure of independence in serving her country.

Ruth had sent Julia a cake for her 22nd birthday; Isabel sent her cookies. I was on the road during most of June and July, and during those hectic days, I had not sent her a letter or a card. How I wished I had!

Julia wrote: "The cookies were gone in no time. They were so good. I am anxious to come home to Florin in a few days."

Those were Julia's last words to us. Little did we know that she was suffering her gravest personal crisis at the time she wrote. Our brother George was a close and dear friend to Julia. She had often talked freely to him and gained encouraging support from him. George had visited her in Pasco during his furlough just before her death. A photo of the two of them from their happy visit was among Julia's things brought back to us by the lieutenant who accompanied the body.

Julia's death was especially painful for George because he could not be with the family during our tears. He was stationed in England at the time. The experience turned into a lifetime hurt and emptiness for the sister he would never see again.

I didn't know then what I know today as an educator about what adolescents and young adults go through and how vulnerable they can be to attacks of depression. Although I had worried about Julia when she was at Kalamazoo, I didn't understand how traumatic it must have been for a sensitive young girl's dignity and self esteem to be discriminated against and humiliated when she found out that advertised job openings were not for her. Even when caring church members walked the streets with her to find daytime employment, Julia could not get a job. I sought help for her from our minister who conducted several counseling sessions which seemed to help. When Julia happily joined the WACS, I felt it was the beginning of adjustment and maturing growth for her. However, it was not to be.

As the older sister, I wish I had known more about counseling and psychology, but, most of all, I wish I had been a better loving friend to her. If only I had written to her about our travels and about coming home to Florin, and if only I had told Julia how proud I was of her, my sister—a WAC in the service of our country.

A military funeral was held. Julia lies buried in East Lawn Cemetery. She ended her life by her own choice. That is the burden of guilt we have lived with these many years.

One by one, our Nisei soldiers returned to Florin. Some took longer than others because they were in military hospitals until their wounds were healed enough to be discharged.

Word came to us of many who would never return. Like Julia, the lives of many Nisei ended in World War II. Gold stars hung bravely in the windows of houses on old strawberry farms, in temporary quarters, and even in barns and chicken coops. The loss of a child brings the same kind of emptiness no matter where one lives.

Finally though, we were home in Florin after our strange adventure in America in World War II.

More Than Half of Nisei Back in Former Homes

By VIC MINAHAN

MORE than half of Sacramento County's pre-war population of Japanese-Americans have returned to their farms, businesses and jobs, and have met a sympathetic, even cordial, reception, a survey by The Sacramento Union disclosed yesterday. The war however, caused 30 per cent of owners to lose their farm, and a number of those formerly in business for themselves are now employes.

Of the estimated 3,500 in agricultural pursuits prior to the war, 2,500 have returned, and, as previously, are concentrated in the Florin area. In the City of Sacramento, it is estimated that 1,000 of the pre-war population of 3,500 have returned.

Japanese-American leaders agreed unanimously that the capital city's citizens are "tops" in their treatment of Nisei returning from relocation centers or war service.

"THE PEOPLE here have been wonderful about it all," said Henry Taketa, local attorney, in a typical comment. "Of course, we didn't expect to be welcomed back with open arms, but the people's attitude here of letting us come back and pick up where we left off without hindrance of any kind has been as fine as in any city in the West."

The valley's Nesei began returning to their homes here last fall, after the president's 1942 proclamation which banned them from the West Coast was rescinded in January, 1945. Sacramento County's Nisei population is estimated at about half its pre-war peak, reached just before the relocation order.

Sacramento Union Nov. 7, 1946

TYPICAL OF THE NISEI who have returned to their homes in the Sacramento Valley are Mrs. Alfred I. Tsukamoto (left) and her mother-in-law, Mrs. Kuzo Tsukamoto. The older woman, born in Japan, can never be a U. S. citizen under present law, while the younger was born in San Francisco, went to American schools and speaks English as her native tongue. The women are shown packing herb tea, grown by the elder Tsukamoto as a hobby, which will be sold in a local store.

Chapter 19

Starting Over

"I never dreamed I would become a teacher. Even though I had once wanted to teach, I knew that I could not because I was Japanese. I guess I thought I'd pick strawberries for the rest of my days . . ."

With the war over, Al and I settled down to raise strawberries and tend to the grapevines planted so many years ago by Ojiisan. Marielle enrolled as a second grader at Florin Elementary School. How glad we were that the school had been integrated since 1939, when Al and I and the newly organized JACL approached the school board. We found to our surprise that there were no objections to integrating the school. That fall in 1945, Marielle's classes were in the very room I had studied in twenty years before when the school had been only for Japanese children.

Florin changed tremendously in the years we were gone. Many old friends and relatives did not return, and we missed them. Some came, looked up a few friends and quietly sneaked away, pained that they could not stay. They grieved over the community that disappeared in our absence.

Some wandered to other communities where friends made during the incarceration years gave them leads into hopeful prospects for jobs. They searched desperately to get back on their feet.

Others spent years trapped in trailer home slums, vainly trying to retrieve what they had lost and with it a sense of dignity and hope. We were all stunned by the ordeal of internment, but we were also

WE THE PEOPLE

silenced by our humiliation. We had no desire to talk about what had transpired. The sooner forgotten, the better for us all. We placed our experiences aside, hid them in closets and deep dark holes, and pretended we were better off forgetting the whole thing. In doing so, we hoped that Florin, California, and the nation too would forget with us. Such shameful years could not bear the light of day; we closed them up with a collective sigh of relief.

We took all kinds of jobs—no matter how menial they were. Some people worked on dairy farms and chicken ranches—anything that could be found. Some lived in barns or shacks, whatever living quarters could be found. With hope still before us, we leased land from friends to try to raise strawberries again.

Many younger ones, who worked in industry when they left camp, found jobs in canneries, frozen food plants, or with county, state or federal governments. Our veterans went to college or trade school on the G.I. Bill when they returned home. We proudly commended their choices knowing that education was the route to better jobs and brighter futures. So too with teenagers who were encouraged by their parents and grandparents to go on to higher education. Somehow they managed to get extra jobs, and the money was found to pay for tuition and books. There were some, however, who missed the opportunities before them, especially with the G.I. Bill. They had not been counseled in camp high schools to take the right classes in preparation for going on to college, and now they sadly found out that it was too late and they could not be admitted.

Day after day we heard of families abandoning their vineyards. The post war price drop caused great hardships for grape farmers and the Florin Fruit Growers' Association.

I had hoped that Al and I might do something other than the endless, back-breaking, stoop labor of strawberries and grapes that never seemed to bring us much financial security. How I longed to do something worthwhile with my life! The frightening feeling of being poor and worries of not having enough to eat brought back memories of shame and degradation from my childhood. I wanted to show my pride as an American citizen; I wanted to express my gratitude and joy as a proud citizen of this great country. Would I ever find an opportunity to serve in some special way? It hardly seemed possible

213

as I surveyed the world from the Tsukamoto berry patch.

My back ached from crawling on my knees and squatting so close to the ground, but it was the only way I could cover the strawberry patch and move aside the leaves to look for hidden ripe berries. My hands and face were grimey and covered with dust. I was ashamed to be seen in my old, faded coveralls and soiled bonnet. If anyone came to look for me, I wanted to hide. But, if this was the only way to make a living, so it must be. There seemed to be no hope that things would improve in the future.

The day came when a decision had to be made. Al and I discussed the sad situation with Ojiisan and Obaasan. We decided that strawberries and grapes could no longer support our family of six. A small patch of strawberries, some boysenberries, quince, and persimmons were all that we would keep. The grapevines were pulled, and in 1949 the thirty-year farming era of our Florin-Perkins farm was ended.

The task of pulling up the grapevines was a painful one for us all. A huge tractor extracted the deep rooted vines from the earth. Sadly we watched as each day, acre by acre, the vines were pulled and stacked to be burned. "It's like pulling teeth," remarked Obaasan, and it was just as painful too.

Sadly we watched the whisps of smoke from the burning of the grapevines all around us. There would be no more wood supply for our Japanese baths from the yearly prunings. We had always gathered up the grape canes after pruning, bundled them up and brought them home to stack up alongside the bath house. The canes served as firewood for heating water for our nightly baths. Every Japanese family had a bath house—a shack built away from the main house. Inside the shack was a redwood tub with a galvanized sheet nailed to it and sealed at the bottom so the fire could be started to heat the water. A wooden float kept our feet from touching the metal bottom.

After a hard day's work in the fields, we washed ourselves with plenty of soap and rinsed, and when we were completely clean, we took a therapeutic dip in the wonderful hot tub. A good soaking did wonders for young and old.

All Japanese Americans in rural communities have delightful memories of being in the tub soaking when someone added fuel to the fire. Suddenly, the heat would shoot up from between the boards and make everyone jump with much laughter as they tried to change their seating position as quickly as they could.

After Al and I modernized our house, we installed a hot water heater and an indoor tub shaped like a deep Japanese tub. We used the shower to wash and then enjoyed a thorough hot soaking each night. How happy Ojiisan and Obaasan were to have the luxury of an indoor tile-lined Japanese bath every night! We were way ahead of the 1970's fad of "hot-tubbing."

We watched the burning of our grapevines with sadness even though we didn't need the yearly prunings for our nightly baths any more. How inevitable was change, and how we humans had to adjust to new ways to live whether we wanted to or not.

Al and I had to think seriously now about getting jobs. Grandpa at 81 could continue with his vegetables and a patch of tea for he needed the joy of puttering at his own speed. We hoped and prayed there would be work somewhere out there for us both.

Getting settled and helping others who needed shelter, food, and support had taken most of our time in the post war years. Al took advantage of the opportunity to remodel our place. We painted and decorated without spending much money for we had the time to do it. The money Bob Fletcher had placed in our bank was a godsend for our days of adjustment. But now it was time to look for jobs.

We were overjoyed when Al found work at the newly opened Sacramento Signal Depot just up the road from us on Florin-Perkins Road. Al's work was repairing electronic communication equipment. First it was simple work, with written instructions to follow, but later Al was sent to classes to be trained to handle more sophisticated assignments. Eventually he was cleaning and repairing electronic and radar equipment to be used by the military during the Korean and Vietnam wars.

My dream for our future began to emerge but there were still some pieces missing. The day that Loren Mee came to call was the start of yet another golden ray that would have a strong effect upon the rest of my life.

Loren had been my classmate at the College of the Pacific. Now he came to call as a Methodist minister, and I have been forever grateful to Providence that such a person was sent to lead us to the

Florin Methodist Church. We had not gone there because we were not sure what our welcome would be. We didn't know who the people were that supported legislation to take our citizenship away from us or who had campaigned to keep us out of California and wanted to send us out of the United States for good. We had no idea who was behind the vandalism of our homes and businesses. When we mingled with the community, we were afraid of running into people who had been party to such incidents.

Most of all though, we were ashamed that it had been Japan that had caused so much suffering and the loss of so many sons in the Pacific. We were afraid of people who blamed us for their suffering though we had nothing to do with Pearl Harbor and the events that followed.

Reverend Mee's invitation came at just the right time and we gratefully accepted it. We took Marielle to Sunday School and encouraged other families, our nieces and nephews who had returned, to go with us to the Caucasian Methodist Church. Gradually, I began to feel more at ease and accepted little responsibilities such as teaching Sunday School and playing piano for services.

Florin had always had two Methodist churches, right across the road from each other. Except for an occasional joint service or party, we had very much stayed apart and done our own programs. The Japanese church closed when we went away, and for several years after our return, the building was filled with crates and personal belongings of people who could not claim them. Having grown up in a segregated church, I felt more at home with Japanese members, so worshipping among all people was a strange, new experience. I knew, however, that going to the Caucasian church was the right thing to do as we had had a happy experience during our brief time in Kalamazoo. I often wondered if we would have been evacuated had we mixed more with our neighbors instead of staying in our Japanese community. Many people did not even know us. Understanding and rapport cannot be established when we do not work together to share problems and enjoy successes.

I started by attending faithfully and regularly. In a few years, in addition to teaching Sunday School, I helped out with Youth Fellowship, served as faculty member for the Tahoe Youth Institute, played piano for church services, directed the children's choir, and attended meetings of the Women's Society of Christian Service. Before I realized what I was getting into, I found myself serving as Spiritual Life Secretary for Northern California-Nevada District of Women's Society of Christian Service where I led services for women in churches all over the district.

In addition to church, I was also concerned about school, so important to my daughter's education and future. I attended PTA meetings and gradually accepted responsibilities there. I helped Marielle's Girl Scout troop leader, Marietta Thomas, who was also the PTA president. We made puppets, and I led fun songs. With a little stage built by Al, the scouts put on Hansel and Gretel. All these experiences led up to the eventful day that took me out of the berry patch forever.

Al and I decided that if I were going out to seek employment, I needed to make myself look presentable. Though we had much we needed to buy, my appearance was a high priority. Al had encouraged me to keep up my sewing, and even though the clothes I sewed looked home-made, it helped out a lot. I was able to sew a new outfit for Marielle each year as she grew taller. For job seeking I made a nice, black coat, and then I bought a dark green, gabardine suit with green hat and purse to match.

On the day I will never forget, I went to the employment office and then made several stops for interviews. I hurried back to Florin School for a PTA meeting. Mrs. Isabelle Jackson, the tall dignified principal, greeted me and commented on my attractive outfit.

"How nice you look, Mary," she said. "What have you been doing today?"

I told her how we were giving up farming and that I was looking for a job. She asked quietly, "Have you thought about going into teaching, Mary?"

I was jolted by the question. My heart jumped and danced. "Do you think I have a chance to teach?" I asked unbelievingly. Back in 1933 when I had registered for college, I was told that a person of Japanese ancestry would never be hired to teach in public schools. Consequently, I had not taken any courses for teaching. What did this mean?

Isabelle Jackson looked right at me with a very professional look and eyes of confidence and said, "Why don't you visit our new Sacramento State College and ask for Dr. Walker. He will have your credits from the College of the Pacific evaluated and tell you what you will need for a teaching credential."

I could hardly believe what I was hearing. My heart pounded wildly at this unexpected release from my prison. Could it be that my dream would become a reality?

I went to visit my friend, Raymond Case, principal of Elk Grove Elementary School, whom I had met through my work with youth at the Methodist Church. Mr. Case was encouraging and rejoiced with me at my new found hope and desire to become a teacher. He gave me a long list of suggestions and names of people to see at Sacramento County Schools' office. He told me how I could get experience working with children by being a substitute teacher in the county.

Roy Learned, another dear friend who had been principal at Elk Grove High School when my sister Ruth attended there, was principal of Mark Twain Junior High School in Sacramento. He and his family had kept in touch with us all these years. They had stored my piano and our wedding gifts when we went to camp. I valued Roy's advice and turned to him to see if I dared break through the web of discrimination by seeking employment in public schools. With Roy's support and encouragement, I found the determination and courage to follow through.

Things began to happen fast. Dr. Walker welcomed my decision, and with his help I enrolled at Sacramento State College. It wasn't easy to get into the discipline of studying after thirteen years of not being a student, but this was an exciting time of my life. My head swam as I plunged into the frightening pace of taking education classes at the college and substitute teaching at the same time.

My first day of substituting, however, was a disaster. I didn't know how to teach the children. I didn't have the background of teaching methods, child psychology, or a million other courses I wished I had taken. I wondered if I had made a mistake by thinking I could become a teacher. I was many units and summer sessions away from graduating and qualifying for a teaching credential. Each day, however, was a little easier, and slowly I developed a routine for stepping into someone else's class and taking charge.

One day an excited Isabelle Jackson drove into our yard to tell me that I was hired for a third grade teaching position if I wanted it. A teacher had decided to retire, and I could fill the vacancy under an emergency credential. Because of the war years, there was a critical teacher shortage—a lucky break for me. I accepted, and within a few days Mrs. Jackson brought me a contract from the Board of Trustees. I could hardly believe my good fortune. I was to make $2570 for ten months of teaching beginning in September of 1949.

To think I was to be a teacher at last! I was thrilled beyond belief. I was to teach in the same building where I had graduated from elementary school. How much the world had changed since my segregated school years in that very building. How much I had changed too from a child of the strawberry fields to a member of the teaching profession.

Isabelle Jackson, who had looked upon the face of a strawberry farmer's wife and seen a teacher, was a legend herself. As teacher, principal, and superintendent of Florin School, she was a brilliant educator who instinctively knew what was best for children and how to reach the goals she set for herself and for her school. How fortunate I was to have this remarkable woman as my mentor and model of what I could become!

I continued to teach the children of Florin both at the Florin School and eight years later at the new school that became the Isabelle Jackson Elementary School. I was invited to join the Delta Kappa Gamma Society, an international society of eminent educators while Mrs. Jackson was president of Beta Pi Chapter. Through the inspiration of educator friends, I began a lifelong association in pursuit of professional growth.

In the early 1950s after several years of "grass roots" lobbying, a long awaited event reached Florin and other communities in the United States. The Walter-McCarran Immigration and Naturalization Act was passed in June of 1952 and finally allowed immigrant Asians to become citizens. At last elderly Issei, who had been born in Japan, could become citizens of the United States. The legislation was a significant milestone for the JACL, led by Mike Masaoka, Sabura Kido, and the national JACL leaders.

For many Issei, however, it was too late; they had lived out their lives without the privilege of American citizenship. For others, going to class and studying civics and English were more than they could manage in the advanced stages of their lives. In Florin, though, sixty men and women stood together on March 16, 1954, and in a touching ceremony, they became citizens at last of their adopted country, the United States of America.

Ojiisan had talked to himself as he worked about the house. *"Yaa Issei ni shiminken ga toreru yoo ni natta. Yokatta! Yokatta!"*

(At last, long last, the Issei can become American citizens. It is good. It is good.)

This gentle Issei, Kuzo Tsukamoto, had, like the venerable pine, withstood the severest travail in his lifetime in 20th century America. Despite harsh treatment, he labored with quiet faith that his dreams would come true. He wanted only to be worthy of a rightful place in his country and its glorious legacy.

No one commanded higher respect than this 86 year old grandfather. He had been a pillar of strength and solidarity in our family and in the Florin Japanese community as well.

Ojiisan joined more than a hundred Issei in the first citizenship class in Florin. Many of them worried that this task might be too great for them to master. Too many years had passed since they had sat in school rooms. Memory and drill had not been part of their life for 60 to 80 years.

The class met once a week all through the cold winter. The teacher wrote in bold letters on the chalkboards, and painstakingly, Issei grandmothers and grandfathers repeated facts that needed to be learned. Their tongues were heavy and unwieldy when they pronounced difficult names and events in American history. Stubbornly, though, Kuzo refused to give up.

"Doryoku suru Yo, Gambatte!"

(I will endeavor with all my might. I will persevere!)

Though he had enrolled in the class with confidence and studied with unfailing persistence, Ojiisan's concentration was lacking. He could not remember what he learned.

Nearing his 90th birthday, it appeared that he could not reach what he had coveted for so long—his American citizenship. The privilege had come too late for him.

One day, with great sadness, Ojiisan announced, *"Zannen da! Moo yame yo."* (I feel a deep regret, but I must quit.)

As I watched his resignation at his sad defeat, I thought of the story of the Daruma, seven times down, eight times up. A well loved Buddhist monk once taught the philosophy that life was full of adversity. "One seldom attains one's first choice goals," he said, "but if you persevere and keep on trying again and again, then success will surely come." The Daruma reminds us of the good luck and happiness it promises to those who persevere. "Though knocked down seven times, get up and try again, for such is life."

Portrayed in the shape of a roly-poly doll that cannot be tipped over no matter how many times it falls because it bounces right back again, the Daruma is a symbol of endurance for the Japanese people. So it was with Ojiisan. He had always bounced back up again no matter how much adversity he encountered. This time, however, he could not reach his goal.

There were no words to express his disappointment. Contrary to the endeavor suggested by the Daruma he had believed in all his life, Ojiisan had to be realistic and accept the inevitable. This was another courageous virtue of his heritage. He continued nevertheless to attend the evening classes for several more weeks.

Others like Ojiisan waged their own private battles with tired bodies, and one by one, they dropped quietly out of the citizenship class. The group of 100 was reduced to 60 by the time they finished and prepared for graduation exercises.

On the evening of the ceremony, Ojiisan dressed carefully in his gray double-breasted suit, a gift from his grandchildren on his 85th birthday. He was not tall nor very stocky, but he seemed inches shorter than I remembered at our first meeting a quarter of a century past. Slightly bent, he walked with dignity and steady steps and commanded the attention and respect of those who saw him. His grayish, light brown eyes were bright with excitement; his rosy cheeks and healthy tanned appearance gave the impression of a much younger man. He certainly did not look like someone who had struggled mightily all his life at strenuous physical labor pioneering on a California farm.

Sixty proud graduates sat on the platform on Issei graduation night. The ceremony began, and everyone sat respectfully at attention. Many were wide-eyed as the Boy Scout troop presented the colors. Everyone stood up to salute the flag of the United States of America. The Caucasian Methodist Church choir led the assemblage in the singing of the Star Spangled Banner. As I crossed the stage to direct them, I saw Ojiisan watch as Al and Marielle took their places in the choir. I heard a deep sigh come from him—a sigh that seemed to envelop him in a sea of emotion. He was so proud!

Isabelle Jackson was one of the speakers. She told about the values brought by education to strengthen citizens of our nation.

"Every group of immigrants brought their rich cultural heritage to make America the finest country on earth in spite of the many shortcomings and wrongs it inflicted upon its people. Tonight we see a part of this country's historic effort to make some corrections. We have finally made the way open for all people barring none from this precious privilege of citizenship.

"Our schools have long respected you. We taught your fine children and grandchildren, and now we anticipate with joy your great-grandchildren. They are outstanding, worthy American citizens because you have nurtured them with noble ideals. We congratulate you on your graduation and welcome you as new American citizens of this wonderful land."

Ojiisan could no longer hold back his tears as Reverend Fujimori interpreted the moving address, and he understood what this outstanding educator had expressed for all to hear on this momentous occasion. His sighing could not be quieted though, for on this great night of citizenship, what he had long awaited was not for him. He listened intently as each name was called and each one walked up unsteadily to receive with shaking hands, the hard-won certificate of graduation.

Then a quiet, scholarly gentleman, 70-year-old grape farmer and produce shipper, Tomosaburo Otani, stood up on behalf of the graduating class and spoke.

"If this great country would let us, we would carry a gun, shouldering the responsibilities of citizenship to the fullest. Even if there was nothing for the aged and weak to do, we would feel honored if we could but be allowed to pick up scraps and dirt to keep America clean. Even though we are tottering with age, we would exert our energies to our last dying moments in sincere appreciation for a nation that has opened its heart to accept us as its own."

The audience was greatly touched by this brief and profound address. We were silent and stunned when he sat down. The impact of his message thrilled us to a standing ovation, and a thunderous applause filled the hall. I felt as though the entire nation rose to honor the Issei, our parents, that night.

Judge Sweeney, who presided at the naturalization ceremony, proclaimed with great admiration, "Never have I heard anything so moving. It was indeed a great speech."

Our choir sang to add our musical benediction to this happy affair. We sang "God Bless America," and I felt as if my whole body was soaring free, joyously over the land. I felt as if I was kneeling once again at the feet of Lincoln, triumphant and proud to be an American, proud of America, the land of liberty with justice and freedom for all.

The internment camp, barbed wire, and soldiers with guns at the watch towers were part of the nightmare of our life, but on this night, this was America as it was intended to be.

Our daughter Marielle seemed to have endured the camp years without any obvious problems to her physical, mental or emotional development. With five doting adults surrounding her with security, assurance, love, and pride, it is a wonder that she didn't come out of her early childhood years a very spoiled child. We marveled at her calm, unassuming manner, her independence, and her respectful awareness of each member of the family. Each of us was treated with a mixture of affection and mindfulness that was truly beautiful.

We sat at a round table—all six of us—three generations. It was a time of our lives when nostalgic, warm memories glowed. We had worried so about the effect of camp life upon the children. How fortunate we were that we were spared the pain and suffering that many parents endured with their children both in camp and when they returned to normal lives.

We once asked little Marielle who she liked the best. She looked intently at all our happy faces around the kitchen table, and then quietly she said, *"Minna suki."* (I like each one the best.) We all grinned with surprise and admiration at how diplomatic she was with the closest people in her life.

Marielle was eight when we returned home to Florin. The heartache of the lost years cut deeply into each of us. We were different from what we had been before our experience. Marielle grew up in no time after our return to Florin, but she was always a happy, self-reliant child. She picked berries for Ojiisan and Daddy in the boysenberry patch at 10 cents a gallon can. She stemmed berries for Uncle Harold in the Florin fruit shed for 25 cents a crate and earned enough money to buy a bicycle to ride to school.

Marielle's first spurt into maturity and a break from the family came when she went away for a three week Girl Scout program at Camp Bear Paw in 1949. She was twelve years old. We were so lonesome for her that we drove up to visit her.

When Marielle brought friends home from school we were always delighted. Across the road from us was a very special friend, Marty Casper. Marielle and Marty were inseparable pals all through their school years. Marty was just a day younger than Marielle but at least a foot taller. We called them "Mutt and Jeff." I dolled them up for Halloween parties, and they went off to Methodist Youth Fellowship camp and performed in variety shows. They did a clown dance and were such a hit! In spite of the difference in their heights, they were so entertaining and comical as both were very well coordinated. We had such good laughs over them and enjoyed their relationship as much as they did.

In no time at all, our little Marielle was a teenager. Bubbling over, full of joy, serious, spunky, and reliant—she was all of these and sometimes all at once too. I tried to teach her to play piano along with the pupils I gave private lessons to, but it didn't work very well. One day, she wished she could play, so I enrolled her in one of the piano studios in Sacramento, but she soon lost interest. I was always sorry I had not found the right way to help her find enjoyment in being a pianist. She sang in our junior choir at church though, so she did find music there.

When Marielle was a high school student in Ann Hunter's English class, she was assigned a project on her family and her life. The project gave her a lasting pride in her roots, and it turned out to be a wonderful project for us too. Fortunately, Marielle's grandparents were able to recall facts and dates important to her research. She studied our family albums and selected choice pictures to help her summarize her search into her roots. It was this spark that ignited for me a gradual search for roots that I tried to instill in young people for the next thirty years. How grateful we were to Marielle's English teacher at Elk Grove High, Mrs. Hunter.

High school was a happy venture for Marielle. She came home bubbling with involvement every day and loved every minute. She was a radio reporter, officer of many clubs, student body secretary, and she entered the oratorical contest. I was thrilled beyond words that after twenty years, attitudes had changed. Marielle was coached by George Nemetz, an outstanding drama coach and English teacher, who made it a memorable experience for her. For me, it was an opportunity to be Mable Barron, coaching Marielle and helping her with the delivery of her speech.

How different this Sansei, Marielle, was from the Nisei I had known. Her self reliance and assurance knew no bounds. She had many teachers she admired and loved, and she learned so much from them. There was a sense of freedom and acceptance at Elk Grove High School far different from when Al and I were students there.

Marielle graduated from high school in 1955. We allowed her to spend the summer with Nami in Benton Harbor and Kalamazoo where she visited her cousins and worked as a waitress at the Kiino Derby Inn of Uncle Hugh and Aunt Ruth.

Marielle was and still is such a joy, but I have always regretted not having a son for Al, the heir to the Tsukamoto family. Except for George (the adopted brother) and his sons and grandsons, there is no Tsukamoto male to carry on Kuzo's name. When Marielle was about eight years old, we asked her what she wanted the most, and she said, "A baby brother." It has always been my secret deep regret that I could not give Ojiisan an heir and that Marielle grew up without brothers and sisters. Often I wished I had twins or triplets of Marielle—and all of them just like her!

More than a decade after Marielle reached adulthood, I discovered to my eternal delight the beautiful story of the Princess Ball. Had I known about it when Marielle was a babe, I would have endeavored to be on my knees every night praying as I wrapped silk threads around the special ball for my precious child, praying for her maturity, her nurturing and growing. Concentrating on qualities of kindness, gentleness, caring and thoughtfulness would help her become a lovely, courageous, and generous woman.

In long ago Japan, when a mother had a little girl, she began a tiny ball with a cotton center and wrapped silk thread around it. She turned it over and worked it to shape it into a perfectly round ball. At every turn of her thread she prayed on her knees and focused her thoughts on health, energy, courage, and gentleness. As the years passed, the mother faithfully spent every quiet hour late at night on her knees, praying that her daughter would become a gracious, gentle, noble, and wise person. Gradually the ball grew in size as the daughter indeed became a lovely person. Each year the growing child as well as the mother knew how faithfully she prayed for the beautiful nurturing of her precious daughter. When the daughter was ready to be married, the huge Princess Ball, embroidered with the most intricate design, was presented to her as the most treasured gift the mother can give—visual evidence of her mother's boundless love and hopes for happy future.

As I humbly cherish my daughter in my twilight years, I realize what a magnificent Princess Ball was created in spirit to represent the life of our daughter, Marielle.

Though we had no son of our own, Al and I are blessed with the friendship of a young man who fills this gap in our lives. Our godson, John Marshall, had been my student at Samuel Kennedy School in Florin. He was an eager learner, very bright and artistic. John became interested in the stories I told about Japanese folk tales and began to study Japanese language so he could appreciate the culture of Japan. On an accelerated program for gifted students, John graduated from high school and went to Japan to study under masters. He became expert in dyeing cloth in beautiful designs using age old methods and natural dyes. Today John is a successful practicing artist in Oakland and creates art that is shown all over the country. John fixes our roof and works up our garden, jobs Al can't do any more, and provides our lives with the joys and love that a son can bring.

Pages from the Tsukamoto Family Album

By fall we were in our new camp, Jerome Relocation Camp in Denson, Arkansas. Row after row of black tarpaper barracks—that was home for 8,000 of us—many from Florin.

My most vivid memories will always be of the guard towers. Soldiers with rifles guarded over us night and day. Barbed wire surrounded the camp.

We weren't allowed to have cameras, so it was always a treat when a soldier who had a camera came to visit. Everyone lined up to get their picture taken—Obaasan, Nami, Ojiisan, Al, me and Marielle.

We took a group picture of all the people from Florin. There were quite a number of us at Jerome.

We worried so about the children. How could we assure them a proper education? How would they turn out after being locked up in this strange existence?

Children are hardy little individuals, however. They amused themselves with simple pleasures, and some adjusted to camp life better than the adults.

We started a USO at camp so that our boys would have a place to come when they were on furlough.

It was a strange experience for them to visit us locked up in camp.

The Tsukamotos and the Ogatas—at Jerome.

Al, Marielle and me—
October, 1942
Block 9-8-E
Jerome, Arkansas.

Our house in Kalamazoo.

Mom and Dad Dakuzaku in Chicago.

Marielle and me.

Here we all are with Harold's green Dodge—ready to head for Florin and home!

Al and I walking down the street in Sacramento.

Al fixing up our house.

Tending to our grapes.

234

The Army notified us of Julia's death just a few weeks after we came home. How I wish I had written to her in those last weeks of her life...

The Years of the Pine

The Golden Years
1970s and 1980s
The venerable pine is rooted in wisdom ,
though bent from ravaging years
it still proudly reaches for the sky.
It is a time of aging, a time for reflection and
reaching out to future generations.
It is a time of needing to be heard
though the sound is only a whisper in the wind.
Twisted and gnarled, the old tree is courageous
and lifts heavy branches always upward.

Survivor of many storms
in its lifetime,
the brave one
will stand with courage
until its end.

Chapter 20

Finding My Roots

"I find it hard to realize that I once hated my Japanese face. My roots are now deep within my cultural heritage, centuries old. Truly I can be the bridge between Japan and America."

In 1956 I began treatment with cortisone medication, a miracle drug for sufferers of rheumatoid arthritis. Marielle had met a professor at State College who told her about Co-Delta, and even though I knew it was potent and caused serious side effects, I decided to use it because it was the only thing that gave me relief. I continued this treatment for fifteen years and was freed from some of the crippling effects of the disease.

I always feared the side effects which I had been warned would affect my kidneys and blood system. I developed blotches of black and blue and red spots on my skin, and several times, I had scares that I might have leukemia because of my abnormal white blood count. I knew I had to discontinue cortisone but when I did, it caused much pain and I had to try desperately to find other means of controlling the crippling arthritis.

I tried acupuncture for four years, but even that did not help. I tried special diets, fasting, and many treatments that were harsh until the doctor prescribed Motrin. So far it has helped.

In Jerome, Mrs. Inori, a dear, dedicated Christian woman, had heard about my affliction and came to try her herbal heating and massaging treatment. She offered some of her herbs for me to continue with this treatment which I did until I left for Kalamazoo.

In Kalamazoo, as I continued to suffer, Al had taken me to see Dr. Alexander, a known specialist, who tried a new treatment of injecting gold salt. I don't remember how long I continued this treatment, but suddenly, my body reacted. I lost my eyebrows and lashes and part of my hairline receded. I developed a terrible itch all over my body and became red and swollen. I thought surely I'd die. Needless to say, this treatment was stopped immediately. I was also sent to a physiotherapist for heat and massage treatment to try to regain back my stiffened joints. Nothing seemed to help.*

Obaasan had a stroke in 1953 and her illness caused us much anxiety. She was a semi-invalid for seventeen years. With Nami's loving care, however, we were able to tend to her needs. Al and I were both working, so we were able to enjoy financial security such as we had never known before. To my great joy, Al agreed to send Marielle to the University of the Pacific (formerly College of the Pacific) where I had been fortunate to spend three wonderful years.

Studying at UOP was just the right experience for Marielle. We had many occasions to visit the campus—football games and events, and just going to visit our daughter. She joined a sorority, was elected president of the associated women students, and won the outstanding senior woman's award.

Marielle graduated from UOP and became a teacher. She had thought of becoming a chemical research scientist, but aptitude tests indicated she should move into a career that allowed her to work with people. I advised her to think about education. She did and was hired by the Elk Grove School District to teach at Florin School where we had all attended and where I began my teaching career. Her second grade classroom was right next door to that of Margaret Knight, Marielle's teacher when we returned from Kalamazoo. What a supportive friend for a new, inexperienced teacher! Her former 8th grade teacher, Glenn Brunswick, was now her principal, another

---

*Dr. Hashiba, a well known physician and surgeon, decided to put my arm in a cast to immobilize it. The next month while I wore this cast my elbow became completely solidified. I have lived with this solidified elbow and my stiffened wrist to this day.

stroke of good luck!

Marielle had special reasons for living at home during her first year of teaching. She had made plans with seventeen of her UOP friends to go to Europe during the summer of 1960. Virginia Short, music professor of the UOP Conservatory of Music, was the tour leader, and it turned out to be a memorable trip. They attended the Passion Play at Oberammergau, concerts in Vienna, lingered at the Louvre in Paris, and spent leisurely days in Florence touching the classic sculpturing art of great artists of the ages. Marielle was delighted with the fairytale-like homes and the clean farms nestled against the Alps in Switzerland and Austria. She came home with amazing purchases: crystals from Copenhagen, watches from Switzerland, cameo pins and necklaces from Italy, music boxes, antique silver pieces from London's silver vault, and inlaid wooden trays. I couldn't believe the spunk and determination of this novice traveler on her first trip abroad.

Marielle grew from the summer's trip into a seasoned world traveler, and she would never be the same again. After her return and teaching in San Jose a few years, Marielle decided to teach in a foreign country. With a little help from my cousin Shizu and her husband Raymond Aka, who worked in the U.S. Embassy in Tokyo, she got a job teaching in Japan. Though more or less isolated from the Japanese people at Nile C. Kinnick Naval Dependent School in Yokohama, Marielle had time to take lessons in flower arrangement and Japanese cooking, and she visited the towns and villages on special days. She learned to speak to the maids and other people who worked at the school. The year had a significant effect upon her life and developed in her an interest and deep appreciation for things Japanese, far more than I had imagined possible in our Sansei Tsukamoto.

During her Christmas holiday, Marielle took a trip to Southeast Asia—Taipei, Bangkok, Hong Kong, Kuala Lumpur, and Singapore. Her letters were exciting. Al and I were drawn to a totally unexpected decision. We decided to go to Japan!

A key factor in our decision was our desire to find our relatives and visit my oldest sister, Masako. Our family had helped to bring Masako to the U.S. for a visit in 1957. My parents had always regretted that their first born child had not come to live in America with them. Masako, who was seven years old, had stayed with her grandmother when my mother sailed for America in 1912. Father had made plans to visit her just before the war, but his passport had been burned in the great San Francisco fire and earthquake, and it took him many months to get a new one. Finally, he received his papers in October of 1941, but the political climate was not good for travel to Japan at that time.

None of us had seen our sister, and we longed to meet her now that the war was over. In 1957, when Father became gravely ill, we pitched in and sent money for her to come visit us. We had a wonderful time with Masa-nesan, older sister. We camped in the December snow in Yosemite and traveled all around California. We tried to show her our world and way of life. She had felt deserted and abandoned when my mother had left her, and she had longed for us just as we had longed for her. This experience made us anxious to know more about the country of our parents, so a trip to Japan seemed the way to do it.

We met Marielle in Yokohama in the summer of 1966 and took her with us to find relatives in Hiroshima and Tokyo. This was the beginning of many enjoyable visits to the land of our ancestors. In Okinawa, we met my uncle on my mother's side, Yoshinaga, and his daughter, Tomiko Matsudo. They provided us with a memorable time as we walked on the ground where the castle of Sho, the last king of Okinawa, once stood. This is where the royal family had lived and where Mom had served the royal family in her childhood years. It was the same ground where Mom and Dad had walked and played so many, many years ago. For me it was the real beginning of my search into myself, the discovery of my deep roots in ancient Japan and Okinawa, a search of joy and pride that would lend immeasurable pleasure to my remaining years.

I retired from my wonderful teaching career in June of 1976, the year of the nation's Bicentennial. Retirement gave me time to reflect, read and assess what my experiences thus far had taught me. I had time to focus attention on imperative goals for the rest of my life.

My years as a member of the Association for Childhood Education International made me realize that peace in this world was what I needed to work toward. This beautiful, God-given world was a place for billions of people to live as friends—free from wars and human suffering, illness, hunger, and premature death. What could I do to bring this about?

I had my training as an educator, my cultural background, and communication skills. How could I put them all together to work for such a great goal?

My church offered hope. I became involved with projects through the Methodist Overseas Relief Work. We worked to feed the world through the Heifer Project and other local projects of the Peace Center in Sacramento.

Then one day in April of 1977, I received a surprise telephone call that changed my plans for a quiet retirement. Kimi Kaneko, my teacher colleague from James McKee School, asked me if I would be interested in taking a position with a group of parents who wanted a cultural heritage school for their children. Called Jan Ken Po Gakko, the school was a non-profit, cooperative, private summer school that focused on parents' participation and community resources to educate children about their rich cultural heritage, Japan, the land of their ancestors.

The school operated on the basic premise that children can be enriched by learning their history and tradition through games, folklore, music, field trips, language, and interaction with the various generations of the community. Most important, however, was the strengthening of their self-esteem as Americans of Japanese ancestry.

The curriculum focused on lessons that stressed the significance of being Americans. We taught the children how they could become proud, respected, and responsible citizens of America, the land of their birth.

How could I say no? I began five busy years of happy involvement, thoroughly committed to my work with the darling Yonsei and a few Sansei. This encounter became a most profound influence upon my life. It was a crowning experience that clearly defined the path I would walk for the remainder of my days.

I was so impressed with the young parents who brought their clear vision, special skills, and intelligence into our pioneering program of cultural heritage for the Japanese American community. They organized, adapted, innovated, and creatively forged ahead, sparkling

242

with dynamic purpose to make a great idea become a reality for their children.

For the five to twelve year olds, we offered a variety of experiences. Students received an introduction to the Japanese language, Japanese cooking and tasting experiences, and Japanese American history. They learned folklore, music, songs, and took part in demonstrations such as ikebana, sumi-e, kimono, martial arts, and musical instruments. We provided art experiences in batik, origami, monkiri, masks, ceramics and much, much more.

I found that many of the children in the school were great-grandchildren of dear Issei I had known and loved in my growing years. I had gone to camp with them; they were old pioneer Florin families even though these young families lived all over the Sacramento area now. Their parents and grandparents had been neighbors, church friends, and even village friends of Kuzo and Ito Tsukamoto from Hiroshima.

Directing the school became a personal mission for me to do something for those I loved. I wanted to give them something that would perpetuate for those who were no longer alive. I wanted a meaningful "passing of the torch" in this privileged task. How I wished I could tell the Issei who were gone what I planned to do, how I would teach their precious great-grandchildren about their hardships, determination, indomitable courage, and the deep love and pride they shared in their cultural heritage. Though Florin was no longer their home, their roots were clearly there, and though we had removed the grapevines of our past, there was still much to learn from the Florin fields and fifty years of toil there.

What I found was that the Sansei parents needed to find out about their roots too. They were Americans, but they knew little about their cultural heritage because they had grown up during a time when it was dangerous to show interest in Japan. It was prudent to forget the island nation where their grandparents had been born. The very name of Japan was synonymous with death, torture, treachery, and deceit, and it had caused much sadness in America. No wonder these young parents could not speak a word of Japanese and some did not know teriyaki from tempura.

Mothers and fathers both took time off from work to take their turns in the summer school as teachers and aides. I began to see changes in many life styles as the adults began to appreciate what the children were learning. They began to show their love for things Japanese in their homes, tastes for Japanese food, interest in Japanese culture. Many took trips to Japan. They remodeled their homes and gardens with Japanese landscaping and decorating ideas. They became involved in church and Japanese cultural festivals in the community.

I composed two songs which I felt were needed to make Jan Ken Po Gakko stronger. I wrote the tune and words to explain the game which gave the program its name, the game familiar to many American children as well as Japanese, Jan Ken Po—Scissors, Paper, Stone. It's a game about winning and losing, and it expresses what children have to learn: there is joy when you learn, and you can't always win no matter how hard you try.

The other song was about how to say good morning—"*Oha yo Gozaimasu*," and we sang it every day. As soon as the musical calisthenics were done outdoors, the children came in to assembly each day for the five week summer session. The first song was good morning in Japanese and then "Jan Ken Po" which we could all play while singing. These became the opening numbers for all our performances wherever we were invited to sing. After ten years, our children are still singing these two songs.

Singing and music were happy, self enhancing parts of the Jan Ken Po program. Children learned a great deal about the Japanese language as well as stories and folktales through the songs.

After only one summer's experience, people in San Jose and the San Francisco Bay area were curious and anxious to find out what we were doing with our summer school in Sacramento. Many came to visit and before long, there were similar programs sprouting up all over the area—the Suzume no Gakko (Sparrow School) in San Jose, the Daruma School in Berkeley, and others in Stockton, San Mateo, and Sebastopol.

We added Saturday extended sessions and the observance of special days. New Year Festival was observed with making special foods and mochi, a pounded sweet rice; the Hina Matsuri or Girls' Doll Festival in March was fun; and then there was Children's Day in May when we made kites, flew them and learned about symbolic carp flying. It was a good way to keep in touch with the children and a fine introduction for new students and parents for the JKPG program. It was also a good time for alumni parents and students to return for little reunions.

Self esteem and a good self image stem from joy and pride in being alive. Eating enhanced that sense of well being and pride. Memorable experiences came from our use of all of the senses including the important sense of taste.

The children learned about the parts of the plants we ate: seeds of rice, sesame, beans, "*azuki*" (a Japanese name for red beans), and peas. They tasted rice balls wrapped in seaweed, and on festive occasions red rice was always served. There were edible parts of plants such as stems, leaves, fruit, roots, shoots, and even flowers. We also taught the children the names for the food they ate.

Eventually, all children took turns preparing delicious Japanese food for everyone in the gakko. Some, of course, resisted trying new things because they were not accustomed to eating Japanese food. Some had never even tasted tofu. We encouraged them all to try, and many developed a liking for the new foods. Recipes were sent home for families to try, and many did. Each class learned to prepare food and taste a tiny serving at the closing assembly. When we made "*Udon*," we cranked the dough and out came long noodles which we boiled and seasoned with a wonderful sauce. Everyone had a taste for a joyful experience. Such pleasures were not quickly forgotten.

The children learned etiquette that our Issei cared about just as we had learned the proper things to say when being served and when eating while we were young. There were lessons in the art of serving food too. The cooks had to remember that they prepared food for eye appeal to delight those who sat around the table. The natural color of the food, whenever possible, is preserved, and an awareness of color combination, variety, and numbers are thoughtfully kept in mind when planning food. Good fortune and joy are expressed in odd numbers. A salad, for example, must be made with three or five things. Color contrast is obtained by combining carrots, green pepper, lettuce, cucumber, and tomato. A sense of gratitude is expressed for the earth's bounty by remembering to serve something from the sea (fish, abalone, squid, sea urchin, sea cucumber, etc.); something from the air (bird, chicken, etc.); something from the mountains (bamboo shoots, mushrooms); and something from the soil (carrots, potato, burdock). The food tasting and nutritious Japanese cooking were very popular and practical as the children took the ideas home to help their families learn to enjoy Japanese eating.

Relying heavily upon my understandings about early childhood education through my twenty years of participation in the Association for Childhood Education International (ACEI), it was easy to build a good Jan Ken Po Gakko program using the ACEI Plan of Action. All that I had gained as an educator in the public schools I was able to assess and pull together. I found myself remembering and using the finest levels of educational thinking and teaching learned from great educators such as Dr. Hilda Taba, Richard Suchmann, Helen Heffernan, and many outstanding Sacramento County consultants: Helen McGinnis, Ursula Hogan, Ethel Rowe, Charlotte Dalrymple, Helen Woods, Mike Weber and many more.

This was also a time to uncover from the distant past some cherished contacts. I made a special trip to La Mirada to refresh my learning from a marvelous, culturally refined teacher from Japan, my mentor of Japanese culture, Kohana Sasaki. Among many things, she taught me a darling song, "*Hyaku Made,*" a counting song to 100 which is still being used in Jan Ken Po Gakko. I gathered information from relatives and friends who had come from Japan years ago and who remembered customs, festivals, and traditions. I dug into old Japanese magazines, assessed my collection of Japanese dolls (and Marielle's too), organized charts and pictures, and put together a huge collection of realia and visual materials for effective teaching.

On weekends we took the children on trips such as a pilgrimage and picnic to Angel Island on the ferry boat to see the place where the picture brides and wives had landed between 1910 and 1923. My mother, Kame Dakuzaku, had stayed there a week in 1911. I felt a deep sense of nostalgia and imagined how she must have felt, lonely and fearful, as she waited to find out what would be her destiny. I saw the pipes that framed the four and five layered bed shelves where the immigrants had slept. I wondered which one had been her cot. I tried to instill these feelings for the past in the children.

We took them to Coloma where a monument had been dedicated during the Centennial celebration of 1969. The little garden monument told of the first Wakamatsu Colony in California in 1869. We placed flowers on the grave of Okei, the 19-year-old nurse maid who died with a fever and was buried in a lonely grave on a hill behind the Gold Hill School. We poured water over her headstone just as people have done for centuries in Japan when they visit cemeteries. The water cleans away dust and grime and is a symbol of purifying the worshipper's soul. It also sends the clean and watered, thirst-quenched spirit joyously to the other heavenly home.

On Fridays, the children performed before happy, smiling, elderly, Issei great-grandparents who listened intently to the songs sung in Japanese. Happy memories of their childhood years in Japan so long ago came floating back to them. They were delighted to see their darling five to twelve year olds sing and dance their favorite folktales dramatized with much humor, American style as well as Japanese style.

The Issei were most impressed when the children made little speeches in Japanese and proudly shared the results of their research about family crests and names. They explained the designs which were beautifully silk screened with stencils crafted by their talented parents who gave of their time to make the children's experiences meaningful.

At the culmination of the summer, an open house was held and all the summer work displayed. The children sang their hearts out. They wore their white "*happi*" coats with family crests on their backs and names written in Hiragana, the Japanese phonetic alphabet. Their white T-shirts were attractive with the bright red, smart looking Jan Ken Po Gakko logo, half of a rising sun. It was symbolic of self image and emerging pride, the morning sun with faith for a brighter tomorrow as Americans of Japanese ancestry.

My favorite story for Jan Ken Po Gakko and one that I still love to tell is the true story of Sadako and the Thousand Cranes. I first introduced the story of Sadako to the children in 1977. It captivated their hearts, which it has continued to do for all the years since. The children listened intently and understood Sadako's fervent cry just as the children and people in Japan were so deeply stirred that it resulted in the great movement of the Thousand Crane Society. But first, let me retell this sad, beautiful story that has by now been carried all over the world.

Sadako Sasaki was a child two years old when the atomic bomb was dropped on Hiroshima. Her family fortunately lived near the outskirts of the city and their lives were spared. They always, however, looked in mirrors to see if ugly, red spots might appear on their bodies as they knew of others getting sick and being hospitalized.

Sadako grew up to be a fast runner. She was an athletic, twelve-year-old, a 6th grade student at Noboricho Elementary School. One day while she was practicing for a field day on the playground, Sadako became ill and was sent to the hospital.

Sadako wanted so much to get well. She saw her friend, who was only nine years old and not even born when the bomb dropped, become critically ill. One day he was taken away never to return to his bed. Sadako knew that death had come to Jiro, her friend.

Sadako's medicine came in folded, white paper packages. The nurses taught her how to do origami by folding the pieces of paper into all kinds of shapes.

One day a friend told her about the legend of a thousand cranes. "If you pray as you make each folded crane and if you fold a thousand cranes, your prayers will be answered. Your dreams will come true with a thousand cranes." Sadako's friend brought her many, pretty, colored origami papers and helped her get started making the cranes.

Sadako wrote in her diary of her prayers and her dreams for a world of peace with no more terrible wars and atomic bombs. She folded her cranes and prayed. She strung them and counted them, but she was beginning to tire easily. One day she wrote a Haiku, a Japanese poem with a single thought:

> *I will write Peace on your wings*
> *And you will fly*
> *All over the world.*

When she had folded 640 cranes, Sadako died.

Her school friends found her diary and her Haikus and they wept as they finished folding the thousand cranes. Sadako's story appeared in the newspapers all over Japan where it deeply moved those who read of her plight and the unfinished cranes. Thousands of cranes were made for her and sent to the Hiroshima officials. The spontaneous outpouring of response to Sadako's story came at a time when the city of Hiroshima was cleaning up and rebuilding after the bomb. Plans were made to build a Peace Park and have in it a children's monument commemorating the lives of all the children who died from the bomb.

When Al and I made our first trip to Japan in 1966, the pilgrimage to the children's monument made a profound impression on me. I could not hold back my tears when our tour guide told us the story of Sadako. I still remember that hot July day when we bowed down in front of the children's monument and wept as we read the inscription:

This is our Prayer; this is our cry;
World peace must be established!

The Mayor's welcome bouquet for our tour group was placed at the base of the inscription. The monument was a beautiful, contemporary, bell-shaped mountain on top of which stood a bronze figure of Sadako, her arms lifting high a golden origami crane. The children's inscription was at the base etched on black marble.

Over the years we made thousands of cranes at Jan Ken Po Gakko. Each summer a new set was delivered to Hiroshima by someone traveling there from Sacramento. Al and I have taken them, and one summer Marielle delivered a set. Former students have been the emissaries as have teacher friends and colleagues. Sacramento's mayor Anne Rudin carried cranes to Hiroshima in 1985 when she attended a world conference of Mayors for Peace in Japan. Al and I were welcomed warmly by Mayor Araki and escorted to the monument in a limousine. I have told Sadako's story everywhere. The urgent need to stop the build up of nuclear weapons makes her story have an even greater impact year by year. My prayers for world peace have found their wings. We surge forward with all humanity's prayer toward a world without war.

I came face to face with the horror of nuclear holocaust when Al's relatives from Japan came to visit us in 1977 and again in 1983. We traveled in a rented mobile home down the Redwood Highway, to Crater Lake, Yosemite, and Shasta Dam, and little by little their painful story oozed out. The Hirose family is the family of Kuzo (Ojiisan) Tsukamoto's second oldest brother, Fusataro. Because Fusataro was not the eldest and therefore the heir to carry on the family name, he was adopted by his aunt, married to Reimon Hirose. They were childless and wanted an heir, so that is how Fusataro Tsukamoto became Fusataro Hirose.

Fusataro's grandson was Shuji, the only son in the family with five daughters. He was married and had two children in 1945; Norio, the son, was five and Miho, his daughter, was three. Yasuko, his wife, was a teacher at an elementary school. It was Shuji's duty to look after his parents as long as they lived. His father had been dead for many years, but his elderly mother lived with them.

The Hirose family lived in Hiroshima, Japan, on the day of the atomic bomb, August 6, 1945. Shuji's youngest married sister, although she lived outside the city, had to visit the dentist that morning, so she came into the city and stopped by to see the family until time for her appointment at 10:00 a.m.

Grandma had a task that all elderly were required to do for the war effort. She had to go into the woods to gather firewood and twigs and bundle them for use by the younger people who were too busy at defense jobs. But that morning Grandma didn't feel well, so the family had urged her to stay at home and rest.

Norio had gone out to fish in a nearby river with his friend, Akio, but his line caught a snag and broke. He had rushed home to get another line and fish hook.

Shuji was in a hurry to lace his knee-length boots and get to work in a defense plant, but his old shoelaces broke in several places. It took him a long time to unlace his shoes and start all over again with a new lace.

Yasuko had already gone to her school. She always went early in the morning so she could prepare her lessons for the day. It was nearly time for morning calisthenics out on the school ground, the customary routine for children in the schools of Japan.

The principal and teachers were ready to join them outdoors, but that morning kind Principal Satow looked at Yasuko, big with child, and said, "Hirose Sensei and Masuno Sensei, you two wait in this room until the morning exercise is over today." Mrs. Masuno was recovering from a recent illness and Yasuko's child was due in a month. Yasuko sat across from her friend who faced the window.

Yasuko recalled, "I saw a sudden flash of bright light. I heard a terrible exploding sound. At the same time, glass sprayed all over the floor. I felt my back full of pain and realized that I was bleeding. I was shocked to see Mrs. Masuno who had sat across from me a moment ago sipping tea, now sprawled on the floor completely burned and brown. I could not wake her.

"I looked out to the yard from the glassless window. Rows and rows of children who had been exercising were gone. They had vanished. I was stunned. I could not understand what had happened. The sky turned dark. Then dark rain poured down. I must have fainted. I don't know how long I lay there shocked, exhausted, and frightened. Finally, I realized I must get home to my family, to my children.

"Some people came looking for anyone who had survived the explosion. They said an atomic bomb had been dropped. I cried and told them I must find my family. Everyone tried to stop me. They wanted me to go to the hospital to be treated for the cuts and the glass that had pierced my back. At the first aid station, they took out the pieces of glass as best they could. I could not wait any longer. I struggled through debris. I stumbled over objects and found they were human bodies charred crisp. I don't know how long it took, but it was dark when I finally came to where I thought my home should be.

"I expected the worst. I thought surely no one would be there. In the crumpled, leaning house that had once stood so sturdily, however, I found the dear faces of my loved ones. I wept unbelievingly. How could they ever have survived the terrible event of this day?

"I don't know how long we talked, but gradually the miraculous happenings of each member were shared. We realized how lucky we had been that our entire family was spared.

"Grandma was safe in the shelter of our home. Shuji had taken so

251

long in replacing his laces in the tall shoes that he was still in the house, so he had been spared. Norio couldn't find another fish hook, so he too was in the house. Itsuye, who had come to wait for her appointment had grabbed Miho and whisked her away out in the field where they hid behind mounds of grass and piles of dirt that served as protection.

"Principal Satow saved my life when he told me to stay inside. Our ancestral gods saved me from the fate that ended Mrs. Masuno's life because she happened to be sitting on the wrong side of the table facing the window. The atomic radiation burned her face and she died. My wounds took a long time to heal. My back was completely burned, but luckily I was sitting so close to the wall, it protected me enough so that I recovered. In a month, I gave birth to a beautiful daughter. We named her 'Shinobu' which means a survivor."

We learned from Yasuko how the family had survived in the days and months afterwards by eating weeds and roots. As we traveled, she noted the sturdiness of the oleander that we saw alongside the roadsides of California highways; Yasuko remembered that often this was the only plant that grew when everything else was completely burned and killed.

When I see today the beautiful, blooming oleander, I think of the anguish and cry of people who have known the horror of war, especially atomic war. I think again of Sadako's haiku: "I will write peace on your wings and you will fly all over the world."

Part of the discovery of our ancestral roots was the finding of lost relatives such as the Hirose family. Their story made me realize how unique each individual is and ponder on why some are chosen to do what they do in their lifetimes. The story has made me work even harder for world peace through my prayers and actions. Though I am but one small individual, I cannot leave this earth until I have done what I can so that others will be free to live their lives to the very fullest. My favorite song has become "Let There Be Peace On Earth and Let It Begin With Me."

Thus I personally found my own roots through Jan Ken Po Gakko and began to appreciate my Japanese heritage. I began to recognize the value of knowing who I was through the foundation of my unique background. I realized that my reliance upon the Japanese American

Citizens League had come about because of my need to be associated with our collective past.

Jan Ken Po Gakko

Chapter 21

From Roots to Redress

*"I always knew the relocation and internment were wrong,
but I never thought I would see the day when so
many Americans agreed."*

How wise and courageous were the leaders of our national JACL and how significant our timing on projects that were to affect many generations. Our president, Shigeo Wakamatsu, a chemist from Chicago, passed the gavel over to Frank Chuman, a Los Angeles attorney, in 1960. Frank named Shig Wakamatsu the head of the Issei History Project and pushed hard for the need to record the history of the Japanese Americans. The urgency for such a project was clear; already it was too late to interview many of our living artifacts, the Issei. For twenty years, however, Shig devoted his time to this project which was later renamed the Japanese American Research Project.

Dr. T. Scott Miyakawa, an eminent member of the Boston University sociology faculty, became the first director of the Issei History Project. He presented an outline which had three objectives:

1)to conduct an in-depth sociological survey of the Issei and Nisei;
2)to publish a definitive, scholarly history of Japanese Americans;
3)to assemble a documentary collection including oral histories.

Later a fourth goal was added—to publish as soon as possible a popular layman's history to be followed in later years by the promised scholarly volumes.

The University of California at Los Angeles was selected as the academic home for the project. UCLA was also JACL President Frank Chuman's alma mater.

The problem of financing such a project seemed impossible, yet a most successful fund raising campaign was waged. Responses came from throughout the entire organization. Many Issei and Nisei and a great many friends of the JACL saw the significance of the endeavor and gave strong endorsement to the project. This enthusiasm was seen in every chapter.

JACL made a grant of $100,000 to UCLA, and a partnership was formed between this major university and an ethnic group "seeking to learn more about itself and to share the knowledge with others (Shig's words)." A $140,000 grant from the Carnegie Corporation and $400,000 from the National Institute of Mental Health gave the project a shot in the arm.

Dr. Robert Wilson, a Japan scholar in the UCLA history department, was named administrator of the funds. Dr. Gregg Stone and his wife, Gladys Ishida Stone, designed a comprehensive questionnaire (72 pages) that probed into the lives and times of more than 1000 Issei and 3000 of their children and grandchildren.

JACL hired Joe Grant Masaoka as an expeditor when the weight of the project began to bog down. Joe and Dr. Wilson traveled widely to collect documentary material and conduct oral interviews. It was a shocking loss to the Japanese American community when Joe Grant Masaoka died in 1970 before he could finish this important work. I had the privilege of corresponding with Joe when I worked to legislate the Evacuation Claim bill and the Walter-McCarran Immigration- Naturalization Act. I also spoke with Joe at various gatherings around Sacramento.

Our Florin JACL worked hard to get some tapes. Al was the chairman of the Florin History Project. There were many meetings to collect data from Issei who could still remember and share their experiences. What a task, though, to stick to the questions; much concentration was demanded in these interviews. For many Issei, it was simply too late. Their memories had failed them in the later years of their lives. Even Grandpa Tsukamoto was not aware of what we were about. Ten years earlier, he would have been a valuable resource for interviewing, but for him it was too late for this too.

Another exciting event that made us aware of our culture and history was the centennial celebration of the first Japanese colonists to come to America, which was held in 1969. Henry Taketa, Sacramento attorney and well known historian, proved beyond a doubt that the ill-fated group of settlers from Aizu Wakamatsu came to the United States with the hopes of establishing a silk and tea colony in June of 1869. They were led by a Dutch or German trader, Eduard John Henry Schnell, a long time confidant of Katamori Matsudaira Lord of Aizu Wakamatsu.

The most exciting part of this story was the discovery of a 75-year-old man named Henry Veercamp who lived in Coloma. Veercamp's mother had given shelter to the young Japanese nursemaid, Okei Ito, and Veerkamp remembered her. His mother had befriended the girl and taken care of her until she died of a fever, lonely, and broken hearted at the age of nineteen. Veerkamp was about 20 years old at the time, and he recalled the tragic story of the colony's hopes, their industry and hardships, and the eventual abandonment of the colony. The foothills of Coloma didn't have enough rain to raise tea and mulberries—that was the tragedy of the Wakamatsu Colony. The plants died, and so did the aspirations of the founders. But we knew conclusively that Japanese pioneers had been in America for 100 years.

We raised a fund to build a monument in which to set a plaque to honor the colony. I was on the committee to write the story of the Issei for the souvenir booklet. A Japanese garden was designed and placed in a corner of the Gold Hill Elementary School in Coloma near Okei's grave on top of the hill.

The Wakamatsu Dedication Ceremony at the Gold Hill School was a memorable one on June 6, 1969. Even Governor Ronald Reagan was in attendance and gave a speech. I taught my Florin students to sing Okei's lullaby in Japanese for the ceremony. Older girls sang in two parts with koto accompaniment. That evening nearly 600 guests were entertained by the children (some Sanseis, some white children from Samuel Kennedy School, and Florin United Methodist Church choir members) at the Woodlake Inn banquet. Remarkably, we all sang in Japanese! I was so proud of them and so pleased with the cultural impact of the event.

The experience of working on the Centennial Celebration committee had a profound effect upon me and deepened my sense of being part of a dramatic history. I found that thought-provoking books were making their appearance as a result of the Issei History Project. Bill Hosokawa had been the featured speaker at our banquet, and his first book, *Nisei, the Quiet American,* was on sale. It was one of the earliest books written by a Japanese American to appear. I was fascinated with what I read.

As I suspected it would, Hosokawa's book sparked a great controversy between conservative older Nisei and the younger Nisei and Sansei. Our young people who had been caught up in the rhetoric and rebellion of the late 1960s which affected the entire nation, objected to the subtitle—"the quiet American." They considered this stereotype noxious and offensive to all Japanese Americans. The controversy continued in the *Pacific Citizen* for a long period and may have helped encourage the sale of the book. It certainly publicized the difference in generational thinking and made me think about things that had never entered my mind before. But this was only the beginning.

Edison Uno was a professor at San Francisco State University who taught a course called "Evacuation and Relocation." For more than 25 years Uno researched and read everything he could find about our humiliating internment experience. In 1971 Uno wrote, "The tide of Japanese American consciousness reached its peak. We took our first pilgrimage to Manzanar. We observed 100 years' celebration of the Japanese in America. We've listened to the hardship and struggles of the Issei in America as the Issei History Project was completed. As we push for Redress, deep feelings find concrete expression...we fully perceived what was in the offing for us, and I began to realize how tragic our past really was."

Uno's article was published in the *Pacific Citizen* and called "Concentration Camp, American Style."

Readers were shocked, particularly Japanese Americans who had struggled to make it after the humiliation of Executive Order 9066. They wanted the episode to be buried and forgotten forever.

Many people were horrified to think we had actually been in prison and that three years of our lives should be referred to as having been spent in concentration camps. They didn't want to interpret their experiences as having been in prison. Their memories were painful, but they were best smoothed over as just another experience, one that was best forgotten. They were tired, confused, and weary of being on the receiving end of demeaning hatred and mistreatment. They hadn't really thought about prison and were not ready to accept it.

It took courage, clear thinking, and dogged determination to wake us up from the lethargy we had fallen into since the dark spring days of 1942. If people thought we had gone to prison because we had done wrong, we had to do something to correct such misconceptions.

Slowly and gradually, Edison Uno and others who felt the same way came together. Ray Okamura and later Dr. Clifford Uyeda and John Tateishi, Min Yasui, Grant Ujifusa, Grace Uyehara, and many more spoke up at every opportunity and eventually whipped the feeling into the full scale redress movement of the 1980s.

Edison Uno deserves the credit for where we are today on the verge of gaining redress. This giant of a Nisei who emerged from a concentration camp, American style, was the very last American citizen to leave the gate at Tule Lake after the longest confinement, totaling 1,647 days. Uno felt the outrage strongly enough to dig into the past and read every available publication since the internment.

> "When we returned from years of internment, the business of repairing our lives, anxious to catch up what we had lost, to catch up with our careers cut short, snatched out of our lives...like victims of rape, we could not bear to speak of the assault, of the unspeakable crime. We spoke only with guarded words; we dared not fully reveal the depth of our feelings about it. The unjust imprisonment was the result of two closely related emotions: racism and hysteria."

Edison Uno's data substantiated the stand from which he spoke. Our Constitution *had* been betrayed. It *was* an outrage! Uno spoke with authority; he was articulate and sincerely intent on the need for redress and attaining vindication for the assault, not only on behalf of people of Japanese ancestry, but because of the unforgiveable violation of our precious constitutional rights. As a lecturer on Asian American studies at San Francisco State University, Uno's words were heard and heeded. But in 1977, Japanese American communities all over the land grieved the untimely death of this fine young professor who spoke out for justice and the need to have our minds and names cleared of this shameful episode of our past. A heart attack took Edison Uno abruptly from our midst.

Talk of some form of reparation had begun even while we were being evacuated. Throughout the years of our incarceration and the post war years when we struggled to get back and catch up on all we had lost, there were discussions and voices speaking out for the unfinished task.

One voice was that of the *Pacific Citizen*, the JACL newspaper. It was the only voice we had to present important issues to Japanese Americans. During the war years when we were sent like lost sheep to ten remote camps throughout the nation, the *Pacific Citizen* brought us news each week of events in Washington and on distant battle fronts. We read what the hate mongers were saying, and we looked to the paper as a valuable source of information as well as a significant morale builder for us.

A great victory took place for us when the JACL leadership successfully achieved the rescinding of Executive Order 9066 by President Gerald Ford in the Bicentennial Year of 1976. How strange that the order had remained on the books for 34 years! Inch by inch, efforts were taking place that would ultimately achieve justice. Ford's statements were welcomed by us: "We now know what we should have known then...Not only was the evacuation *wrong*, but the Japanese Americans were and are loyal Americans...! I call upon the American people to affirm with me this American promise...that we have learned from this tragedy of that long ago experience to treasure liberty and justice for each individual American and resolve that this kind of action never again be repeated." This took place on February 19, 1976, exactly 34 years after the order was signed by President Roosevelt in 1942.

The Civil Rights movement of the 1960s contributed greatly to the change in thinking over the next two decades. I noticed it in my relationships with the parents of the children in Jan Ken Po Gakko. I marveled at their ability to question and speak out. The thinking of the entire nation was affected, and the discussions that took place on campuses of colleges and universities vastly enlarged our understanding of democracy. Voices of young Sansei and Nisei from such environments emerged to speak out in the 1970s. They greatly shocked the Japanese American communities where the vast majority of people were silent about what had happened during the war, and they wanted to stay silent and let it all be forgotten so they could go on with their lives.

In 1978 the JACL leadership made an important stand. At the national convention in Salt Lake City, a daring decision was made that had great historical impact. A resolution was passed seeking $25,000 for each of the 120,000 persons forced out of their homes and incarcerated by General DeWitt's actions in 1942. This meant a staggering sum of three billion dollars! The proposal was finally adopted even though there was strong opposition and there were some who felt too much emphasis had been placed on the monetary compensation. Before the convention was over, everyone realized that the road ahead would be a strenuous one that required monumental effort.

As early as 1943, an eminent professor of constitutional law at Yale University, Eugene V. Rostow, had called the internment "America's worst war-time mistake." Reminders of the First Amendment to the U.S. Constitution called attention to the guarantee to citizens of the right to petition the government for a redress of grievances. Redress—it was a new word for us, but we certainly had a grievance. We had been deprived of our constitutional rights, imprisoned without due process; surely we had a right to redress for these grievances.

Judge William Marutani stated our position clearly: "We are in an American society where any redress of grievances is customarily recognized by monetary means...We must refocus our sights upon the central theme of vindication of suffering endured by our Issei and their offspring. We are just plain Americans and continue to be so. As any red-blooded American worthy of his salt would, we seek to have our names, our reputations cleared. We want our country and our fellow citizens to openly recognize that our Issei parents and the Nikkeis (Americans of Japanese ancestry) were not disloyal. As proud Americans, we want the record cleared." Cases involving Fred Koramatsu, Min Yasui, and Gordon Hirobayashi, previously denied by the courts, were brought forth once again.

As I read the reports I was encouraged to think and widen my outlook beyond the Japanese American communities. I realized that we older Nisei needed to listen and change our old ways. We had been saddled by our Issei cultural heritage to such an extent that it was difficult to see any other views. The redress movement made sense to me when I realized that the young parents I had worked with in our Jan Ken Po Gakko school were saying the same thing.

A little child's question made me a believer. He was a bright little fellow, about ten years old, and the great-grandchild of a dear Issei friend I had known most of my life. "What did Great-Grandpa do wrong that they put him in the prison camp for so long?" he asked. I was stunned. We had been talking about internment and the wartime relocation for several weeks. I had no idea that the children would think crimes had been committed. I thought we had told them over and over again that we were innocent and had been imprisoned unjustly.

I wondered where I had erred in my thinking and teaching. The children still thought we had done something wrong. Redress meant fair play and a reversal of discrimination. What a beautiful country this would be if racism and prejudice could be set aside to no longer warp our minds and sap our energy. Justice and hope for a brighter America could only come about with continuing education. What an amazing document, our Constitution. To think that our founding fathers had had the wisdom to foresee confusing situations such as this. My task as a teacher was clearly laid out before me. Now I know what redress really meant.

In 1979, JACL, with an eye to political realities, shifted its thrust for redress to a request for a fact finding commission to investigate the circumstances surrounding the evacuation and internment. In August of 1979, six senators jointly introduced Senate Bill 1647 entitled, "The Commission on Wartime Internment and Relocation of Civilians Act." The following month a similar bill was introduced in the House of Representatives, HR-5499.

Redress for 120,000 persons (this figure includes the 110,000 West Coast evacuees as well as the Hawaiians and those who were detained by the FBI) whose constitutional rights had been violated some 40 years ago, was finally underway. It was realistic to determine whether or not a wrong had been committed, and then to propose a form of redress if it had.

Criticism and ridicule, however, came from many who felt that the wrong was obvious. They felt the investigation was a meaningless and wasteful way of avoiding the issue. Even JACL members were divided over the issues.

The thought of reparations was unacceptable to many Nisei. It carried the connotation of payment demanded of victors in a war of defeated nations. It was too harsh for the Issei—they were uncomfortable with such an insensitive demand. Even I recoiled for a long time at the thought of redress. I could not bring myself to point my finger at the U.S. government and all our distinguished leaders in Washington and accuse them of wrongdoing.

I could hear my father's voice reminding us children, "Don't hurt other people. Respect and learn from your elders—your teachers, leaders, your president, and country. Don't bring shame upon the family and the Japanese people. Even if you are hurt, struggle and continue to do good. Endure!"

But the innocent questioning eyes of Yonsei children who wanted to know the truth convinced me that as a conscientious educator and as a responsible Nisei citizen of America, I owed them an honest answer. In an effort to be a confident, faithful, caring person who had gone through the evacuation and who had access to the history that had been written about us, I had to take a stand. I had to use my hidden outrage to help us all become proud, happy citizens in an America that was willing to correct its own mistakes and continue striving to reach the dream and great principles upon which our country was founded.

Unless we older Nisei who remember vividly the shame and hardship suffered by Japanese American people are willing to tell our stories, it is impossible to win redress. We need the courage and stamina in our declining years to assume our responsibilities as caring, mature citizens of a wonderful country. *WE THE PEOPLE* need to show by our actions that we sincerely believe this is the best country in the world. We need to show our faith and confidence in a constitutional democracy for all the people. We need to be vigilant and in the words of Hiroshi Kashiwagi, "become fierce guardians of our Democracy." That's what our U.S. Constitution is all about.

Thus Al and I joined the ranks of those who supported the redress movement. On July 31, 1980, President Jimmy Carter signed Public Law #96-317 creating the commission to study the internment and relocation of 1942-45. "It is with a great deal of pleasure I sign this legislation into law. The commission study is adequately funded. It is not designed to be a witch hunt. It is designed to expose clearly what happened in that period of war in our nation when many loyal American citizens of Japanese descent were embarrassed during the crucial times of our nation's history. I don't believe anyone would doubt that injustices were done, and I don't think anyone would doubt that it is advisable now for us to have a clear understanding as Americans of this episode in the history of our country...We also want to make sure their (the commission's) efforts will prevent any recurrence of this abuse of the basic human rights of American citizens and also resident aliens who enjoy the privileges and protection of not only American law but of American principles and ideals."

President Carter named Dr. Arthur S. Flemming, Chairman of the U.S. Commission on Civil Rights; Judge William Marutani of the Philadelphia Court of Common Pleas; and Joan Bernstein, former general counsel of the Department of Health and Human Services, to serve on the Commission.

The Senate selected Edward W. Brooke, former senator from Massachusetts; Hugh B. Mitchell, senator from Seattle; and Father Ishmail Vincent Gromoff, a Russian Orthodox priest who was one of the evacuated Aleuts from Alaska. The House appointed Arthur J. Goldberg, former ambassador to the United Nations and a U.S. Supreme Court justice; Congressman Daniel Lungren of Long Beach, California; and the Reverend Robert F. Drinan, a Jesuit priest and congressman from Massachusetts. Joan Bernstein was elected by the Commission to serve as its chairperson, and Paul Bannai, the first

Nisei to be elected to the California legislature, was chosen as the executive director of the Commission.

Word went out across the land that former evacuees were to be encouraged to testify before the Commission. Various community groups assisted JACL leaders and church groups in reaching out to the entire Japanese American community. Many orientation meetings and practices were held for those who were reluctant to speak but had unique stories to tell.

The first hearing was held on July 14, 1981 in Washington D.C. My heart was in my throat as I wondered how I could dare stand before such a distinguished group of Americans to tell my story.

We learned that the Commission would hold hearings in San Francisco on August 12, 13 and 14. I struggled with my testimony trying to get it down to the five minutes allotted. I felt that I should speak for the 2500 people of Florin who found that their community disappeared while they were behind barbed wire fences. I wanted to represent the families, the grandparents and elderly Issei as well as the tiny Yonsei tots in our care.

We rode to San Francisco from Sacramento in buses. Teams of television people and reporters had met us at the Japanese Methodist Church as we gathered to board the buses. Cameras and notebooks were everywhere. It was a momentous day!

My throat was dry and my entire body a bundle of nerves as I listened to the heart breaking testimony of others while I waited my turn to speak. The hearing room at Golden Gate University was filled with families and friends and people of all races and ages. Jan Ken Po Gakko parents and children from Florin had come too. I felt a sudden urge to speak for them as well as my generation.

There were 750 people who eventually spoke before the Commission, and I was only one, but I felt that I spoke to the entire nation. At last my country cared about what had happened and wanted to know how I had been hurt and what the terrible wrong had done to me. I was proud of my country; she had not disappointed my faith in her.

I set my notes aside and spoke extemporaneously. I spoke up for Ojiisan and Obaasan, my mom and dad, Mrs. Kurima, and the children in the camps. I spoke for the Yonsei and other children following us and how they depended upon us to make the most of this momentous opportunity to tell the truth and thereby prove our innocence. I knew I was going over my time, but I felt that the Commission members were really listening. I came away disappointed and frustrated that I had so little time to say what was on my mind. I felt I had done poorly, but I was reassured by the smiles around me and the nodding heads. Al said I talked for eight minutes, so I had taken an extra three minutes and no one stopped me. I felt good about that, but I wondered if my message had come across.

"Our redress and reparation endeavor has finally given us our first ray of hope of clearing the years of secret humiliation and guilt. At long last, I feel this is our chance to model Nisei confidence, courage and hope in American democracy that our Sansei and Yonsei and all Americans need to see. Today, I am here to speak for them, the children of the future.

"These children need to know that America will be fair in the long run and that their grandparents really didn't deserve to be put in concentration camps, that they were never guilty of any crime. For forty years, invisible in America's history books, we endured this injustice unchallenged. Unless we who were victims cared enough about our America to correct her errors, there will be no one to clean up this sordid episode in our history. And it could be repeated! We need to be sure that every generation will be taught the truth, that books will be written for schools to clear the record of our tragic experiences. Everywhere people must learn that our government erred but had the greatness to correct her mistakes, and the educational process moved ahead to pave the way for more freedom, justice and fair play for all its people. That finally even the Supreme Court of the land would review the case and set the record straight."

Things were different after the Golden Gate Hearings. There were reports in all the local newspapers and television. Almost every day there was a call from a TV station or a paper. They wanted to do special programs, and there were hours of interviewing and taping sessions.

I felt like Ron Wakabayashi did in an article he wrote for the *Pacific Citizen's* holiday issue in 1981 entitled "Year of Tears:"

"I have seen more Japanese American tears in 1981 than in all the prior years of my life combined. I have seen Obaachan tears, Ojiichan tears and my own.

"It is not that Japanese Americans do not cry easily. Stoicism is a stereotype. We cry at all the ordinary human pain that must touch all of our lives. But in 1981, we cried for ourselves. We cried for each other's pain of 39 years ago.

"Thousands of tragic stories were told. Thankfully, we survived and have worked through much of the adversity that faced us. But we cried for that adversity. It was so unnecessary. We know more than anyone else, how unnecessary the injustice was. Others can recognize the injustice. We can feel how unnecessary the injustice was.

"There is something about this mass crying that is remarkable. In the hearing rooms you could tell that we felt each other. We touched each other. We went through an experience of knowing how each other felt. The proper presentation that we have known was laid aside, and we took the time to cry together.

"The Nikkei man addressing the commissioners paused. His voice was starting to break. In silence, our hearts knew exactly what he was feeling. In silence, we knew each other's rage. In silence, we thought about the young Nisei, barely 18 years old, forever a veteran and how much we missed him. During the intermission, when another panel of fellow Nikkeis were taking their seats to give their testimonies, we think about what Ojiichan would say if he were here."

My life was never the same again after speaking before the distinguished members of the U.S. Commission on Wartime Internment and Relocation of Civilians in August of 1981. The urgency of my bold commitment took precedence over everything else in the days that were left for me on this earth.

After 750 testimonies and the monumental task of research and deliberation, the Commission reported to Congress and the American people their conclusions from the two year study. Their report is entitled *Personal Justice Denied*, and its message is clearly that Executive Order 9066 *was not* justified by military necessity. Further, the report claims that the broad historical causes which shaped the decisions of 1942 were race prejudice, war hysteria, and the failure of political leadership. These recommendations were implemented into the Civil Liberties Act of 1987, the Redress Legislation.

Chapter 22

A Legacy for the Future

*"What would Obaasan say if she knew her old suitcase
was at the Smithsonian?
What will all the great grandchildren of the future say
when they see it there?"*

While we prepared for the hearings, Al and I were busy making preparations for our first Florin homecoming reunion. Our committee of forty people worked for a full year to make this memorable event a reality. Nearly 850 former Florin residents gathered happily to remember and experience a nostalgic and unforgettable reunion. They came from all over the U.S., and some even came from Japan. We honored fifty Issei, and many families echoed with repeated little reunions in the weeks that followed.

We were inexplainably drawn to that reunion. Thousands of tears were shed at the strange homecoming which was more like a pilgrimage, for many had not been back to Florin since their abrupt departure so long ago.

In 1982 we dedicated a monument at the Buddhist Church grounds in Florin. We wanted our Issei to be remembered for the struggles and hardships they had endured, and we wanted their legacy of faith and devotion to duty to be remembered by future generations. Our parents were not spies, traitors nor criminals! They had made significant contributions to the history of Florin and south Sacramento County as pioneer farmers of strawberries and grapes. That is how we wanted them to be remembered in the community where they had toiled and lived.

The monument stands there today as a symbol of our past. Not so with another monument placed in Florin in 1985. Al and I worked with the committee that put together the "Once in a Lifetime Reunion" for all people who had ever lived in or gone to school in Florin. The outgrowth of this activity was the formation of the Florin Historical Society, a much needed organization. The monument that was unveiled on the day of the reunion left many of us with sad feelings in our hearts, not for what it said, but for what it did *not* say. A tribute to grape and strawberry growing, there is no mention of the contribution of Japanese Americans at all. Reminders of forty years ago rushed through my very soul, time and time again during the preparations for the huge parade and festivities. I heard about comments that were made that were simply unbelievable. I could hardly believe that people still carried such prejudicial and ignorant attitudes. Some people, apparently, still want to believe that we *were* dangerous 45 years ago, that some of us *were* spies, that radios and guns *were* found in secluded areas, and that we knew about the invasion of Pearl Harbor before it happened. My heart was heavy each time I heard such outrageous claims.

The speaker on Reunion Day was U.S. Congressman Robert Matsui who represents the Sacramento area. His grandfather and father were fruit growers in Florin just as we were. How ironic that Bob was the speaker and that the monument did not mention his heritage nor ours. And even more ironic was the fact that the monument was placed on the very grounds of the old Florin East School where many of us had attended a segregated public school.

I do not wish to offend the many wonderful people of Florin I have known all my life, but the bigotry of 45 years ago that allowed us to be placed in concentration camps is still alive today. It is hidden in dark closets, but it is there; and it will continue to come out when least expected for that is the way of racism and bigotry no matter where it is hidden away. We must all be zealous in providing the education that will break through those barriers once and for all.

FLORIN

FLORIN COMMUNITY ESTABLISHED IN 1875 BY SUGDEN AND JOHNSON, NAMED BY E.B. CROCKER. RAIL SERVICE STARTED IN 1875 FOR SHIPPING OF TOKAY GRAPES AND STRAWBERRIES. JAMES RUTTER PLANTED THE FIRST TOKAY GRAPES IN CALIFORNIA ON HIS RANCH. STRAWBERRIES PLAYED A MAJOR ROLE IN FLORIN HISTORY.

IN 1897 FRASINETTI'S WINERY WAS ESTABLISHED. IT IS THE OLDEST ORIGINAL FAMILY OPERATED WINERY IN NORTHERN CALIFORNIA.

DEDICATED JULY 20, 1985 BY LIBERTY PARLOR NO. 211 N.D.G.W. AND ELK GROVE PARLOR NO. 41 N.S.G.W.

It is time, however, to set these thoughts aside. There have been many wonderful experiences to counteract them. For the past five years, the Elk Grove Unified School District has adopted a resolution to commemorate February 19 as a day of remembrance. With many others, I have organized an extensive display of materials and artifacts for the school children of Elk Grove and south Sacramento to view. Hundreds of students of all ages from primary to high school visit the display with their teachers. I have also each year assisted with a workshop for the teachers so they will be better able to teach this part of American history to their students. Our Florin JACL has held a community evening for the past five years—an evening to thank the many people who have supported us and to continue educating the wider community. Our speakers have been John Tateishi, National JACL redress director; Judge Marutani who was on the Congressional panel; Eric Saul, curator of the Presidio Museum in San Francisco; Chester Tanaka, author of *Go For Broke*; Dr. Howard Langley, curator at the Smithsonian Institution in Washington D.C., and Dr. Peter Irons, author of *Justice at War*.

Dr. Langley's discoveries in Florin will be featured in the Smithsonian exhibit scheduled to open on October 1, 1987. I am honored to be one of the persons chosen to have their voices on tape in the exhibit. Al and I sent many artifacts from Florin and the Sacramento Valley to Washington—some were ours and some belonged to friends, neighbors, and relatives. It is amazing how many things we found in garages and barns—even in trunks that had not been opened since people came back from camp.

TO THE SMITHSONIAN FROM FLORIN, CALIFORNIA

A. OBAASAN'S WOVEN SUITCASE

It was a fine woven suitcase lacquered deep brown color, reinforced on the corners with leather and finished with a sturdily- set handle. Unlike the usual suitcase with a hinged cover to open, the upper basket was lifted from the fitted bottom. It was well-lined with blue printed fabric to keep the woven basket together as well as to protect its content.

This was the suitcase Obaasan and Ojiisan brought back from their nostalgic trip to Hiroshima in 1934 after nearly thirty-five years that Kuzo had been away from his native land. Grandma packed her treasured things from Japan in this suitcase.

When Executive Order 9066 drove her from her farm home, Grandma packed a few of her precious items among her clothing in this suitcase and traveled to Fresno Assembly Center; to Jerome, Arkansas; to Gila, Arizona; and finally back to Florin again.

When Obaasan passed away in 1970 at age 91, we found all the pictures of her family, her grandchildren, and great-grandchildren packed away in this suitcase. There it remained in our closet for fifteen years until we learned about the Smithsonian's search for artifacts. Al and I decided that if the Smithsonian could use this suitcase from Hiroshima that Obaasan had loved, we would donate it. The proof that this suitcase traveled on the tragic journey of the Tsukamoto experience was the tell-tale 3" wide band of light-green paint Alfred had used to mark all the luggage that belonged to the Tsukamoto family.

Chet Tanaka, Executive Director for the "Go For Broke, Inc.," wrote a fictional article about "Mary's Suitcase" and its travels to publicize the need for such items for the Smithsonian Exhibit and to highlight the untold story of the internment years. "Go for Broke" is an expression used in the game of dice. It means to give all you have or bet everything. The 100th and 442nd Nisei soldiers of Hawaii felt that in World War II the Niseis had to "Go for Broke" and give all they had to win confidence in their loyalty. The veterans formed "Go for Broke, Inc." to preserve their history and their heroic record to tell the story of the Japanese American experience and help bring understanding.

271

B. OJIISAN'S PACKING CRATE

To: Kuzo Tsukamoto #22076
Rt. 1, Box 173
Florin, California

This was painted on the crate by Kuzo's son-in-law, Harold Ouchida. It was made of unpainted hard wood, about 2 x 2 1/2 x 3 and made in Arkansas when the remaining residents at Jerome were preparing to be dispersed to the nine other camps or to new jobs on farms and communities all over the Midwest and Eastern USA in June, 1944.

Every family was busy getting crates ready. Many converted their tables and desks that had been made out of scrap lumber into crates to pack the necessities they had accumulated in the two years since their departure from their California homes.

Ojiisan's crate was smoothly sanded and well made with a lid that fitted well. After his return to Florin from Gila, Arizona, we packed away my souvenir collection of the weekly "Grapevine" from Fresno; The "Denson Dispatch" from Jerome, Arkansas; my old JACL news, "Pacific Citizen;" reports, letters, diaries and journals; memorabilia from Kalamazoo; scrapbooks and books accumulated all these years away from home. This was truly my "gold mine" for research when I was ready to write my book.

When the old barn was torn down to make way for our new garage, the crate was kept under the table where I had my collection of potted cactus and succulents. Water seeped into the crate and soiled it, leaving water marks on the faded, yellowing papers. Mice had gotten into the crate over the years and left their tell-tale destruction of valuable written material. This is the crate we sent to Washington D.C. for the Smithsonian exhibit.

C. OTHER ITEMS ACKNOWLEDGED BY THE SMITHSONIAN

(a) A photo of Mom picking berries in the field. It was a snapshot which was enlarged for the Historical Exhibit collection. Mom was busy in the fields, wearing her home sewn, white bonnet, moving along the berry plants in a crouching position and pulling her strawberry basket carrier along to fill ripe berries into the baskets.

(b) A vase made of hard wood, carved, shaped, and varnished by Joichi Nitta for his wife, Shizuko, who loved to make Japanese flower arrangements. The vase was about 12" tall, 12" in diameter at the top, sloped and narrowed near the bottom of the vase. It had an attached base which was about one inch thick and extended out about twelve inches to give adequate support for the heavy vase to stand upright.

(c) Two handmade bonnets, made of bleached, discarded rice sacks by Masao Taniguchi's mother. They were given to me by Glenn Taniguchi and had been put away by Glenn's grandmother after she stopped working in the fields in Florin when she was 88.

(d) Travel permit issued by the U.S. Employment Service, Sacramento, California, dated April 21, 1942. Issued to Nami Tsukamoto for permission to travel beyond five miles from Florin to see a doctor.

(e) Blue identity card used by Mary Tsukamoto for the mess hall admission in the Jerome Relocation Camp, Arkansas.

(f) Christmas card from T/Sgt Richard Itanaga of the 442nd RCT from Italy, 1944.

(g) Snapshot of USO Committee Hospitality Center, headed by Mary Tsukamoto (standing in the doorway of the camp building). Mary Tsukamoto and the USO Committee organized dances, the Social Center for GIs and took bus loads of girls to Camp Shelby, Mississippi to entertain the soldiers of the 442nd.

(h) Copy of the Souvenir Edition of the Newsletter from Camp Harmony, temporary detention center, dated August 14, 1942 (vol. 1, no. 12).

(i) Mimeographed notice of E.P. Pulliam, manager of the Fresno Assembly Center, dated July 23, 1942.

D. PHOTOGRAPHS
(special panoramic photos of people in Florin)

These photos are on loan to the Smithsonian.

(1) Japanese Methodist Church Sunday School group photo (circa 1933-34). (7" x 29")

(2) All Florin Picnic, taken in 1935. It is the only photo of most of the community, particularly the youths who came to the first JACL picnic sponsored by the newly organized Florin JACL. It brought together the cluster settlements in the ten mile radius surrounding the town of Florin. (6.5" x 41")

(3) One photo of the Taisho Language School dedication of the Taisho Hall, 1924. (7.5" x 30")

(4) Uchida farm on Florin Road. It shows the young Tokay grapevines planted in rows, the tractor, the farm home and in the inset, the Uchida children. This photo and all other panoramic photographs were taken by Mr. Kuroko who had a photo studio in Sacramento on 4th Street. (7" x 35")

E. SHELL JEWELRY FROM TULE LAKE
(On five year loan to Smithsonian)

Loaned by sister Isabel Oshiro, given to her by Mrs. Kishaba; given to me by Mrs. Kishaba who made them while at Tule Lake.

(1) Necklace made of tiny white shells. (9" in length)

(2) Corsage make of larger flat shells. It looks like a miniature camellia. (3.2" x 5")

(3) One corsage with yellow bow. (8.5" x 2.5")

(4) One corsage made of tiny white shells. (5.5" x 2")

Florin Chapter J.A.C.L. and
Florin Japanese-American Community

Presents

**TIME OF REMEMBRANCE RECOGNITION NIGHT
"SALUTE TO THE NIKKEI VETERANS"**

Japanese Buffet Dinner

Saturday, March 9, 1985
Dinner 6:00 PM ● Program 7:30 PM
Donation $5.00

Florin YBA Hall ● 8320 Florin Road ● Sacramento, California

N⁰ 292

FLORIN CHAPTER JACL
FLORIN AREA JAPANESE AMERICAN COMMUNITY
RECOGNITION NIGHT

**TIME OF REMEMBRANCE
EAST TO THE SMITHSONIAN**

SATURDAY   6:00 PM   MARCH 15, 1986
FLORIN YBA HALL

SPEAKER FROM THE SMITHSONIAN INSTITUTE

Exhibits, Memorabilia, Artifacts
Music by James Rutter 7-8th School Band
Light Refreshments   Donation: $5.00

N⁰ 331

FLORIN CHAPTER JACL
FLORIN AREA JAPANESE AMERICAN COMMUNITY

TIME OF REMEMBRANCE
"Preserving Our Fragile Constitution"

Featured Speaker. Professor Peter Irons
Sacramento Valley Premiere Showing of.
"Conversations: Before the War/After the War"

Saturday, March 28, 1987   Florin YBA Hall
8320 Florin Road

Doors open at 6 PM for exhibit viewing
Program begins at 7 PM   Donation:
Asian Hor d'Oeuvres $8 Adult

N⁰ 1278

Japanese Community Recognition Dinner
HONORING MRS. MARY TSUKAMOTO
Sponsorship of Florin Chapter JACL

Friday, January 9, 1987 at Sheraton Sunrise Hotel
(Located: Sunrise and Highway 50)
TIME: 6:00 p.m. - No Host Cocktail, 7:00 p.m. - Dinner
Dinner Reservation: $15.00 per person (tax deductible)

1987 CHAPTER INSTALLATION TO FOLLOW

Chapter 23

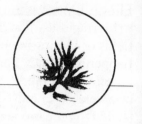

On the Wings of a Crane

"Let there be peace on Earth and let it not end with me."

This is my story; I am but one American, speaking out in 1987. I, Mary Tsuruko Tsukamoto, whose Japanese name means crane, have found my roots, and now like Sadako's little cranes, I too have found wings and can soar from the highest mountain peaks. In my sunset years of the pine, I see bright horizons for all people of the world. I particularly see bright horizons for Americans in this wonderful country of ours.

It is true that I have lived a life of adversity, but I have been fortunate to have had many wonderful experiences. I am grateful to warm, affectionate friends who gave me the courage and determination to do what I felt needed to be done. I know I have had more recognition than I deserve, but I am thankful for the opportunities that were placed before me, and I only hope that I made the most of them.

High up in the California redwood forest near Meyer's Flat, is a redwood tree with my name on it, the Mary Tsukamoto tree. It was dedicated for me by my colleagues in the Northern Section of the California Association of Childhood Education International in 1976. In the same Avenue of the Giants, stands another tree, this one dedicated to Marielle; we are the only two so honored from a single family. Our trees will stand there forever, and so too, I hope, will the spirit remain in our public schools to encourage children to reach their greatest potential for they are the foundation of our future, our great hope for the America of our dreams.

In July of 1986 the National JACL recognized me in Chicago as the JACLer of the Biennium. Imagine me being honored along with

Ellison Onizuka, the astronaut, who was awarded posthumously due to his tragic death with the "Challenger!" As a child in the strawberry fields of Florin, I could not have imagined such a wonderful thing happening to me. I am deeply humbled.

In November, 1986, Al and I celebrated our 50th wedding anniversary. Hundreds of friends and relatives from all over the U.S. shared the occasion with us. I am grateful to have been so blessed with family and friends and my beloved partner, Al. I cannot sit back though, for our work must go on, and there is still much to do. In a way, we have only begun.

Almost half a century has passed since 1942. Americans know now that our relocation and internment was a mistake made by our country's leaders. They know that the U.S. Constitution was ignored by the racists who called for our removal after Pearl Harbor, but they also know that the seeds for these actions were planted long ago in California's fertile soil. It is recognized now that our rights as citizens were thrown to the winds during that time of hysteria– our rights, guaranteed by the U.S. Constitution and including rights of property and due process. Al and I were only two of thousands who suffered these wrongs, but the story is much the same for us all.

I have summoned up the courage to tell my personal story because I believe that Americans deserve to know the truth. When I hear of those who say that the internment never happened, and that only those who wanted to live in camp were given that protection, I know how vital it is that the truth be told. Truth will assure us a government of the people, by the people, and for the people.

As an American of Japanese ancestry, I believe that all children should know what happened during this chapter of our country's history. That is the only way we can be assured that what happened to us will never happen to any American ever again. Truth is our assurance!

We the People of the United States, in order to form a more perfect Union, establish justice, insure domestic tranquility, provide for the common defense, promote the general welfare, and secure the blessings of liberty to ourselves and our posterity, do ordain and establish this Constitution of the United States of America.

This noble document has survived intact and served us well for two hundred years. Let it speak for at least another two centuries for all people in this free nation.

As I reflect upon the ideas of the Great Emancipator, the thought comes to me that if America ever chose to live by a government of "We, *some* of the people" instead of "We *the* people," at that very moment, a great idea would begin to perish from this earth. How terribly fragile our democracy is, and how necessary it is that we all become fierce guardians of our constitutional form of government.

The end

Pages from the Tsukamoto Family Album

I could hardly believe that I was actually teaching school. I tried hard to teach my students to think as well as to read and write and do math.

Our Issei mothers and fathers finally became citizens after weeks and weeks of study. Many could not complete the course because they were too old.

We toured Japan, China, and the Far East as well as Europe. Al was a great tour guide, and we always had plenty of friends and relatives to join us.

A highlight was finding the family of Al's cousin in Hokkaido. We all posed for a family picture.

We hosted three young boys from Japan— Masahiro Ando (on my left); Sachiya, Mr. Kume's grandson; and Tatsuya Fuji, grandson of Al's cousin.

Imagine having three teenagers around to keep track of! They were so interested in learning English that it was easy to keep them busy.

281

The Week of Remembrance gave us an opportunity to educate the public as well as school children. We were grateful to the Elk Grove Unified School District for allowing us to set up the exhibit in the Board Room.

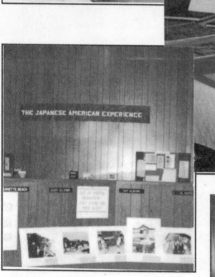

We constructed an entire barrack room just as it had been in camp. Children were always so amazed to think of an entire family living in such a little bit of space.

Our sleepy little town of Florin had never seen anything like the Once-in-a-lifetime Reunion of July, 1985.

Congressman Bob Matsui was our speaker.

We built our float in the Tsukamoto back yard. So many helped!

Kiyo Sato-Viacrucis marched with the Sacramento Veterans of Foreign Wars, Nisei Post 8995. Kiyo was a captain in the Air Force Nurse Corps.

283

Dr. Harold Langley, Curator at the Smithsonian Institution, spoke to us at the 1986 Time of Remembrance.

On Sunday morning, Illa Collin invited us into the Sacramento County Building so that Dr. Langley could see the mural by Yoshio Taylor to commemorate the Japanese experiences in the U.S. Hiroshi Kashiwagi's beautiful poem is a perfect complement to the splendid mural.

That's Supervisor Illa Collin next to Dr. Langley, and Marielle between Al and me.

284

We were surprised at what was found in people's barns and garages. Some trunks had not been opened in forty years—since people came back from camp.

To think that this "junk" is needed in Washington for the Smithsonian exhibit—It is hard to believe! We are part of American history.

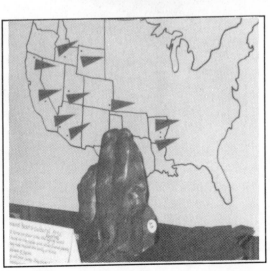

Al and I boxed up clothes, furniture, farm tools, and camp art and took it all to San Francisco where the Smithsonian people went through it and decided which objects they needed for the exhibit. Moon Kurima donated a lot of family things. Al is holding Grandma's suitcase. The wooden box was used to ship Grandpa's belongings from camp to Florin.

Sacramento Bee photo

Al and I are enjoying our last days on our little farm. We own the acreage, but soon our quiet fields with the quail and jackrabbits will be part of Sacramento's development as the city moves southward. Except for camp, Al has lived here ever since he was a little boy...68 years. Now it will soon be time to move.

287

WE THE PEOPLE OF THE UNITED STATES IN ORDER TO FORM A MORE PERFECT UNION, ESTABLISH JUSTICE, INSURE DOMESTIC TRANQUILITY, PROVIDE FOR THE COMMON DEFENCE, PROMOTE THE GENERAL WELFARE, AND SECURE THE BLESSINGS OF LIBERTY TO OURSELVES AND OUR POSTERITY, DO ORDAIN AND ESTABLISH THIS CONSTITUTION FOR THE UNITED STATES OF AMERICA.

AMENDMENT I. Congress shall make no law respecting an establishment of religion, or prohibiting the free exercise thereof; or abridging the freedom of speech, or of the press, or the right of the people peaceably to assemble, and to petition the Government for a redress of grievances.

AMENDMENT V. No person shall be held to answer for a capital, or otherwise infamous crime, unless on a presentment or indictment of a Grand Jury, except in cases arising in the land or naval forces, or in the Militia, when in actual service in time of War or public danger; nor shall any person be subject for the same offence to be twice put in jeopardy of life or limb, nor shall be compelled in any criminal case to be a witness against himself, nor be deprived of life, liberty, or property, without due process of law; nor shall private property be taken for public use without just compensation.

AMENDMENT XIV. Section I. All persons born or naturalized in the United States and subject to the jurisdiction thereof, are citizens of the United States and of the State wherein they reside. No State shall make or enforce any law which shall abridge the privileges or immunities of citizens of the United States; nor shall any State deprive any person of life, liberty, or property, without due process of law; nor deny to any person within its jurisdiction the equal protection of the laws.

NOTES FROM MARY'S JOURNAL

1867   Kuzo Tsukamoto is born; he is the 9th one, Misasa Machi, Asagun, Hiroshima.

1879   Ito Kadokawa, 4th child, is born, Midorii, Hiroshima.

1885   Japan approves emigration; first ship leaves with laborers. Kuzo orphaned; at 18, he leaves on the second boatload recruited for labor in the sugar cane plantations of Hawaii.

1888   Kuzo sails on a Russian fishing vessel to Vancouver, Canada; labors for several years in salmon fishing and canneries; coal mines in Montana, Wyoming; railroad repair and maintenance jobs in Idaho, Utah; plants grapes in Central Valley of California.

1892   Kuzo Tsukamoto arrives in Florin; leases land, and tries to raise berries.

1894   Kuzo returns to Hiroshima to seek a wife; His sister, Chiyone, is married to Jinkichi Segawa. Kuzo's niece, Sen Segawa, marries Ito's oldest brother. From that bond, Kuzo marries Ito Kadokawa, a fifteen year old. Ito is unwilling and too young to leave her family. Kuzo goes on to Florin to find a place to settle.

1902   Ito arrives in Florin with her six year old nephew, Etsuzo Kadokawa, child of Toraichi and Sen (Segawa) Kadokawa. They adopt him as George Tsukamoto and love him dearly.

1907   Ito and Kuzo are overjoyed; their first born, Hatsuko Margaret, arrives; Kuzo is forty years old.

1909   Hisako Edith, is born.

1912   Iwao Alfred, the first son, is born.

1913   Y. Tsuda entered into the lives of the Tsukamotos and the people of Florin. He starts the first Sunday School and a Japanese language school.

1914   Japanese Methodist Church is started, meeting in homes.

1915   Kuzo leads the congregation in a fund drive; a new Japanese Methodist church building is constructed.

1917   Namiyo (Nami) is born.

1920   All these years Kuzo and Ito leased land from John Reese and share cropped on Gerber Road. Reese decides to triple the rent because farmers are making good money after World War I. The Tsukamotos move to their new property purchased by the three older children on Florin- Perkins Road; Kuzo, as their legal guardian, draws up the papers with a lawyer to make sure the Alien Land Law is abided by.

1921   George marries and Kuzo takes out a mortgage on the Stockton Road property to start him out on his L and M Garage in Sacramento; Al and his sisters ride on the Traction Line to visit the dentist and enjoy George and Sawayo in Sacramento.

1923   Kuzo and Ito's first grandchild, Percy, is born to George and Sawayo.

The Florin School is separated into East and West-separate schools for white and Japanese children.

1925   Hatsuko Margaret marries a baseball player, second baseman for the Florin Champs: Charles Ogata from Seattle.

Chosei Taro Dakuzaku brings his family to Florin and enrolls his three older daughters at Florin East School. Taro had left Okinawa at the age of 17 after marrying Kame Yoshinaga; he worked in Hawaii and then in San Francisco where he was during the Earthquake. Taro labored all over the Valley; got a job with the Southern Pacific Railroad as a cook; started the Capital Laundry on Geary Street in SF with his brother Choshin and friends. Called Mom in 1912; daughter Masako left in Japan to care for her grandmother; Ruth born in 1913, Mary in 1915, Isabel in 1917, Jean in 1920, Julia in 1922, George in 1925.

1928   Hisako Edith graduates from Elk Grove High; first Nisei student body treasurer.

1929   Edith marries Harold Yasuji Ouchida, a bright young businessman, president of the new Northern California Farms Company, one of the strawberry shippers. Al goes to work for his brother-in-law at the age of 16; is soon a key berry salesman at the Y Street Market.

1931   Al graduates from Elk Grove High; a star halfback on the varsity football team; baseball player; star basketball player.

1933   I, Mary Dakuzaku, graduate from Elk Grove High; I won medals as the top scholar in the freshman and sophomore classes. Ella Yoshinaga won the freshman medal when I took the sophomore medal; practice was discontinued the next year.

I enroll at College of the Pacific because of the determination of Mable Barron, my caring teacher.

1934-35 Important, exciting years full of expanding world experiences for a country girl going to college.

Kuzo and Ito visit Japan. They sell inherited land and treat relatives to a wonderful vacation.

I receive a beautiful kimono from Kuzo and Ito; I am Al's girl. I use the kimono for dramas and dances at COP.

My arthritis becomes very serious. I drop out of dancing; it is unbelievable to be nineteen and so crippled.

1936   I drop out of college unable to finish my senior year.

Al and I are married on a very special day, November 22. My sweetheart of three years and I share our gladness with our family and friends and begin our life together.

1937   A darling little girl comes into our lives as we become a family. We coin her name from both parents, Marielle Bliss, and she is destined to become just that, full of life and enthusiasm for making the world a beautiful place for all.

1939   Young JACL members integrate the Florin School; contacts are made with the county superintendent R.E. Golway, Isabelle Jackson, and the school trustees: Harry French, Chris Frasinetti, and Frank Stewart. Ten years have passed since my graduation, and now finally, it is integrated after 16 years of segregation.

1941   December 7—Pearl Harbor is bombed. Our hearts are torn apart!

1942   February 19—President Roosevelt signs Executive Order 9066. We do not yet understand what it means nor what is to follow.

March 21—Congress passes Public Law 77-503 legalizing Executive Order 9066; it is now a crime punishable by a $5000 fine and one year in jail if we disobey.

1942   April—I am hired by the Florin JACL as a secretary, while others work frantically to keep the last strawberry crop from being a total loss. We buy war bonds, write letters to cheer our worried Nisei boys in the Army, roll bandages and try to organize a Red Cross group. We enroll in First Aid classes.

Mr. Iwasa commits suicide; FBI harassed him to talk; they didn't know he had had a stroke and his speech was impaired.

Mrs. Nishimura gets scarlet fever and dies; leaves a family of six children and a husband who always relied upon his strong willed wife; none of us are allowed to congregate so cannot even get to the funeral.

Curfew frightens us. Mrs. Shintaku has a painful ear infection; her son runs over in the dark; it is past eight and none of us of Japanese ancestry are allowed out; Al sneaks his truck out and drives with dimmed lights to get Dr. Ito. We are fearful.

To get to town we have to go beyond our five mile travel restriction. We are on pins and needles every time we do it for fear of being caught.

Isabel gets caught without a driver's license on her way to Motor Vehicle to get it renewed. Police stop her and we send a friend to help.

We are told to report for registration, seat assignments, and word of our destination on May 24 and 25. We leave in a few days.

May 29—Our day of departure; we are prisoners in our own country, imposed upon by our own government for being Japanese, nothing more.

Late afternoon, in the sweltering heat of Fresno, we enter behind barbed wire enclosure and see manned watchtowers and men at attention with machine guns in their hands. We are interned at Fresno Assembly Center.

October 14—we are driven out of Fresno and wait almost all day in a hot, stuffy train. Toward evening, the train heads south past Bakersfield and across the state boundary. By dawn we see the Colorado River and view the Grand Canyon in the distance. We are enroute to Jerome Relocation Camp.

For five days and nights we ride to our sad destination on a cramped train.

October 18—we arrive exhausted on Sunday night. We have not had any food all day because the dining car never made it to our train in Arkansas.

December 25—our first Christmas away from home; I write a Christmas letter to the President and Eleanor Roosevelt; hundreds of messages are mailed from Denson, Arkansas, 9-8-E, the place we call Jerome. Cold and frosty, we face our first critical emergency—there is not enough fuel for our needs.

1943   Christmas and the New Year are bleak, but our children learn there are good Christians on the "outside" who care about us. We are grateful.

Trouble brews. There are beatings and riots reported from other camps.

The military announces that they will accept volunteers to form an all Nisei fighting combat unit. They write up a questionnaire with yes, yes or no, no answers. Only those who are loyal and totally pro-American will be allowed to relocate as free people. Families and friends are divided.

Spring, summer and into fall, the complicated problems generated by the government blunder on and mushroom into an ugly tragedy. Finally, when we are segregated and the dissidents sent to Tule Lake, we are free to breathe again and be ourselves.

Quietly, in my sanctuary, other things are developing.

In January I mailed my first story to the *Christian Herald*. It appears in the April, 1943 issue.

Eleanor Roosevelt's letter to me arrived in January. I could not believe my good fortune to have the First Lady write to me.

Brave souls organize a YWCA in the camp. I become the first director of Denson Y.

March—I go out of camp for the first time for a week—to Jackson, Mississippi to attend a leadership workshop.

May—I am invited to lead a seminar at the Hollister Student Christian Conference. I take Marielle and experience a great week in the Ozark Mountains, but I feel like a fish out of water and greatly inadequate.

July— Al and I go to Indiana with Jessie Trout, a missionary from Canada who spent 20 years in Japan. Jessie's idea is to bring a team of three "Exhibit A" Nisei (Al, I and Paul Sato, a farmer from the Stockton area) to agricultural Indiana to convince people of the need for our resettlement.

It is a year of parting as we say goodbye to family members and friends who leave camp. I continue my work with the YWCA and work to build a strong USO in Jerome.

October—Al leaves camp with a group of young men and fathers who travel to Indiana, Ohio, Chicago, and finally settle in Kalamazoo. Al gets a job in a paper mill.

November—Al wires for me and Marielle to come to Kalamazoo We leave our friends sadly, but joyously become free and leave Jerome.

Ojiichan, Obaachan and Nami are separated from us for the first time as they stay in camp. Marielle, Al and I become a family again in Kalamazoo. Al gets a night job at the Peter Pan Bakery where Hugh Kiino works. We celebrate our second Christmas away from Florin, but we are free in Kalamazoo; it is a white Christmas, the first for us all.

1944

February—Father Dakuzaku and family come from Chicago to live with us at Lay Boulevard. Mom, Julia, and George are all with us now. They all work at the Peter Pan Bakery except Mom and me.

March—We miss our family and friends very much. They write that Grandpa Ouchida is dying of cancer. Jerome will be the first of the ten WRA relocation camps to close.

Al, Marielle and I take a week to visit Jerome and attend Grandpa Ouchida's funeral. It is a strange but wonderful feeling to visit and see how the USO is doing its work.

April— We have had many happy new experiences, made new friends and come face to face with harsh reality. Wonderful church friends have made us feel welcome.

July— We move to a big house at 410 Dutton, a block away from school and in a nice neighborhood, close to stores and church.

August—George is drafted into the U.S. Army. He goes to Reno on a furlough and brings back Harold's green Dodge. The tires are bad and we can't get new ones.

December—President Roosevelt must lift the ban on persons of Japanese ancestry. The Mitsue Endo case has finally made it to the Supreme Court. It has been determined that "the government cannot detain a citizen without due process and without a cause." Finally, we can return home.

1945

January—A few friends anxiously go home to Florin so they will be able to harvest their 1945 crop. It is a disaster; the public is not ready. There are burnings and beatings. The agitation to keep us out is bad news.

Spring—Julia finds out the hard way that being Japanese has drawbacks. She is not allowed to work days at the bakery. She becomes depressed and joins the WACS in desperation.

April— President Roosevelt dies. The nation is shocked.

Our all-Nisei fighting combat team blazes a trail of victories that reach front page news. We are so proud of our boys!

May— War in Europe is over. Hitler is dead! The allies have won the war Our boys will be returning home.

The Ogatas leave Gila and settle on a peach farm in Eau Claire, Michigan. They bring Kuzo and visit us in Kalamazoo.

Al decides to take our two fathers to visit New York and Washington. The war is not yet over with Japan, so we travel carefully. People think we are Chinese so we are safe.

June— We prepare to pack again and leave for California; Mother, Jean and Father are anxious to return to Florin; they leave on the train. George is in the Army in Europe, and Julia is now stationed in Pasco, Washington.

July— We drive away in Harold's Dodge. head for Gila, Arizona.

July 5— We reach the hot desert city of Gila. Everyone has deep sun tans and is very brown. We hardly recognized our relatives and Florin friends.

July 9— We drive off—Harold, Edith, Little Sonny, Hitoshi (Harold's younger brother), Al, Marielle, and I. We head for our homes in Florin.

July 10—We drive almost non-stop afraid of what may happen to us if we do more than stop for gas. In the early dawn, we arrive home in Florin. The town is changed–so many buildings are no longer there.

August—Grandma, Grandpa, and our neighbors, the Okamotos and Nittas, return to Florin.

We are devastated by the news of Julia's death.

Marielle enrolls in Florin Grammar School and attends school in the same room I was once in. It is no longer segregated.

We help Bob Fletcher harvest his grapes. The 1945 crop is his.

Families continue to return all fall and winter. Some have places to stay; others manage somehow.

1946   We struggle to make it on the farm.

October—We take time to celebrate the 50th wedding anniversary of Ojiisan and Obaasan. Relatives and friends gather with us.

Marielle and I are busy with church and MYF, children's choir, Girl Scouts, PTA, Women's Society.

1948   We learn to put into practice Mike Masaoka's Japanese American Creed and learn how to become politically active. I write letters, make speeches and tell about our Nisei veterans home from the battlefields as heroes. We win the Evacuee Claims bill, but it is a monumental disappointment. Without proof of ownership, only a few qualified for their claims of loss.

1949   District Spiritual Life Secretary for Women's Society of the Methodist Church; I attend a summer program on missions at COPandmeetMarjorie Poole, a nationally renown speaker and writer. She feels my message needs to be told.

Al decides to pull out our grape vines and quit farming.

Isabelle Jackson looks at me and asks me if I would become a teacher. My entire life changes as I go back to college.

Fall—I sign a contract to teach in the same school I graduated from when it was segregated. I enter the teaching profession as a proud American.

Al is hired at the Sacramento Signal Depot, only a few minutes away from our home.

1950

March—I go to Cleveland, Ohio, to the World Conference for Methodist Women and speak at a seminar group chaired by Marjorie Poole. It is my first airplane ride.

1952 We campaign to win Issei citizenship rights; McCarran-Walter bill is passed.
January—Florin School moves to new building on Kara Drive.

1954 Issei Citizenship class graduates; they become citizens. I am initiated into the Beta Pi Chapter of Delta Kappa Gamma.

1954 I begin demonstrating at workshops—Better Teaching Conference sponsored by CTA; my class does two part singing at Sacramento State and on television.

1955 Ojiisan and Obaasan go on their first plane ride to visit their children and grandchildren in Chicago and Benton Harbor.

Marielle is a popular Elk Grove High student—an orator. She graduates.

Marielle and Nami take a train to Chicago and visit relatives and friends. Marielle works in Kalamazoo during the summer at Ruth and Hugh Kiino's restaurant.

I become president of the Sacramento County branch of ACE; new friends, ACE, workshops, demonstration meetings; my teaching is focused upon my interest in social studies and music.

1956 Al is flown to Las Vegas to do special repair work on radar equipment for the Army—all expenses paid.

Marielle goes to Sacramento State; she discovers Co-Delta, a life-saving cortizone derivative that helps me cope with my rheumatoid arthritis.

1957 Marielle transfers to UOP, my school (now a university). We visit Stockton often and keep in touch with her.

Surprise of my life! The PTA gives me an honorary life membership, an unforgettable "This is Your Life" presentation. Mable Barron, Marielle, and my brother George are there.

1958   Chairman of committee and M.C.--we plan a surprise "An Evening for Isabelle Jackson;" nearly 250 friends, former pupils, parents, and teachers attend to honor this great lady.

Board of Trustees announce a new school to be named Isabelle C. Jackson Elementary School on Orange Avenue. Glenn Brunswick is the principal; I am transferred to the new school.

1959   Marielle finishes a busy year as AWS president; is selected as the outstanding senior woman; she graduates.

Our life with Florin Methodist Church takes on a renewed enthusiasm as R. W. Reneau and Helen come to Florin. A miracle happens as we plan for a new church on Palmer House Drive.

I begin my work on the state board of the California ACE as legislative chairperson.

September—Marielle gets a job teaching second grade at Florin School.

1960   Marielle goes to Europe with 17 former college classmates; a fabulous thrilling experience.

1962   I am scheduled to teach at the new Samuel Kennedy School, but the building is not ready. I volunteer to travel 20 miles each day with my class to Pleasant Grove while we wait for our classroom to be finished.

December—We make mochi; purchase a Volkswagen, our third car (family passenger car and a pick-up truck); I drive the new car to school.

1963

April— Finally my students and I are able to move to Kennedy School on Briggs Drive; we say good-bye to faculty and principal Robert Fite at Pleasant Grove.

June— We rent a trailer and drive north to Kent, Washington with Marielle, Esther Shikuma, and a friend to attend the Seattle World's Fair.

July— Demonstrate social studies teaching at Hillborough Elementary School with Helen McGinnis directing; made many wonderful friends including Hilda Taba, an expert in teaching children to think.

1963   We cancel our anniversary plans on the fateful Friday when the nation is saddened by the shocking news of our young and bright president slain!

1964   Much sadness and many deaths: Harold Ouchida dies after being ill for years with TB, cancer and diabetes—Edith is left with six children including Wayne who is still in grammar school.

I am devastated with the shocking news of tuberculosis. I am sent to Ross Sanitarium and embarrassed that all my students at Kennedy School must get skin tests to see if they have contracted the disease from me. Fortunately, they have not.

September 26—Ojiisan quietly breathes his last at the age of 97. I am okay and released from Ross on the day of Kuzo's funeral.

I rest and remain idle during the winter months. On the day we make mochi, December 22, my father, Chosei Dakuzaku, dies at the age of 77, after 17 years of being paralyzed with a stroke.

1965

January—My sister Masako flies from Tokyo to visit Mom and all of us. We convince Mom to go back to Japan with her to meet her grandchildren, her only brother, Anmei Yoshinaga, in Okinawa, and her sister in Miyagi in northern Japan. Mom enjoys her visit immensely and stays several months.

Take six units at Sacramento State and spend an easy, enlightening spring still resting.

August—Marielle is able to fulfill her dream of teaching abroad. With the help of Ray Aka, she gets a job in the Naval Dependent School in Yokohama. We send her happily off to a new adventure.

September—I am back once again at Samuel Kennedy School after a year's leave of absence. John Marshall, a bright ten year old eager student, is in my class.

October—Two shy youngsters, unable to speak English are placed in my class because I speak Japanese. Reiko and Tadakazu Hatch change my style of teaching and affect my attitude and philosophy. I begin to reach into the Japanese culture for bits and pieces to intertwine into my teaching. It seems okay to do this and the children are very interested.

Notes From Mary's Journal

1966   Marielle's glowing report of her experience in the Orient convinces Al and me to go abroad. We take a month's trip to Japan and extend our visit to include Taipei, Bangkok, Hong Kong, Singapore, and Okinawa. I meet my sister's family for the first time; we find Al's lost cousin Wasaku Tsukamoto in Tokyo; we meet the Hiroshima relatives who survived the atom bomb; we meet my mom's brother in Okinawa and see the castle we had heard so much about where Mom had lived and played.

1967   I take more classes in critical thinking and begin to search for my own roots.

1968   Lead our first tour group to Japan; Edith, Nami, Charlie, and Kadokawa cousins, Gladys Halverson and many friends from school, church and the Army Depot. We go to Manila and are in an earthquake on the last day of the trip.

1969   April—Go to the ACEI Study Conference in Atlanta, Georgia and report on "The Value of Literature in Understanding Different People of the World." I am a member of the standing committee on Intermediate Childhood Education.

Because I speak Japanese I am asked to interpret when the Tokyo ACE is organized with Mrs. Hatsue Iida as president.

Centennial Year for the Japanese immigrants to America; served on the committee and dedicate the Wakamatsu Colony at Coloma; direct my children in song; my first doll presentation.

Take a trailer trip up north with Mrs. Otani, Grace Kawai, and Marielle; we camp at Crater Lake, Mt. Rainer, Olympia, Victoria; take Mrs. Miki along and go the Prince Rupert on the ferry up the channel; beautiful Banff, Jasper, Glacier, National, Yellowstone—a wonderful trip.

1970   Attend ACEI Study Conference in Denver, Colorado. Hatsue Iida and other educators from Japan also attend; we become penpals.

Al and I take a trip south to Hearst Castle and Ensenada, Mexico. We visit relatives and friends in L.A. on our return. George Tsukamoto, Al's adopted brother, has cancer surgery and is failing fast.

September—Obaasan has an accidental fall in the bathroom and breaks her hip. She is in the hospital for several weeks.

October—Obaasan dies at the age of 91 and goes on to join Ojiisan.

December—George Kadokawa Tsukamoto dies at the age of 75.

1971

July— Al and I lead our second group to a wonderful tour of the Orient. We take Arlene and Ted, Nami, Judy Oshiro, the Alton Halversons, Roy Wilsons and other friends. We include a trip up north to Hokkaido and contact Shige Tsukamoto who later leads us to find our long lost relatives.

September—I am given a new assignment at James McKee School in Elk Grove—a third grade.

1972

May— Meet the young Andos from Tokyo with their two year old son, Masahiro; she is a kindergarten teacher, daughter of my ACE friend, Hatsue Iida. They plan to tour America.

June— Take Edith and Mrs. Otani and the rented trailer to visit relatives in Oregon, Vancouver, and Victoria.

August—A wedding for Nami--we drive to Reno to a Catholic church where Nami marries John King. All the nieces and nephews are there and Edith is matron of honor.

1973

March—CACEI study conference with program on intercultural education; a thrilling evening of music and dance with many ethnic groups represented.

Summer—Our first trip to Scandinavia, a two week tour through lovely fjords, mountains and lakes.

I fly to Washington to serve on the International-Intercultural committee with Dr. Leonard Kenworthy.

My story "An American With a Japanese Face" and an article, "Realia for World Understanding" are published in Childhood Education Magazine.

My arthritis becomes more painful. In desperation I try a diet and eating habits suggested by Dr. Collin Dong.

1974 I begin acupuncture treatments with Dr. Dong in San Francisco's Chinatown. Al takes me to appointments every five weeks (for four years); we take many different friends with us to spend the day in the lovely city by the Golden Gate.

301

I organize and put on a doll festival in the James McKee multipurpose room for the entire school and the public; I share my dolls and the values of the Japanese cultures.

March—Marielle and I fly to Washington and display our dolls and kimonos at the ACEI conference. I make a special presentation on "I am Somebody."

July—We rent a motor coach and drive to Spokane for the World's Fair; Hideo and Dorothy Kadokawa go with us; we continue on to Lake Louise and Victoria.

1975   Isabel and Tom Oshiro's son, Neal, is married in a beautiful garden wedding at the Prost's garden in Concord. The bride, Kiyo, beautiful in a flowing wedding gown, changes into a magnificent kimono sent from her family in Fukuoka, Japan.

The Andos come for two weeks; we rent a huge 21' motor home and take Masako, grand daughter Yukari, and the Andos to Crater Lake, the Oregon coast and the redwood highway.

August—Ray and Shizu Aka bring Kyo Machiko, the movie star, her manager Ichikawa-san and friend, Katie Kamikubo, to our home which they use as their headquarters as they travel in a motor coach to Canadian Rockies and travel all around. We have a memorable experience with such great guests.

September—Mom (Kame Dakuzaku) slipped away—her heart gave out. Her brave working days are over.

1976   January—I am not improving with Dr. Dong's treatments; have lost a lot of weight and am in great pain. I can't open the door of our Buick, so Al gets me a Mercury Marquee Brohme; I can at least lift the latch.

June—I am honored at a retirement tea by the James McKee PTA and a great party at Valley Hi Country Club; my last day of school on the 9th—I finish my 26th year of teaching and am now retired.

July—We travel all over the British Isles and western Europe in a Volkswagen minibus—Alice Behm, Eleanor Brunswick, Roy and Nonnie Wilson—an unforgettable summer.

September—a beautiful day in Williams Grove on the Avenue of the Giants. I touch a tree named after me! I am honored for my contributions to International-Intercultural Education.

WE THE PEOPLE

1977   I am hired by the Jan Ken Po Gakko parents as the director of their language and cultural school. It is a summer session and the encounter with Sansei parents and their darling Yonsei children is a turning point in my career as an educator.

August—The Hiroses from Hiroshima come to visit; we rent a giant motor home and with Marielle and Al driving, we travel all around California. They deliver the first thousand cranes (from Sadako's story) to the mayor of Hiroshima.

October—I have surgery–a replaced teflon and plastic elbow.

1978   Jan Ken Po Gakko plans a New Year extended session with a wonderful Japanese New Year potluck.

John Marshall and many exciting young people serve on the board of Jan Ken Po Gakko; the involvement is exciting. We put together the first camp art display. The second thousand cranes are made. Al and I deliver them to the mayor of Hiroshima.

March—We honor Mrs. Kohana Sasaki, the wife of our former minister; 150 former church people gather for a wonderful reunion—the first reunion in Florin.

April— Sudden emergency gallstone surgery; Methodist Hospital for five days.

October—Another great tour; Al and I lead the Orient Paradise Tour; 22 of us visit Japan, Taipei, Hong Kong, Bangkok, Penyang, Singapore. Hiroses, Yasuko and Shuji help us get together with relatives in Hokkaido—Kuzo's brother's family—six generations!

May—Take a two day bus trip to Tule Lake for dedication and pilgrimage sponsored by the JACL and the NCRR (National Coalition for Redress and Reparation).

1979   Al retires after 32 years of service, including camp, from the federal government.

We adopt Buster, our dog, from the Adams family; Al enjoys fishing, Buster, and a new style of living.

We attend the first Sakasa Jinsei demonstration at the Buddhist Church's Obon Bazaar by John Marshall, our godson.

August–Begin serious plans for a book with Elizabeth Pinkerton; read a great deal, research; find journals, diaries and letters from camp.

Finish three years of Jan Ken Po Gakko as the director.

Tear down the leaning barn built so long ago by Kuzo; Hire J. T. Ross to build a fine new garage.

Marielle brings us a stray cat named Hungry. She is transformed into a lovable ruler of our household.

A great step is taken by the JACL and redress becomes a word to reckon with. We witness John Tateishi become national JACL redress director; much is accomplished as he pushes to get legislation passed in Washington; we want a commission to study the entire tragic episode of the internment of 1942.

1980   Charlie Ogata creates a beautiful Japanese garden in our yard. Mr. Nitta gives us choice plants from his farm which is sold—pines, azalias, camellias, and others.

April—Marielle is in charge of a great banquet entertainment in San Francisco for ACEI Study Conference.

Al and I enjoy season tickets to Music Circus and Arm-chair Cruise.

September—We fly to communist China for 19 days with the American-China Friendship Association; a most enlightening experience into an ancient culture.

Send article "Seven Times Down" to Mission Magazine of the Methodist Church; published.

1981   Our third annual Open House for friends and family; following in the old Japanese New Year's custom.

February—Sacramento JACL and NCRR ask me to be their speaker for the February 19th Day of Remembrance.

Speak at the Walerga Dedication.

Plan for the First Homecoming Reunion of former Florin residents who were evacuated in 1942; send out thousands of letters.

The fifth year with Jan Ken Po Gakko, a happy and exciting summer; trip to visit the opening of the "Go For Broke" exhibit at the Presidio; sadly retire from JKPG but it is time to move on to other things. Families surprise me with a memorable surprise party and a magnificent handmade banner made by the loving hands of 88 families. I will cherish it forever.

August 13—An historic day – two buses leave Sacramento to take us to San Francisco and the hearings at Golden Gate University—the Commission on Wartime Relocation and Internment of Civilians; I testify for 8 minutes—way over my time; the beginning of a new phase of my retired years.

1981   August 14—We fly off to Alaska for ten days of touring including a cruise down the channel with a stop at Ketchikan; all very special with dear family and friends.

Finish my writing of Florin's history requested by Sam Tsukamoto for the Sacramento County Soil Conservation Project. It becomes an important source for our later reunion booklets and is published in the *Elk Grove Citizen* and the *Pacific Citizen*.

October—800 return to experience the nostalgic pain of leaving Florin in May 1942; we have a wonderful reunion; they are so surprised to see how Florin has changed.

1982   My arthritis continues to be a trial. I discontinue cortizone and try a new diet using Dr. Airola's book; fast with natural foods; lose 15 pounds and go down dangerously to 100 pounds.

Serious work on writing; strict discipline of getting up at five or six and writing every day; pages and pages.

June—Feel guilty for not working harder for JACL and redress effort.

Begin planning for an event next February 19.

August—Visit Jessie Trout in Owen Sound, Canada, a fond visit with this impressive woman who meant so much to us while we were in camp.

John Tateishi comes to interview me for a chapter in his book *And Justice For All*. I spend three hours talking into a tape recorder.

Notes From Mary's Journal

September—Fred Barbash of the *Washington Post* calls for an interview after hearing my testimony at the San Francisco hearings; this is later published in a ten part series that receives wide public atention. A reporter from the *Dallas Herald* also interviews me.

October—I go to Mercy Hospital to have knee replacement surgery.

A historic monument is dedicated on a beautiful autumn day at the Florin Buddhist church garden; good media and news coverage; the dedication is participated in by an Issei, Riichi Satow; a Nisei, Mary Tsukamoto; and a Sansei, Tom Nakashima. Symbolically, the torch is passed.

1983   February 19—Town Hall meeting on the Day of Remembrance; John Tateishi is our speaker; this is planned by the Florin JACL and the Sacramento NCRR (National Redress and Reparations).

Sacramento City Board of Education adopts the Day of Remembrance for their school curriculum; Betty Pinkerton, Al and I go to the Elk Grove Board to seek such action; they formally pass a resolution to have appropriate observances in classrooms.

We set up an impressive historical exhibit in the YBA Hall and invite students to see it; also open it to the public; a workshop for teachers too.

February 24—The Commission's report is made public; I get many requests for interviews.

April—Illa Collin calls a group of us together to prepare a county ordinance to memorialize the injustice of county workers losing their jobs when the war started; George Matsuoka, Henry Taketa, Al and me.

I meet Senator John Garamendi at the reception to honor Glenn Houde, Elk Grove superintendent of schools; I present Dr. Houde with a Daruma doll.

May—A five day tour of the Grand Canyon, Bryce, Zion.

John Marshall moves to Oakland to pursue his career. We shall miss him.

September—We go to New England to see the fall colors; stop in New York to have lunch with Grant Ujifusa at Random House. My story is the first chapter in John Tateishi's book.

October—Very involved in the redress movement; invited to San Francisco to plan how we can be more effective.

December—Masahiro Ando comes to spend two weeks with us; Al takes him fishing and the Pinkertons have a party; he spends a day at Elk Grove High School with Betty and Sarah

Mochi making, becoming an annual event.

1984   January—New Year's Day—invited Pinkertons, Ubaldes, Herburgers, Fossgreens, Yabes as well as our usual guests; a good feeling of sharing our culture with dear friends.

February—Our second Day of Remembrance with the Honorable Judge William Marutani as our guest speaker; again the exhibit and recognition of Isseis and their veteran sons. We set up the exhibit in the Elk Grove Board Room and then move it to Florin for Saturday night; for the whole week, school children tour the exhibit and I speak to them; we even have a space set up to look like our barrack room in camp.

March—This is the year for 1000 cranes; made them for wedding gifts and to take to the Peace Park in Hiroshima to hang at the children's memorial; Sadako's prayer for peace and long life and dreams becomes a meaningful symbol.

April—Assigned as Area 1 redress coordinator, a contact person for Reno, Marysville, Placer, Sacramento, and Florin chapters; attend many meetings in San Francisco; vigorous letter writing campaign; my computer is wonderful!

May—A book signing party in San Francisco for John Tateishi's book *And Justice For All*; all of us who have our stories included are invited to be there; Pinkertons go with us.

July—Edith suddenly becomes ill and passes away; we meet to make funeral plans; Al and I are scheduled to leave for Germany to attend the famous passion play at Oberammergau; Marielle and Christine are already in Frankfurt waiting for us. The children urge us to go even though we are a day late for the tour.

We hurriedly catch up although we are grieving for Edith and sad not to be able to attend her funeral; we meet the tour in Berne, Switzerland; visit sunny Italy, Austria; the passion play is a glorious experience.

Autumn—We continue to grieve for Edith and miss her very much; I write a tribute for her as I did for Charlie; it will be something for the children.

I serve as M.C. for Sacramento Asian Legal Services and the Asian Community fund-raiser for Coram Nobis.

1984   November—The Florin Historical Society is organized; something new and exciting is planned–a once in a lifetime reunion of everyone who has ever lived in Florin; Al and I are involved in regular meetings.

1985   February 19—We dedicate the mural at the Sacramento County Build ing; Illa Collin has been instrumental in bringing this about; Hiroshi Kashiwagi's beautiful poem "1942-45" is magnificently transferred to a colorful mural by Yoshio Taylor; lovely Japanese symbols explain the travesty of justice as well as the hope and courage and noble effort to become better Americans in a greater America.

March—We hold our third gala Time of Remembrance with our exhibit even better; Eric Saul is our keynote speaker, the curator of the San Francisco Army Presidio museum and creator of the famous "Go For Broke" exhibit now touring the nation. We pay tribute to all veterans and show the film "Nisei Soldier"; the place is packed with more than 400; we honor 17 Issei.

April— Al's dear friend and classmate, Sam Tsukamoto, dies and leaves a great void. It is a sad day; our JACL and the Florin Reunion Commit tee lose an enthusiastic worker.

I am the M.C. at the Angel Island dedication of the East to America exhibit and meet Congressman Norman Mineta who is the speaker; it is a cold, but memorable day.

Spring and Summer—Much research and many contacts are made to collect family histories for our souvenir booklet for the reunion; we discover stories that have remained unknown for the past forty years.

June—A great surprise! I receive a phone call from Go For Broke Inc.; guests from the Smithsonian are coming to Florin to see our artifacts; we hurriedly call everyone to help; Hannah Satow, Henry Taketa, Gene Itogawa, Mike Umeda—they all bring things and help set them up; our usual crew cooks a small dinner for more than 20; it is amazing what we collect in such a short time; the Smithsonian visitors including Dr. Harold Langley, the curator, are pleased to find so many artifacts in Florin—we have farming implements, camp objects, clothing and much, much more. People are finding things in dusty corners of barns and attics; it seems like there was a need to keep things even though we didn't know what that need was. I never could have dreamed that it would be for the Smithsonian.

Our yard is a busy place as we construct a float for the great Florin parade. We make a huge globe with large grapes and strawberries on top; One of Sam Tsukamoto's last grape vines decorates a corner; it is beautiful and such a wonderful symbol of everything we once knew and lived.

July 21-22—The reunion is memorable with a parade, picnic, dance, and the dedication; Congressman Matsui is there; we have souvenir T-shirts, caps and booklets; Florin has never seen such a gala affair.

Gladys Halverson, whom I had adopted as my dear Gladys Halverson Tsukamoto suddenly passes away. We are deeply saddened.

August—I am on TV frequently with interviews and documentaries.

October—We celebrate the 50th anniversary of Florin's JACL; scholarship recipients are honored as well as past JACL presidents; there is a huge surprise for me—Mary Tsukamoto Day; I am recognized by the mayor, Anne Rudin, and Illa Collin for the Board of Supervisors; I am overwhelmed.

1986   A happy New Year's day even though it is not the same without Edith and Gladys. I enjoy preparing foods with Marielle, passing on to her what my mother used to do each New Year.

January—Florin JACL installation at Frasinetti's new restaurant where the winery used to be; Dr. Ken Ozawa is our speaker.

Beta Pi Chapter of Delta Kappa Gamma Society has a luncheon to honor me. It is a special event with Mayor Anne Rudin there.

February 19—Day of Remembrance—the rain goes on and on; roads are closed due to flooding, but the crew sets up the exhibit from Go For Broke at the Capitol; we crowd into the Governor's meeting room; he flies in after surveying flood damage and presents the proclamation.

March—Al and I make many contacts searching for artifacts hidden in barns.

Christine Umeda is our hostess to greet Dr. Langley at the airport; he is duly impressed with what we have found—clothes, books, furniture. Many are marked to be taken to San Francisco where Smithsonian exhibit builders and researchers will check them and select carefully.

Notes From Mary's Journal

Our theme is "On to the Smithsonian in 1987; History forgotten is history repeated." The next morning Illa Collin, Pinkertons, Marielle, Al and I have breakfast with Dr. Langley; Illa shows him the prized mural at the County Building before we take him to the airport.

April— A great surprise call from Grace Uyehara; I am to fly to Washington and testify before the House sub-committee on HR 442; I have to write my 5 minute testimony and also mail a more detailed one to Washington.

July—My red letter year—I cannot believe so much is happening in my 71st year I am called from San Francisco's National JACL headquarters to be at the Chicago convention to accept the award as the JACLer of the Biennium. Imagine! Al takes me to Chicago and everything becomes a whirlwind; July 21 is a high moment of my life!

August 29-31—Florin Homecoming Reunion II for 400 happy people; it is a time of healing and gladness; banquet, picnic, memorial service, dance, and fellowship.

September—Five days with Bill Matsumoto's tour to the 1986 World Expo at Vancouver; full of exciting memories.

November 22—Al and I have been married for fifty years; Nami, John, and Marielle have a wonderful dinner for us. Ruth and Hugh come from Michigan; Isabel, Tom, Jean, Art, George, Grace and cousins Jackie and Neal, Tom and Dorothy—make the evening full; 220 dear friends and relatives join us; there is a slide show program of our fifty years and surprises galore! John Marshall, 1000 cranes, a tiered cake, and special decorations.

December—The exciting year catches up to me with flu and a nagging cough that keep me confined for most of the month; missed four Sunday church services; I sing in the Christmas Eve service, but should have stayed in bed.

1987   January—For the first time in many years, we cancel our New Year's Open House; my cold lingers on; enjoyed the platter of delicious food brought over by niece Arlene.

Florin-Perkins Road is undergoing drastic changes; the old Benedict house is demolished and familiar landmarks are disappearing; the acreage around our farm to the west has a completely new look with giant warehouse buildings which are rented to small business; street lights and a widened four lane smooth road are replacing our old country road. The

entire land around us is changing; toward Elk Grove are new subdivisions with hundreds of new houses going up in what used to be strawberry farms and grape vineyards.

Florin JACL has had a secret committee working to honor me as the National JACLer of the Biennium; I am surprised that they kept it so quiet; it is a wonderful evening at the new Sheraton Sunrise Hotel. All my dear friends and relatives are there along with Betty Barron Nelson, Mary Barron Berganz and John to represent the family of Mable Barron, my mentor who transformed a shy frightened child into a brave spokes person and activist of the 1980s.

Joy is multiplied when cousin Shizu and Ray Aka come from Tokyo; Ray is the recipient of the coveted medal from the Emperor and the Japanese government; it is called "The Third Medal of the Rising Sun on a Maroon Ribbon" and is given to only a few distinguished persons outside of Japanese nationals. Ray has been honored for nearly forty years of service to improve and establish harmonious relations between Japan and the United States.

What a busy month—Al quietly and faithfully helps me dress and drives me to every JACL installation dinner meeting throughout the Valley; I speak for our redress legislative effort at French Camp, Merced, Placer, Marysville, and Reno—every weekend we are on a busy schedule!

Something new and significant is developing. Mayor Rudin and Illa Collin are organizing a commission to help celebrate the 200th birthday of the U.S. Constitution in the city and county. It means many meetings, a sub-committee on education, meeting with clubs and other organizations, but a valuable and meaningful effort.

February—My 19th year as exhibitor of my dolls at the Japanese Cultural Fair sponsored by the Florin Japanese Language School connected to the Florin Buddhist Church. It is a significant cultural education event for the entire Sacramento area and it is for the public.

I speak to the Elk Grove Board of Education requesting their support for our Bicentennial project and our presentation of our internment experience; there is unanimous support and a resolution is adopted.

March—A truckload of fabricated barrack parts is greeted by our crew of workers; our exhibit is once again constructed for the children; it gets better and better each year; Anna Kato is the coordinator for the school district; Al and I get the workers and the items to be displayed. Each day bus loads of children come with their parents and teachers to hear my

1987   presentation and see the exhibit. We do this for an entire week. Letters
from the children make me realize what an emotional and intellectual
impact we are making. More than 750 children visit the exhibit—from
fourth graders to high school seniors.

March 28—A beautiful and exciting day—our Time of Remembrance
with Dr. Peter Irons as our speaker; Dr. Irons is author of *Justice at War*;
he makes us think about ordinary people who speak up for their beliefs
as many have done in America. We serve Asian food to 400; books are
displayed along with the entire camp exhibit including the barrack; many
dignitaries honor us with their presence: Elk Grove school district
superintendent Robert Trigg, Board president Kay Albiani, Dr. Bartley
Lagomarsino; Roy Herburger of the *Citizen*, Rick Abrams and Judy
Tachibana from the *Bee*, Sandra Gin Yep from Channel 3, Dr. Linbaugh
from UOP, Dr. Carlson from American River College, Illa Collin, Terry
Kastanis (City Council) and Judge Frank Richardson, Chairman of the
Bicentennial Commission.

April— We make exciting plans to attend the opening of the exhibit at
the Smithsonian on October 1; many of us plan to be in Washington D.C.
for the great event.

It is time to finish the book.

BIBLIOGRAPHY

Bosworth, Alan. *America's Concentration Camps*. New York: W. Norton and Co., 1967.

Brookman, Phillip. *The Other Side of Infamy*. Stockton: Stockton JACL, 1983.

Chuman, Frank. *Bamboo People—the Law and Japanese Americans*. Del Mar, California: Publisher's Inc., 1976.

Conrat, Maisie and Richard. *Executive Order 9066—the Internment of 110,000 Japanese Americans*. Cambridge: MIT Press, 1972.

Daniels, Roger. *Concentration Camps U.S.A.: Japanese Americans and World War II*. New York: Rinehart and Winston, 1971.

Daniels, Roger, Taylor, Sandra, and Kitano, Harry, (editors). *Japanese Americans from Relocation to Redress*. Salt Lake: University of Utah Press, 1986.

DeWitt, General John L. *Final Report—Japanese Evacuation from the West Coast*. Washington D.C.: U.S. Printing Office, 1943.

Drinnon, Richard. *Keeper of the Concentration Camps: Dillon Myer and American Racism*. Berkeley: U.C. Press, 1987.

Duus, Masayo, *Unlikely Liberators, Men of the 100th and 442nd*. Honolulu: University of Hawaii Press, 1987.

Embrey, Sue Kunitomi. *The Lost Years—1942-46*. Los Angeles: Moonlight Publications, 1972.

Fisher, A.R. *Exile of a Race*. Seattle: Ford T. Publishers, 1965.

Fukei, Budd. *The Japanese American Story*. Minneapolis: Dillon Press, 1976.

Girdner, Audrie, and Loftis, Anne. *The Great Betrayal*. New York: Macmillan, 1969.

Grodzins, Morton. *Americans Betrayed: Politics and the Japanese Evacuation*. Chicago: University Press, 1949.

Harrington, Joseph D. *Yankee Samurai, Secret Role of Nisei in America's Pacific Victory*. Detroit: Pettigrew Enterprises, 1979.

Hironaka, Peter. *Report From Round Eye Country, a Collection of Sketches, both Verbal and Visual, by a Transplanted American*. Dayton: Graphic Concept Center, 1981.

Hosokawa, Bill. *Nisei: the Quiet Americans*. New York: William Morrow and Co., 1969.

Hosokawa, Bill and Mike Masaoka.. *They Call Me Moses Masaoka, an American Saga*. New York: William Morrow and Co., Inc., 1987.

Houston, James and Jeannie Wakatsuki. *Farewell to Manzanar*. Boston: Houghton-Mifflin, 1973.

Irons, Peter. *Justice at War: the Japanese American Internment Cases*. New York: Oxford University Press, 1983.

Ishigo, Estelle. *Lone Heart Mountain*. Los Angeles, UCLA, Hollywood JACL, 1972.

Kikumura, Akemi. *Through Harsh Winters*. Novato, California: Chandler and Sharpe, 1981.

Kitagawa, Daisuke. *Sansei and Nisei; the Internment Years*. New York: Seabury Press Inc., 1967.

Kitano, Harry. *Japanese Americans, the Evolution of a Subculture*. Englewood Cliffs, New Jersey: Prentice Hall, 1969.

Levine, Dr. Robert and Colbert, Dr. Rhode. *Japanese American Community—Three Generation Study*. New York: Praeger CBS Educational Professional Publishers, 1983.

Leighton, Alex. *The Governing of Man—General Principles and Recommendations Based on Experience at the Japanese Relocation Camp*. Princeton: Princeton University Press, 1945.

McWilliams, Carey. *Prejudice: Japanese Americans, the Symbol of Intolerance*. Boston: Little, Brown and Co., 1944.

Myer, Dillon S. *Inside Story of Uprooted Americans*. Tucson: University of Arizona Press, 1971.

Noda, Kesa. *Yamato Colony: 1906-1960 Livingston, California*. Merced, California: Merced JACL Chapter, 1981.

Okada, John. *No, No Boy*. San Francisco: Combined Asian American Resources Project Inc., 1976.

Penrose, Eldon. *California Nativism—Organized Opposition to the Japanese, 1890-1913*. Saratoga, California: R. And E. Research Associates, 1973.

Rodino, Peter, *Chairman of Committee on the Judiciary. Hearings Before the Subcommittee on Administrative Law and Governmental Relations of the Committee of the Judiciary,* House of Representatives, 99th Congress. Washington: U.S. Government Printing Office, April 28 and July 23, 1986.

Saiki, Patsy Sumie. *Gambare! An Example of Japanese Spirit.* Honolulu: Kisaku, Inc., 1982.

San Mateo Chapter of the Japanese American Citizens League. *1872-1942: A Community Story.* San Mateo, 1981.

Sarasohn, Eileen Sunada. *The Issei—Portrait of a Pioneer, an Oral History.* Palo Alto: Pacific Books, 1983.

Sone, Monica. *Nisei Daughter.* Boston: Little, Brown and Co., 1953.

Spicer, Ed. H. Hansen, Asael T., Luomala, Katherine, Opler, Marvin K. *Impounded People.* Tucson: University of Arizona Press, 1969.

Tanaka, Chester. *Go For Broke, a Pictorial History of the Japanese American 100th Infantry Battalion and the 442nd Regimental Combat Team.* Richmond, California: Go For Broke Inc., 1982.

Tateishi, John. *And Justice For All.* New York: Random House, 1984.

tenBroek, Jacobus, Barnhart, Edward N., Watson, Floyd W. *Prejudice, War and The Constitution.* Berkeley: U.C. Press, 1954.

Thomas, Dorothy Swaine, Nishimoto, Richard. *The Spoilage.* Berkeley: U.C. Press, 1946.

Uchida, Yoshiko. *Desert Exile.* Seattle: University of Washington Press, 1982.

Uchida, Yoshiko. *Journey Home.* New York: Atheneum, 1978.

Uchida, Yoshiko. Journey to Topaz. New York: Charles Scribner's Son, 1971.

Uchida, Yoshiko. *Samurai of Gold Hill.* New York: Charles Scribner's Son. 1972.

Weglyn, Michi. *Years of Infamy, the Untold Story of America's Concentration Camps.* New York: William Morrow and Co., Inc., 1976.

Wilson, Robert A., and Hosokawa, Bill. *East to America—A History of the Japanese in the United States.* New York: William Morrow and Co., 1980.

EPILOGUE

Our book was ready just in time for our first book signing party on September 20, 1987, where we experienced the thrill of being authors. The Florin JACL, thanks to the dedicated leadership of Andy Noguchi and Twila Tomita, sponsored our party with Tom Nakashima as a wonderful master of ceremonies. Anne Rudin, Sacramento's busy mayor, took time from her last hours of campaigning to join us. (We celebrated her re-election two days later.) Friends, relatives, and colleagues came – more than 200 hundred of them! Suddenly, *We the People* was off and running.

And, we've been running ever since! Already we are going into our second printing, a step we never dreamed we would take so soon.

Our big day was October 1 in Washington, D.C. when the Smithsonian opened its new exhibit to celebrate the two hundred years of the U.S. Constitution. There we were on the steps of the Capitol and later with special tickets for the exhibit - "A More Perfect Union-Japanese Americans and the U.S. Constitution." What a surprise to see Mary featured so prominently; we knew they were using her voice, but we were unprepared to see her on video monitors and such an extensive display featuring Florin as well. The Florin exhibit is one of the first to be seen - the entire history of strawberry and grape farming with the artifacts we found in old barns and garages. A huge poster-sized picture of Mary's mother in her berry bonnet working in the strawberry field covers one wall of the display. We wonder how they ever created such an excellent copy from that tiny, faded snapshot, the same one we used in our book.

The entire exhibit is an emotional trip through American History, the story of injustice and the continuing struggle through the courts, slow and painful, but yet, one tiny step forward all the time. From the moment you reach the top of the escalator on the third floor of the Museum of American History and find yourself face to face with a huge photograph of the Constitution framing a camp photo of little children pledging allegiance to the flag, you know this is no ordinary exhibit. There is something about those prisoner children, hands across their hearts and faces so trusting and sincere, that jars you uncomfortably. Immediately you realize that "A More Perfect Union" is going to be different from what you expected. By the time you

316

walk out and see Mary Tsukamoto again on a final television monitor, you have been totally immersed in the story, trying to absorb hundreds of messages, some subtle, others boldly challenging your thoughts. You find yourself saying, "Could this really have happened in America?"

Dr. Roger Kennedy's words rang in our ears as the Director of the Smithsonian Institution explained: "The reason for doing this kind of show is to make it clear that we don't always get it right, but we keep on trying. It is a show that deals with Americans behaving toward other Americans."

Chester Tanaka summed it up: "After 45 years, they are finally telling the whole story with all the credibility and majesty of the U.S. government behind it."

The exhibit will be at the Smithsonian for at least the next five years - long enough to educate thousands of Americans and visitors as well.

We had two more book signings in Washington - one at the Rayburn House Office Building on Capitol Hill, thanks to our Congressman, Robert Matsui; the other was at our hotel. These were our first opportunities to introduce our book to people who did not know us. Their response was wonderful and a taste of what was to come.

Reporters and television cameras followed Mary all over Washington and resulted in numerous interviews and articles in newspapers across the nation. Shortly after our return to Sacramento, she was invited to return to Washington to be filmed for the TODAY show. There was our book, only two months old, and already on national television! How lucky could we get?

That's the way it's been ever since. We have been deluged with cards and letters from all over America and even some from other countries. Many families and long-time friends have found the courage to talk to one another about their experiences. Often our book orders are for entire families - parents and grandparents wanting to make sure that those who come after them will know how it was for them during this chapter of their lives.

On September 17, the actual birthday of the Constitution,

EPILOGUE

HR 442 (aptly named for the famed World War unit), the Civil Liberties Act of 1987, passed the House by a significant vote of 243 to 141. We are still waiting for the Senate vote*, and then hopefully, the President's signature to bring the story to an appropriate end.

In February of 1988, Dr. Thomas Crouch, Chairman of the Department of Social and Cultural History and supervisor of the Japanese American exhibit, came to Florin and Elk Grove for the Week of Remembrance sponsored by Elk Grove Unified School District and the Florin community. Dr. Crouch spoke to high school students, and under the leadership of teacher Mary Kashing, a videotape was made for use in history classes. Included was an interview with Mary Tsukamoto so that students would understand the connection of national events to the live of people in their community.

"Florin at the Smithsonian" - it's like a dream come true, and for Mary Tsukamoto it *is* a dream come true. Her life will never be the same!

COMMENTS FROM OUR READERS

PIERRE MOULIN wrote to us from France: "You deserve congratulations. You did a fine job." Pierre is the author of a new book. *U.S. Samurai en Lorraine*, the story of the Battle of Bruyeres and the incredible friendship between Bruyeres, France and its liberators, American soldiers of Japanese ancestry.

ROY TANIGUCHI, writing from Tokyo: "I read with great interest and find that your book is just the kind of book I wanted someone to write before the memories fade away."

GARY LAWSON, principal of Jessie Baker School in Elk Grove: "You have written a most powerful account on a subject which has been neglected for far too long. I could hardly put it down. Your account of your experience as well as those of your family and friends was written so vividly that I felt every emotion possible...Lots of luck...I hope you sell a million copies and that justice finally arrives for so many of you who suffered."

*The Senate passed S1009 on April 20, 1988.

HARRY IIDA: "I have read the book through and have been inspired much. Best of any so far on how it was inside. I was in Tule Lake until November 1942 when I volunteered."

ROSIE TANI: "Congratulations on your beautifully written book. I enjoyed reading every word, every page of it. It brought back many memories. All kinds of feelings emerged: sadness, pride, anger, compassion, laughter, pain, but most of all, I felt so proud of you, a person of such faith, patriotism, and courage..."

MADGE MARTIN, member of ACEI: "I have read your book with genuine interest. It's something that needed to be written and is done without rancor, but with feeling and conviction for justice and love of country."

NOBY YAMAKOSHI, founder and chief executive of NOBART: "Thank you for writing all your memories...and congratulations on the masterpiece! I especially enjoyed the day to day encounters of camp life which I have never seen in any other book."

MARVIN URATSU: "Your story has appeal for all humanity which aspires and for the ultimate triumph of truth over evil. You have done so without bitterness and self-pity, which is refreshing."

LOIS SHELLHAMMER, educator: "I have read and cried over your wonderful book and your wonderful life several times now, and if I read it again tomorrow, I would respond the same way. Now after almost forty years, I can see evidence of how you have always inspired those who know you. With your book many more will be so influenced. Thank you for being you, and thank you for giving us your book."

HARTLEY PHILLIPS: "I just finished reading your book and felt compelled to write the first letter of my life to an author. Thank you for sharing this part of your life with me. As a white person who was born in 1948 and grew up in a white middle class neighborhood,

EPILOGUE

I was given little knowledge about the internment period or other impact of the war on Americans of Japanese descent. I lived on Reese Road in Florin for six months in 1975 and never knew anything about the bigotry and hardship which went on there."

KIMI HOWELL, Margaret Ogata's granddaughter: "I want to thank you for my book. By the time I reached Chapter 1, I had tears in my eyes. I will treasure your book always. There was so much I didn't know or understand. I'm very proud to be a part of this heritage."

MABEL ROSE (JAMIE) VOGEL, art teacher in internment camp: "Oh, how I've enjoyed reading your book...I want to read it all over again. Of all the many things I've read on relocation, *yours* is the one which magically takes me back immediately to those days inside."

Well, that's what we are hearing from our readers. We are grateful to each and every one who has taken the time to let us know their thoughts.

Arigato...

Elizabeth Pinkerton
April 14, 1988

"A sense of great serenity and peace overwhelmed me as I cried with gratitude for the superb exhibit. It clearly expressed to me our great Democracy's dauntless endeavor to corrrect itself. My blind faith in my country and the unwavering loyalty I clung to while I wept behind barbed wire confinement more than forty years ago has at last been nationally confirmed. I am liberated from the stigma that has shrouded my honor and dignity for so long."

Mary Tsukamoto

320

FLORIN AT THE SMITHSONIAN

September 20, 1987
Mayor Anne Rudin joins us at our first
book signing.

Washington D.C.
October 1, 1987

Dr. Harold Langley, Curator of the Smithsonian, and Congressman
Robert Matsui join us at our second book signing at the Rayburn House

A MORE PERFECT UNION

JAPANESE AMERICANS AND THE UNITED STATES CONSTITUTION

SMITHSONIAN INSTITUTION
Washington D.C.

A Celebration of the Constitution

MARY TSUKAMOTO

Florin at the Smithsonian!

Index

323

324

Sacramento Bee Photo

MARY TSUKAMOTO, a resident of Florin, California and a retired public school teacher, has devoted most of her life to political action and setting history straight. She and her family were among the 110,000 Japanese Americans who were sent to prison camps during World War II because of their ancestry and without due process in direct violation of the U.S. Constitution. This is her story, the story of internment in America, written in the spirit of justice by one who demonstrates in her daily life, her love for country and her people.

ELIZABETH PINKERTON, a writer based in Elk Grove, California, has researched the history of northern California and Sacramento County. A graduate of Wisconsin State College and California State University at Sacramento, she also attended the Principal's Institute at Harvard University. As a teacher and principal in Elk Grove schools for the past 25 years, she has worked to improve education for all children. She presently holds the position of Director of Special Projects for Elk Grove Unified School District.